THE HORNBY BOOK OF TRAINS

THE FIRST ONE HUNDRED YEARS

PAT HAMMOND

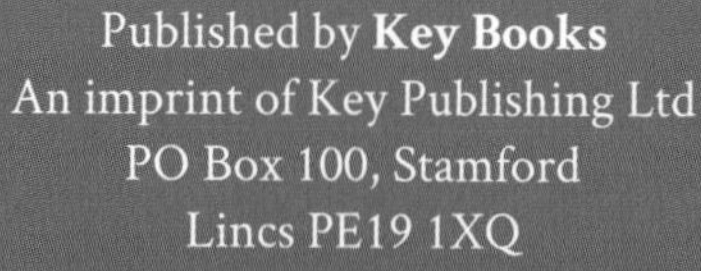

Published by **Key Books**
An imprint of Key Publishing Ltd
PO Box 100, Stamford
Lincs PE19 1XQ

For **Hornby Hobbies plc**
Westwood, Margate
Kent CT9 4JX
United Kingdom

The right of Pat Hammond to be identified as the author of this edition of 'The Hornby Book of Trains – The First One Hundred Years' has been asserted in accordance with the Copyright, Designs and Patents Act 1988 Sections 77 and 78.

Typeset by Aura Technology and Software Services, India.

Copyright © Pat Hammond

ISBN 978 1 913295 21 9

2020

CONTENTS

FOREWORD

I was ten years old when I received my first and only Hornby Dublo locomotive. It was Christmas Day, 1960. The model was a 2-rail BR Black 0-6-0 R1 Class locomotive and, in a separate parcel, was a Hornby Dublo 2-Rail TPO Travelling Post Office. The previous Christmas my brother was given one of the first Hornby Dublo 2-Rail sets, which included a BR light green R1 locomotive, two wagons, a brake van, plus a basic oval of 2-Rail track. By the following Christmas he had added a few more lengths of track and a siding and was supposed to let me run my locomotive when he was not playing with his. Of course, there was definitely some sibling rivalry between the two of us so, more often than not, I had to wait until he had either become bored with playing trains or wandered off to do something else.

Being a widow, I am not sure how my mother could afford to buy such luxuries for both her sons but she did, and for her boys she wanted Hornby, because Hornby was to her the best and, in her words, was certainly made to last.

Some years later we moved to Northampton and I quickly made friends with Nick whose father owned The Model Shop in Wellingborough Road. Fast forward to 1971, and after Nick's father had sadly passed away, Nick asked me to join him in the shop. With that, my career in the model and hobby industry began. Some seven years later I found myself as an Area Representative for Hammant & Morgan, a transformer and controller company that had been purchased by Hornby Hobbies Ltd, Margate, and three years after that I became the Brand Manager for Hornby Railways.

During my many years at Hornby I have seen numerous changes, some good and some questionable but, throughout, there has always been a passion generated by those who have been working on the Hornby brand. Designers, engineers and those who manufacture the models all share a common passion, not only for the products but also for the name 'Hornby'.

This latest edition of *The Hornby Book of Trains*, superbly written by Pat Hammond, traces the history of Hornby Trains as well as Tri-ang Railways up to and beyond their amalgamation, highlighting the ups and downs that have characterized so much of Hornby's one-hundred-year history. However, throughout the brand's evolution, be it from the original founder or via the Lines Brothers' Tri-ang Railway brand, their joint ethos continues to be maintained, which is to produce quality products for the enjoyment of all.

Times may change but the heart and soul of Hornby is still the same as it was one hundred years ago and I, along with all of those at Hornby, are proud and privileged to continue the tradition.

Simon Kohler
Hornby Hobbies Ltd
January 2020

ABOUT THIS BOOK: ONE HUNDRED YEARS OF HORNBY

When talking of model railways, the name Hornby means different things to different people. To some it is the large 0-gauge metal trains mainly of the inter-war period. To others it is the 00 scale Hornby Dublo trains which were at their peak in the 1950s. To modellers it is the highly detailed models they find in shops today. Although they share a brand name, they are all very different products. The Hornby brand has been owned by four different companies and while it has been carried by three quite different systems they have had three things in common: they have been British, they have been quality products and they have all carried the name 'Hornby' with pride.

The story starts with the Hornby 0-gauge system, first introduced in 1920, and follows the Hornby name year by year over the century. When we reach 1938 the main attention switches to the new Hornby Dublo which, in the 1950s, became the company's main model railway product.

In the 1950s we start to feel the challenges of other systems; principal amongst these is Tri-ang Railways made by Rovex Scale Models Ltd., a member of the Lines Bros. group of toy manufacturing companies. In the book we have briefly shown the development of this system from its birth in 1950, through to 1965 when it switches to the top of the page as the new carrier of the Hornby name. In 1972 the Hornby brand had yet another owner and in 1981 we see 'Hornby' as the name of an independent company for the first time in its long history.

As the book follows the story year by year, at the end of each decade we stop to review the previous ten years. These decade summaries are also intended to offer the reader a shortened history, enabling them to take longer strides through the book when the finer detail is not required. Milestones of the decade are also listed there in note form.

So, let us begin at the beginning with the man who started it all, and his company.

FRANK HORNBY AND MECCANO LTD.

Frank Hornby's signature.

Frank was born to John and Martha Hornby on 15 May 1863 at 77 Copperas Hill, Liverpool, near to the site of Lime Street Station. He left school at sixteen and started work as a cashier in his father's business. In 1887 he married Clara Godefroy, a schoolteacher, and they had two sons, Roland and Douglas, and a daughter, Patricia. On his father's death in 1899, Frank became bookkeeper to David Elliott, who ran a meat importing business in Liverpool.

Frank and Clara Hornby with daughter, Patricia, in 1913. (Courtesy *Liverpool Echo*)

'Mechanics Made Easy' tin. (Courtesy New Cavendish Books)

In his spare time Hornby enjoyed inventing things, and it was at home that he developed what was intended to be an educational toy for his sons. Using strips of metal drilled with holes at regular intervals, which allowed them to be joined with nuts and bolts, he created interchangeable parts that could be used again and again to build different structures.

Hornby called this toy 'Mechanics Made Easy' and, understanding its potential, he borrowed money from his employer and took out a patent, dated 30 November 1901, under the title 'Improvements in Toy or Educational Devices for Children and Young People'. David Elliott also saw the potential of Hornby's invention and set him up in business in a vacant room next door at 17 James Street. Hornby and Elliott became partners and on the the top of the tin containing the parts is the inscription *'Elliott & Hornby, 18 James Street, Liverpool'.*

'Mechanics Made Easy' sets went on sale in 1902, each tin containing sixteen different parts and a leaflet detailing the construction of twelve models. Some 1,500 sets were sold in 1903, but the business was not yet profitable. New parts were introduced and by 1904 three different sets, A, B and C, were available. However, the business was not in profit until 1906 and by then there was a developing overseas market. Instruction books were now in French as well as English.

By the following year, Hornby was ready to give up his day job with Elliott and set up working full-time on his own. Until now parts had been manufactured by outside contractors, but in the summer of 1907 Hornby found a suitable workshop at nos. 10–12 Duke Street, Liverpool and started producing some of the parts himself. At this time Hornby changed the name of his product to the more marketable 'Meccano', which was registered on 14 September 1907. To raise more money with which to expand, Meccano became a limited company in 1908 and Elliott decided it was time to retire from the partnership.

As demand grew more space was required and in 1909 the Meccano factory was relocated to a former carriage works at 274 West Derby Road, Liverpool. Many more staff were taken on and now virtually all the parts were produced in-house. However, demand for Meccano was quickly outstripping production again and a further move would be necessary. Its next home would be the purpose-built Meccano factory in Binns Road, Liverpool, which was in full production by September 1914. The same year Hornby's friend and former partner, David Elliott, died aged fifty-nine.

It was in 1909 that the name 'Hornby' had first appeared on a product and this was an expensive educational Meccano set called 'Hornby System of Mechanical Demonstration'. The first railway toy (possibly developed by Märklin) was released by the company in 1915 under the name 'Raylo'. It was a fixed-track game with a clockwork 00-size locomotive that had to negotiate a complex

BOYS MADE HAPPY
WITH MECCANO
MECHANICS MADE EASY.
You can make your own Models of Cranes Windmills, Railway Trucks, Signals, Flying Machines, and many others.
FULL INSTRUCTIONS WITH EACH OUTFIT.
Send Post-card for Illustrated List.
OF ALL BEST TOY DEALERS, OR
MECCANO, LTD., 12, Duke St., LIVERPOOL.

Meccano advertisement from 12 Duke Street, Liverpool.

Meccano advertisement (1910) from 274 West Derby Road, Liverpool.

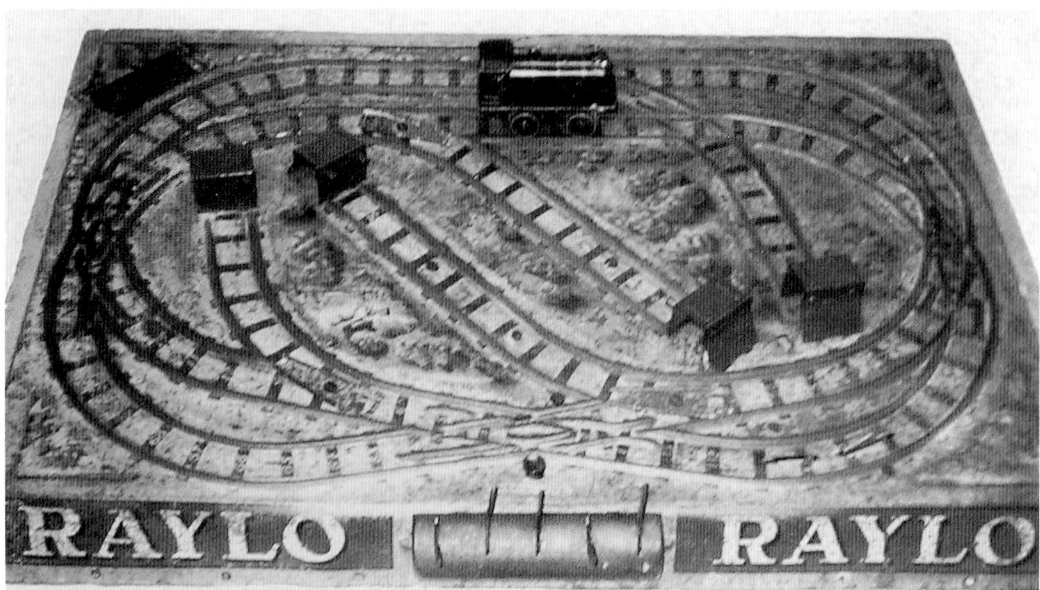

Raylo, sold by Hornby (c. 1915). (Courtesy TCS)

network of points switched with levers by the player. The name 'Hornby' was not used to market a loose-track model railway system until 1920.

The Meccano factory's products were being sold in many countries and Meccano Ltd eventually had agents in Argentina, Canada, Denmark, France, Holland, New Zealand, South Africa, Sweden and Switzerland, and a working relationship was established with the German company, Märklin, allowing it to produce Meccano in Germany under licence. The first Meccano headquarters in France opened at Boissy in 1921, but French Hornby trains were initially made at Binns Road. By the late 1920s trains were being finished and packed at the French premises, but it was not until the new Meccano (France) Ltd factory opened in Bobigny in the early 1930s that a 'made in France' range was developed.

Early on Hornby engaged two men who would become important to the success of the company in the years ahead. These were a Birmingham engineer friend named Ernest Beardsley and the other was ideas man, George Jones. Beardsley would become head of production while Jones would be head of marketing. We will hear more of them later.

In 1922 Frank Hornby was elected President of the British Toy Manufacturers' Association, a post he rightly held with pride. He was a millionaire by the 1930s and owned a mansion called 'Quarry Brook' in Maghull, north of Liverpool, into which he had moved his family in 1920. He owned a limousine and was chauffeured to work each day.

In 1931 Hornby entered politics, being elected as the Conservative member for the Everton constituency. During his time at Westminster, he left the running of the company to his co-directors and staff. It may have been his failing health that led to him resigning his seat before the 1935 elections. Frank died at home in September 1936, of a chronic heart condition which had been complicated by diabetes. He is buried in the grounds of St Andrew's Church, Maghull.

Hornby's Quarry Brook, Maghall, Liverpool. (Courtesy Peter Hodge)

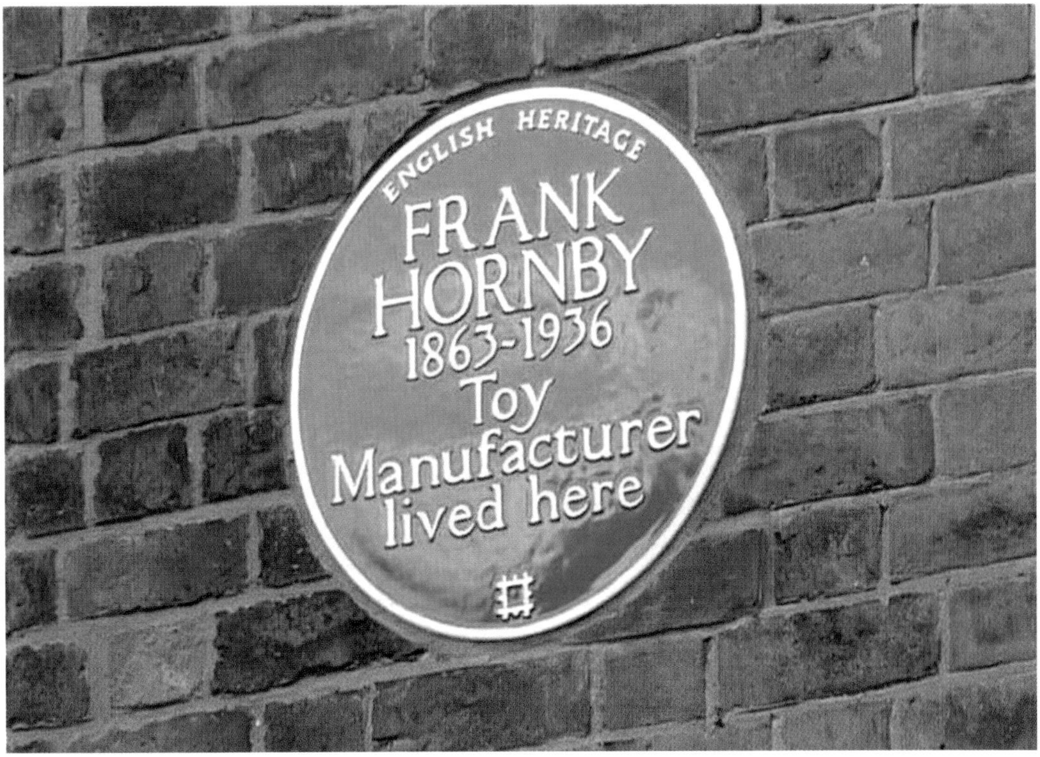

Blue plaque on the wall of the former home of Frank Hornby in Maghall. (Courtesy *Liverpool Echo*)

MECCANO MAGAZINE

The next number of the Meccano Magazine will be published in November. Readers who wish to have the Magazine posted to them regularly should send us **2d.** in stamps for postage for one year.

VOL. 1. No. 1 SEPT.-OCT., 1916

THE MECCANO MAGAZINE

TO HELP MECCANO BOYS TO HAVE MORE FUN THAN OTHER BOYS

A Fine New Meccano Crane

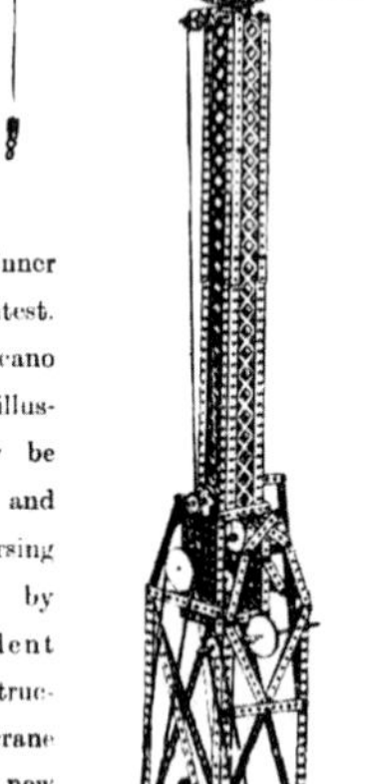

This is a Prize Winner in the last Meccano Contest. When run with the Meccano Electric Motor, as illustrated, the jib may be swung, the load raised and lowered, and traversing movement obtained by means of independent mechanism. Full instructions for building the crane will be found in the new Manual of Instructions.

A Message to Meccano Boys from the Inventor of Meccano

Since I first took out patents for Meccano in 1901, the hobby has made remarkable strides. I look back upon those days with keen pleasure, because even then boys recognised the merits and usefulness of Meccano parts and bought them eagerly. In those early struggling days, I had no factory to make the parts, or in which to work out new ideas. The difficulties were numerous and often almost insurmountable. Now Meccano is manufactured in the largest toy factory in the British Empire, equipped with the latest machinery, operated by many hundreds of skilled workpeople.

During these eventful fifteen years, a million boys of all nationalities and ages have bought and played with Meccano. Once they have started the hobby they have continued with it, buying the new parts and the new manuals as they came along. More boys play with Meccano than play football or cricket or any other hobby. I have corresponded with so many boys about Meccano, and I have got to know them so well, that I have come to look upon every Meccano boy as a personal friend, and I do not think that since the world began any man was so blessed with boy friends as I am. It is a great happiness to me to be able to send to them all a message of good-will through the Meccano Magazine.

In future issues I want to tell you of some of the early struggles and experiences which I had in gaining opportunities for you to buy Meccano and in getting it manufactured, how some of the best parts and models were suggested to me, and plans which have been laid for the future development of the hobby. I want to know you all better, and I want you to know Meccano and myself better. My determination is the same now as it has been for fifteen years: to keep Meccano the happiest, most pleasurable, and most instructive toy which boys ever had.

F. Hornby

Managing Director Meccano Ltd.

The Meccano Loom

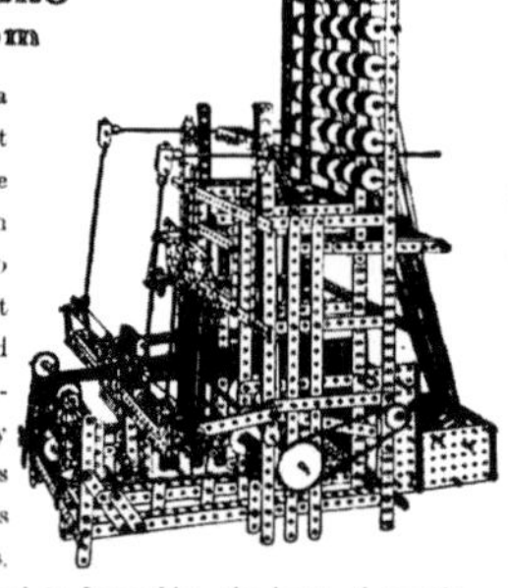

This is a magnificent new Prize Model which every Meccano boy will want to build and use. It automatically weaves ties and belts in all colours. It was designed in Lancashire, the home of weaving, by a Meccano user, who took for his patterns the great looms at which he worked to earn his living. It is perfect in every detail, and, like all other Meccano models, the work of an expert. Every boy should build this wonderful model, and learn all there is to know about weaving.

Our First Number

Meccano boys have been asking us for some years now to start a Meccano magazine, and here it is at last. This is a modest little first number, but it will achieve its purpose if it makes all you Meccano boys feel that you know us a little better. We have a lot of interesting developments in store, all of which will be announced in the *Meccano Magazine*, and we want you boys to look out for them, as they will all mean more fun and pleasure for you. Some of you are apt to get into a rut and to think that you are having all the fun it is possible to get out of Meccano, whereas, as a matter of fact, we are going ahead all the time and discovering new models, new ideas, and new fun for you. Write to the Editor as often as you like; he is just a grown-up boy with a lot of experience, and he knows how boys feel about things, and how to help them out of their difficulties. If your letters to him are interesting enough, you will probably find them printed in the *Meccano Magazine*.

The Editor.

The New Meccano Manual of Instructions

If you want to really taste the joys of Meccano, you must obtain this new edition of the Meccano Manual of Instructions. For the first time it reveals the great possibilities of the hobby. It contains hundreds of prize-winning models with instructions for building them. There are models in this book which have taken years to bring to perfection. Models to play with, like the Helter-skelter, the Automatic Billiard Player, Joy Wheel, and Box Ball Alley; models to work with like the Meccano Loom, which automatically weaves ties and belts in all colours just as good as any you could buy in the shops, the Meccanograph for making thousands of exquisite designs with years of interest in it for children or grown-ups; engineering models like the Jack Knife Bridge, Stone Sawing Machine, Weighing Machines of various patterns, new Cranes and Bridges, scientific models, models of Guns, Armoured Cars, and others of war interest. By the time you have made all these models, you will have learned many useful engineering things, you will be a much brainier fellow than when you started, and you will be ready for the new supplementary editions of the Manual of Instructions which are in preparation. Every Meccano boy should keep himself up to date with new manuals. It is only by doing this that he can get the full value from his Meccano outfit. The new edition contains 326 models and costs 1s. 3d. or 1s. 6d. post free. You can obtain it either from your regular dealer, or from us if you have any difficulty.

First issue of the *Meccano Magazine*, September 1916. (Courtesy *Meccano Magazine*)

Meccano Magazine (MM) was launched by Frank Hornby in the autumn of 1916 as a bi-monthly publication for Meccano builders and was edited by him until 1924. The first copies were given away free but in 1918 readers had to pay twopence for the postage on four issues. It was also published in the USA as *Meccano Engineer*. In 1919 it doubled its size to eight pages and now cost one penny. New Meccano products were advertised for the first time in 1920 and in 1922 the magazine became a monthly publication.

It was in the March/April 1920 issue of *Meccano Magazine* that Frank Hornby announced that before the next winter he planned delivery of *'the finest series of clockwork railway trains ever made, all designed on a new principle'.*

As new products were developed at Binns Road they received magazine coverage, each being allocated its own regular series of articles aimed at getting the most enjoyment from the company's products. There were sections of the magazine devoted to Hornby 0-gauge trains and later to Hornby Dublo. In these, readers were shown how to perform manoeuvres seen on the real railways.

The magazine was also famous for its technical articles on real engineering wonders and transport systems. In the autumn of 1922 *Meccano Magazine* predicted a public broadcasting service and prepared readers for it by offering them a Meccano crystal radio-receiving set for fifty-five shillings or you could buy the parts from Meccano and build it yourself.

There were also frequent competitions for photographers and regular features for stamp collectors, which brought in a lot of advertising revenue from stamp dealers. Later there was also 'Fireside Fun', for which readers were encouraged to send in their jokes. Another major function of the magazine was to report on the two membership organisations, 'The Meccano Guild' and 'The Hornby Railway Company', for the members of which competitions were run.

Although Frank Hornby took an active interest in the magazine its later success was also attributed to Ellison Hawks, who had been put in charge of it. An amateur astronomer and author of many books, Hawks had an ability to make science interesting. He was also responsible for the company's highly successful advertising.

From May 1924, the magazine, now edited by Hawks, had full-colour covers, and the December 1924 issue contained ninety-six pages and cost threepence. By the 1930s *Meccano Magazine* had a circulation of 70,000.

The Meccano Crystal Radio Receiving Set

For Broadcasting and Morse Reception.

START RADIO NOW

WHAT can be more delightful than—having erected your aerial and connected it to your receiver—to place a 'phone to your ear and hear land stations signalling to ships at sea and ships signalling back; to hear the human voice in song and speech, and music of all kinds with perfect clearness. Broadcasting stations are now installed in London, Birmingham and Manchester, and we understand that the erection of additional stations in Cardiff, Newcastle, Plymouth and Edinburgh (or Aberdeen or Glasgow) is being proceeded with, and that these stations will be in operation shortly.

Efficient and Inexpensive.

Meccano crystal radio set, No. 1 non-constructive type, December 1922. (Courtesy *Meccano Magazine*)

In 1932 W. H. McCormick became editor, followed by Frank Riley late in 1940.

The magazine's success would not last for ever. With losses showing in the early 1960s and the company itself in financial difficulties, publishing of the magazine passed to IPC in 1961, and in 1963 was sold to its printers, Thomas Skinner & Co. From 1965 the magazine featured Tri-ang Hornby as well as Meccano Ltd. products. In 1968, after a five-month break in publication, it was acquired by Model & Allied Publications (MAP) and edited by John Brewer, who, at the end of his career, was editor of

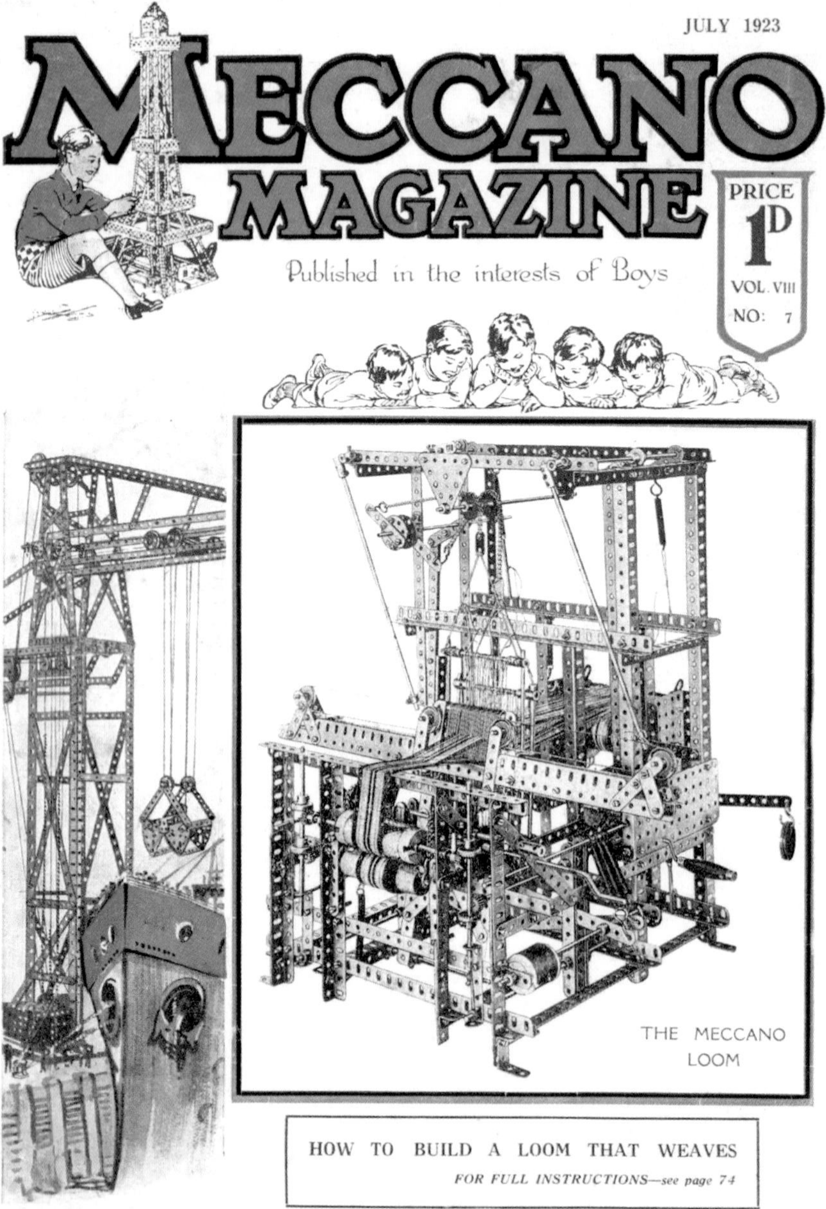

Meccano Magazine, first cover with colour, July 1923. (Courtesy *Meccano Magazine*)

Railway Modeller. MAP published *Meccano Magazine* monthly until the end of 1972 when it was taken over again by Meccano Ltd. (by then owned by Airfix Industries). From 1977 it incorporated *Meccano Engineer* and the *Meccano Woman's Journal*, but finally disappeared in the spring of 1981.

In its heyday, *Meccano Magazine* was an institution and copies of early or rare issues are sought by collectors today. It was not only a superb marketing tool, but was entertaining and educational, setting a standard for others to follow. Apart from a few early issues, good-quality copies may now be downloaded free from the internet.

Meccano Magazine, first multi-coloured cover, December 1923. (Courtesy *Meccano Magazine*)

1920
FIRST TRAIN SETS

HORNBY 0 GAUGE

Hornby 0-gauge trains were initially a development of the Meccano system. It is said that the idea developed out of a new piece of Meccano, a corner bracket called an 'architrave', which could be used to form cab sides when building a locomotive out of Meccano. This had been produced during the First World War, and a small model locomotive was made up with it in the factory.

Whether or not this inspired the Hornby trains, the first train sets were put on the market in 1920 and the models were advertised as being 'constructional', i.e. held together with nuts and bolts so that they could be taken apart like Meccano. This, no doubt, was what Frank Hornby was referring to in *Meccano Magazine* as 'designed on a new principle'. The steel pressings which formed the parts were purpose-made to look like real railway engines and rolling stock when assembled, and not like something built out of Meccano. These train sets came with track and were in strong cardboard boxes.

During those early years the method of construction was different from that of German trains imported before the First World War, as the latter were usually tinplate and the parts joined together with tabs that passed through

The first No. 1 Great Northern Railway (GNR) train set. (Source unknown)

slots before being bent over to hold the pieces together. More expensive models were soldered together. In 1925, Meccano Ltd. would abandon nut and bolt construction and adopt tab and slot for the Hornby 0-gauge range.

Locomotive made at the factory from Meccano during the First World War. (Courtesy *Meccano Magazine*)

This is perhaps the place to point out that probably the very first train sets to be made at the Binns Road factory in 1920 were cheap copies of pre-First World War German sets made by Bing, and were in fact made in tinplate and not the enamelled pressed steel that would be used for the main products. Arriving in the shops in June 1920, the cheap tinplate sets came in a choice of three liveries. An 0-4-0 tender locomotive could be in lined black livery for London & North Western Railway (LNWR) and named *George the Fifth*, green and red for Great Northern Railway (GNR) or maroon for Midland Railway (MR), the last two being un-named. The locomotives had an undersized tender, and each came with two very short four-wheel coaches appropriately liveried.

An original cheap tinplate set with *George the Fifth* and coaches. (Courtesy Vectis Auctions)

The No. 1 London & North Western Railway (LNWR) locomotive. (Courtesy Vectis Auctions)

The No. 1 Midland Railway (MR) open wagon. (Courtesy LSK)

It is not known how well those tinplate sets sold, as the main attention was focused on the enamelled sets which, if the reports in *Meccano Magazine* are to be believed, the public were clamouring to get their hands on. In 1920, work started on doubling the size of the factory and initially work on the new 0-gauge trains was undertaken in the works canteen – other eating arrangements having to be made.

The locomotives, which had a four-wheel clockwork mechanism and a tender, were available in a choice of three colours – red (MR), green with red valances (GNR) and black (LNWR) – and while they carried no company lettering, adverts explained the companies they were meant to represent. The locomotives had steel rod handrails either side of the boiler, held in brass fittings. The domes, buffers and coupling hooks were also in brass, whereas the chimneys were painted metal castings. The cab-side numbers were embossed brass plates and the number carried was 2710.

Each set had a single grey open wagon carrying the appropriate company lettering MR, GN or LNWR. Strangely, the letters were separately stamped out of metal and painted white. Each letter had tabs that fitted through slots in the sides of the wagon. This seems an expensive way of lettering wagons; later ones were stencilled and later still transfers were used. The wagons also had turned brass buffers and coupling hooks.

The rail sections in the sets seem to have been a copy of those made before the First World War by Bing in Germany. There were four quarter-circle curves with a nine-inch radius. The sets also had two straight rails, each about ten inches long. Each rail section had three sleepers and the rails themselves were made from folded strips of metal sheet; they plugged together.

1921
NO. 2 LOCOMOTIVES AND COACHES

By 1921, a larger 4-4-0 locomotive (called the 'No. 2' engine) was already in production and there were also long bogie coaches to go with it. The locomotive looked like a longer version of the No. 1 locomotive in the original sets, with the same brass dome and other fittings including the embossed brass number plate that carried the number 2711. The tender was more substantial and had six wheels instead of four.

It was announced that sets in Caledonian Railway (CR) and in London Brighton & South Coast Railway (LBSC) liveries were to be made. I recall playing with a blue tender locomotive when I was a boy, around 1950, as it was in a collection of second-hand Hornby my father had bought from boys at his school in the 1920s.

Although blue locomotives were made for a short time, it is thought that brown ones for the LBSC sets were not made at all. However, wagons from LBSC sets do exist, lettered as such, and it is assumed that black locomotives were used instead of brown ones, as black would be appropriate for an LBSC goods train.

There were also suggestions that two more liveries might appear, these being the Great

The No. 2 locomotive in London & North Western Railway (LNWR) black livery. (Courtesy Vectis Auctions)

The No. 2 locomotive in Midland Railway (MR) maroon. (Courtesy Vectis Auctions)

The No. 1 Midland Railway (MR) coach. (Courtesy Vectis Auctions)

Eastern Railway (GER) and the South Eastern & Chatham Railway (SECR). It is assumed that the locomotivess would have been blue and green (or grey), respectively, but these did not materialise.

As with the larger locomotives the new bogie coaches were referred to as 'No. 2', and this term would apply to future bogie coaches and bogie wagons, whereas mainstream four-wheeled rolling stock was classified as 'No. 1'. The early Hornby 0-gauge bogie coaches always looked strange. Being of nut and bolt construction each coach had four conspicuous screw fixings on its roof. Both versions of the coach looked like Pullman cars and one carried Pullman transfers. The other was marked as a 'dining saloon' and carried the crests of one of four railway companies: GNR, LNWR, MR or CR. Four-wheeled (No. 1) coaches were also released during the year in the livery of each of the above four companies.

The rather flimsy 9-in. radius track initially used was replaced with better track, which had 12-in. radius curves, more sleepers and clips to stop track accidentally separating when in use. A second wagon was now also available: a covered luggage van in GNR, LNWR or MR livery. The first lineside accessory arrived in the form of a lattice footbridge.

With both No. 1 and No. 2 train sets in at least four liveries and in either passenger or goods format, the range of sets available to the public was already large – and this was only the second year!

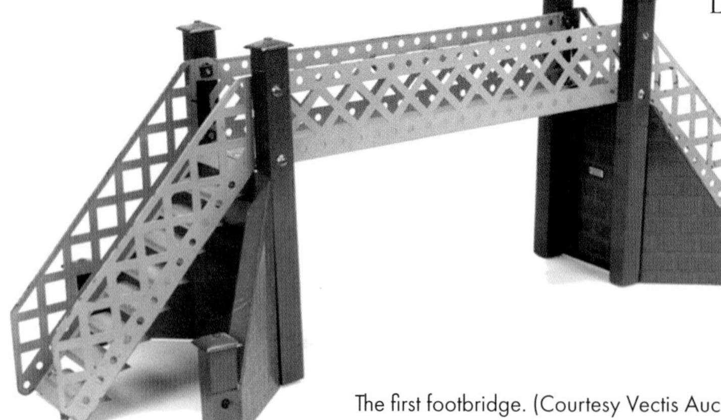
The first footbridge. (Courtesy Vectis Auctions)

The No. 2 Pullman coach. (Courtesy Vectis Auctions)

1922
WAGONS AND ZULU LOCOMOTIVES

It was in 1922 that the range of wagons really took off. All we had so far had been an open wagon and a luggage van. Now there was the addition of a cement wagon, gunpowder van, timber-carrying wagons, two styles of goods brake vans and a tank wagon, which in years to come would brighten up the railway with a whole range of colourful liveries. One of the timber wagons had a long base carried by two four-wheel bogies (making it a No. 2 wagon). The four-wheel wagons now had a new base, with open axle-guards similar to those of the four-wheel coach. Points and a buffer stop were now also available.

Other important additions were the two lower-priced locomotives which formed the Zulu range; the name, it is said, came from a train service, which ran into Liverpool.

One Zulu locomotive was a tender 0-4-0 and the other a 0-4-0T (the first tank engine in the series). These models would

The No. 2 timber wagon. (Courtesy LSK)

The No. 1 London & North Western Railway (LNWR) brake van. (Courtesy Vectis Auctions)

The No. 1 LNWR gunpowder van. (Courtesy Vectis Auctions)

introduce a new 'No. 0' range to compete with other inexpensive toy brands such as Whitanco, Wells and Brimtoy, all of which were the result of the government's call for British toys to replace those supplied by German companies before the First World War.

Hornby's Zulu locomotives were similar to their existing models, but were cheaper to make, and particularly popular was the Zulu tank engine. Like the No. 1s both the new locomotives had a simple four-wheel clockwork mechanism, and an important difference was that they were not of nut and bolt construction but adopted the tab and slot method of assembly to keep costs down. They may also be identified by the plain un-embossed front of the smoke box, as the end of a tank wagon was used to form this.

The Zulu tank engine. (Courtesy The Saleroom)

The Zulu locomotive. (Courtesy The Saleroom)

The Hornby G0 Zulu train set. (Courtesy SAS 1)

1923
POST-GROUPING LIVERIES

At the beginning of 1923 the large number of railway companies in Great Britain now became just four by a process of geographical grouping. The largest of these was the London Midland & Scottish Railway (LM&S or LMS) with 7,500 miles of track. Next was the London & North Eastern Railway (L&NER or LNER) with 6,700 miles of track. The two smaller companies were the Great Western Railway (GWR), with 3,800 miles, and the Southern Railway (SR), with just 2,200 miles of track, respectively.

HORNBY 0 GAUGE

Of the railway companies that Hornby had been representing with their train set liveries the CR, LNWR and MR had all been absorbed by the LMS and so the red and black locomotives were now used for LMS train sets. The GNR was now part of the LNER and so the green GNR locomotives became LNER. Furthermore, the locomotive models now carried company lettering, either on the splashers or on the tender. At the 'grouping' in 1923, none of the four railway companies had adopted blue for a locomotive livery, consequently blue locomotives disappeared from the Hornby range. The Zulu locomotives now carried LMS lettering. While these changes were taking place with British train sets, Hornby sets exported to France carried PLM (red), Nord (green) and Etat (black) liveries. These stood

The No. 1 LNER locomotive. (Courtesy Vectis Auctions)

The No. 2 LMS locomotive. (Courtesy Vectis Auctions)

The LMS Zulu tank locomotive. (Courtesy Vectis Auctions)

The No. 1 Chemins de Fer du Nord (NORD) locomotive. (Courtesy Vectis Auctions)

The No. 1 Paris à Lyon et à la Méditerranée (PLM) locomotive. (Courtesy Vectis Auctions)

The No. 2 LMS tank engine. (Courtesy Vectis Auctions)

The No. 2 LMS tank engine. (Courtesy LSK)

for Paris à Lyon et à la Méditerranée, Chemins de Fer du Nord and Chemins de Fer de l'État, respectively.

A new locomotive in 1923 was a large tank engine, a 4-4-4T. It was based on the 4-4-0 tender locomotives (No. 2) with a four-wheel bogie beneath the cab and coal bunker, but was of tab and slot construction. The new large tank was released early in the year, before the new real railway liveries were known and so the green

The No. 1 GWR gas cylinder wagon. (Courtesy Vectis Auctions)

The No. 1 hopper wagon. (Courtesy LSK)

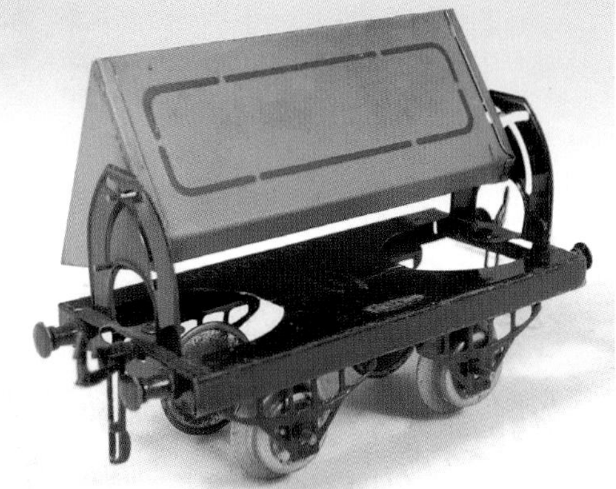

No.1 side-tipping wagon. (Courtesy LSK)

The Hornby turntable. (Courtesy Vectis Auctions)

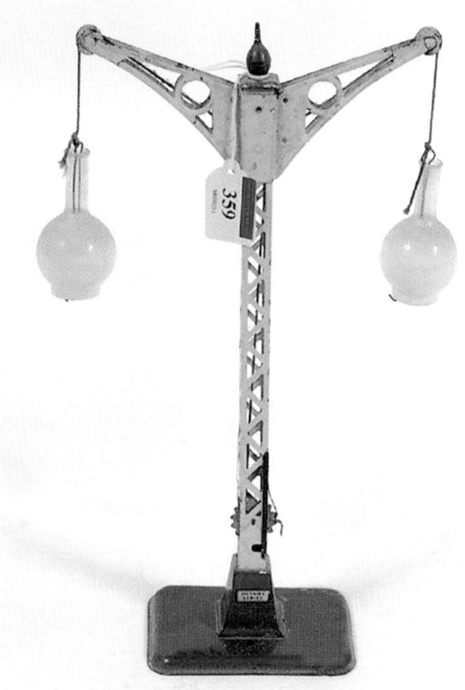

The No. 2 globe lamp standard. (Courtesy LSK)

L&NER version initially has red valances like GNR locomotives.

Both black and red LM&S versions were also made.

New wagons added during the year included both side and rotary tipping wagons, two lumber wagons (No. 1 and No. 2), a hopper, bogie luggage van, two cattle trucks (No. 1 and No. 2), gas cylinder wagon, milk traffic van, refrigerator van, trolley wagon (bogie well wagon) and the first of a number of private owner vans – the short-lived 'Colman's Mustard'.

New lineside accessories included the 'Windsor' station, turntable, telegraph pole, signal, twin globe station lamp and a loading gauge. For one year only there were also two presentation sets of different sizes which contained a selection of accessories.

1924
PRIVATE OWNER VANS

HORNBY SERIES

The name 'Hornby Series' was adopted for the whole of the Hornby 0-gauge range, including the Zulu sets. The Zulu tank engine was promoted to become the No. 1 tank engine. 'Hornby Series' decals were applied to everything and so too was a liberal coat of varnish to protect the paintwork and give them a glossy appearance.

LNER and LMS lettering was now appearing on most of the wagons and locomotives.

The No. 1 LNER former Zulu tank engine. (Courtesy Vectis Auctions)

The No. 1 Carr's Biscuits van. (Courtesy Vectis Auctions)

The No. 1 Crawford's Biscuits van. (Courtesy LSK)

The No. 1 Jacob & Co.'s Biscuits van. (Courtesy W&W)

The No. 1 Seccotine van. (Courtesy Vectis Auctions)

The No. 1 LNER snow plough. (Courtesy Vectis Auctions)

The No. 1 LMS passenger guard's van with long thin base and clerestory roof. (Courtesy LSK)

Following the success of the Colman's Mustard van there were further private owner vans, including Carr's, Crawford's and Jacob's biscuit vans, and one advertising Seccotine glue.

Another new wagon was a snowplough with a large working blower fan driven from one of the axles.

The four-wheel coaches were replaced with a different design which represented a clerestory

Platform accessories Set 2. (Courtesy SAS)

The Hornby Series tinplate signal cabin. (Courtesy Vectis Auctions)

Hornby Series clockwork and electric level crossings. (Courtesy Vectis)

roof, typical of gas-lit coaches. There were tin-printed LMS and LNER versions that were longer and narrower than the ones they replaced. The new coaches were now used in the No. 1 passenger train sets and a new long thin open wagon, which used the coach base, was now made for the No. 1 goods sets. This new rolling stock for sets was no longer of nut and bolt construction but clipped together with lugs and there was now a (separately purchased) passenger guard's van to go with the coach.

Also new in 1924 was a host of lineside accessories. These included a tunnel, a level crossing, a new footbridge, a junction signal, viaduct, signal cabin and three sets of platform accessories such as luggage, milk cans and platform machines.

1925
ELECTRIC TRAINS

The introduction of the Metropolitan electric locomotive provided the first Hornby electric train set and it came with two Metropolitan bogie coaches. The locomotive was also the first by Hornby to have its body modelled on a real prototype and the fact that it was an 0-4-0, and not a Bo-Bo, was concealed by the low skirt. It is probably best remembered for having a high voltage motor. The set contained a rheostat which reduced the mains voltage through resistances and a light bulb, but children still risked receiving an electric shock if they touched the new three-rail track when it was operating. The locomotive was withdrawn the following year and when it returned in 1926 it had been fitted with a 4 V motor.

The cheap tinplate trains of 1920 were called 'No. 00' from 1925 (not to be confused with 00 scale) and the Zulu train sets were renamed 'No. 0 Goods Set' and 'No. 0 Passenger Set', thus losing the Zulu name. The unpopular new slim wagons of the year before were replaced with better-proportioned ones. Larger goods sets were introduced, one for the 0-4-0T and the other for the 4-4-4T, each with a selection of wagons.

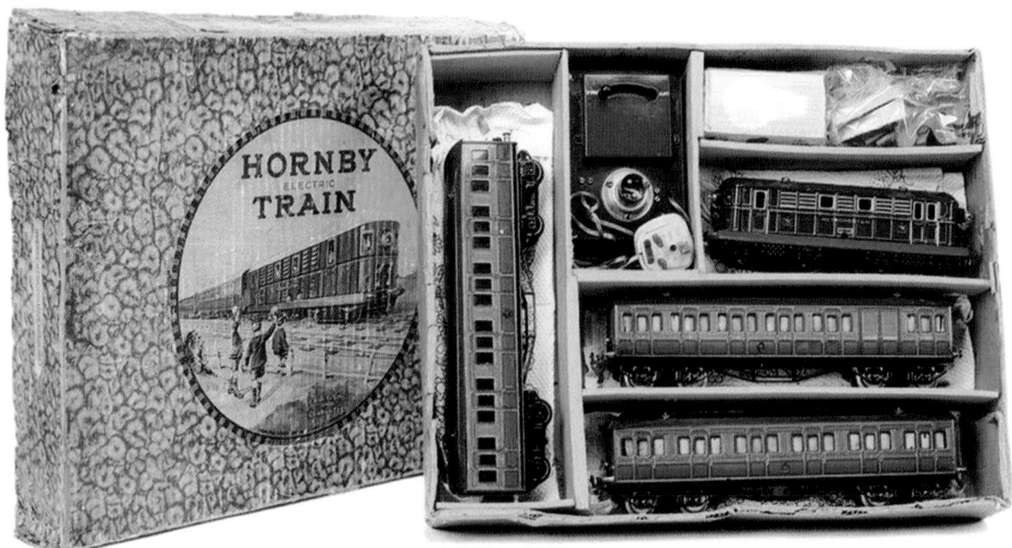

Metropolitan high-voltage train set with extra coach and no track. (Courtesy Vectis Auctions)

Hornby Metropolitan electric locomotive. (Source unknown)

The No. 00 Midland Railway (MR) train set. (Courtesy Vectis Auctions)

A three-rail viaduct. (Courtesy LSK)

The Hornby Book of Trains, first edition. (Courtesy LSK)

With the electric locomotive came three-rail track, with the centre rail providing the live supply. A three-rail viaduct was added and extensions to it were also available now for both two- and three-rail tracks. There were also new two-rail track points in both 1-ft and 2-ft radiuses as well as three-rail parallel points.

The Hornby Book of Trains was first published in 1925. This was an enlarged Hornby Series catalogue that also contained several articles about the real railways.

1926
BLUE TRAIN, GREAT WESTERN RAILWAY AND M SERIES

Early on Meccano Ltd. had seen the potential of the nearby French market and from the beginning of Hornby trains had produced train sets in three French liveries, referred to above, for sale there. It was the importance of this market which led to the design of a French locomotive at Binns Road, which was based on a Nord Pacific but had a 4-4-2 wheel arrangement (instead of 4-6-2). The Nord and PLM locomotives were produced with either clockwork or 4 V electric motors and sold in two- and three-rail Riviera Blue train sets. These sold well in France and the French colonies, but also in the British overseas dominions.

The bogie coaches were bulkier than the existing Pullman cars and were painted blue and lettered 'Compagnie Internationale des Wagons-Lits et Des Grande Express Europeens'. The coaches in the train sets were a sleeping car and a restaurant car and were the first Hornby coaches to have a flexible corridor connector and an end plate for the rear coach. The locomotive was the first of the 'No. 3' range.

Since 1923 only LNER and LMS liveries had been produced on the British range. That was now about to change with the addition of GWR locomotives, coaches and wagons. This was acknowledged with a picture of *Pendennis Castle*

The No. 3C PLM locomotive for the French market. (Courtesy Vectis Auctions)

E320 Riviera Blue train set for France. (Courtesy Vectis Auctions)

The No. 1 GWR composite and full brake. (Courtesy Vectis Auctions)

The No. 1 GWR tank engine. (Courtesy Vectis Auctions)

The No. 2 GWR 20 V large tank engine. (Courtesy Vectis Auctions)

The No. 2 GWR locomotive. (Courtesy Vectis Auctions)

M1 green and M3 maroon locomotives. (Courtesy Vectis Auctions)

on the cover of *The Hornby Book of Trains* for 1926. The locomotives were the same as the LMS and LNER ones, but in darker green and with typical GWR safety-valve covers in place of the domes. Also, during 1926 the 'LNER' lettering on wagons was replaced by the more correct 'NE'.

The locomotive from the 1920-copied German tin-printed train set (which had become the No. 00 set the year before) became the M3 locomotive (now with a larger tender) and, along with the simpler but sturdier M1 locomotive (another Bing copy with a narrow tender), formed the new M series which would develop into a quite extensive budget range.

Control system with six-lever frame. (Courtesy LSK)

The M1 locomotive was referred to as the M1/2, presumably because it was used in both the M1 and M2 train sets. In 1926 these included a four-wheel Pullman car and the obsolete 1924 slim train set open wagons that had been replaced in 1925. Both passenger and goods sets were available.

The main range of lineside accessories now included a goods depot, an island platform, paling fence and a platform extension for the Windsor Station, which could also be used to turn it into a terminus station. It was also in 1926 that the less than popular Hornby Control System was introduced. This allowed mechanical control of clockwork trains, points and signals from a lever frame in the signal box via a network of rods.

1927
NO. 3 LOCOMOTIVES

Having produced the Nord and PLM 4-4-2 No. 3 locomotives for the French market, it was decided to make use of new tooling to produce a range of locomotives in LMS, LNER and GWR liveries. Both 4 V electric and clockwork versions of each were made and, although they were not authentic models, this time they carried famous names.

The light green LNER locomotive was 4472 *Flying Scotsman*, the red LMS locomotive was 6100 *Royal Scot* and the darker green GWR locomotive was 4073 *Caerphilly Castle*. None had the correct wheel arrangement for the prototype, but this was 1927 and at that time such things did not carry the same importance that they do today. These were shown in the catalogue as No. 3 locomotives and the newly built real *Royal Scot* would

The No. 3 LMS locomotive, *Royal Scot*. (Courtesy Vectis Auctions)

The No. 3 GWR locomotive, *Caerphilly Castle*. (Courtesy Vectis Auctions)

adorn the cover of *The Hornby Book of Trains* the following year.

To make up new train sets with the new 4-4-2 locomotives, a better-quality coach was required. This was a Pullman car based on the coaches produced for the Blue Riviera sets. The windows were made larger and the window surrounds embossed. Like the French ones they had the correct recessed doors, which early Pullman models lacked, and they now also had corridor connectors and corridor end plates. Also, unlike the early Pullmans, which had been painted green and cream, these had the usual brown and cream Pullman livery.

One invention was a brake and reverse rail that, when set, would trigger a switch on the locomotive's clockwork motor, which would put it into reverse. One possible use for this was on an end-to-end layout if you wanted the locomotive to change direction when it was running out of track.

During the year many of the wagons received brighter colours, the downside of which was that they looked less realistic. This also affected some lineside accessories, on which black was replaced by blue for bases. At the same time, gold transfers replaced stencilled company letters on wagons.

New additions during the year were two French-style wagons, another platform accessory set and the start of a series of inexpensive

The No. 3E LNER set with the *Flying Scotsman* and new Pullman cars. (Courtesy Vectis Auctions)

lineside accessories to go with the M series sets. The first two were a wayside station and a small turntable.

Further afield a factory Meccano Ltd. had opened in Elizabeth, New Jersey, USA came into production during the year with a range of products for the US market called 'Hornby Lines'. However, the venture was not to survive for long and the business was sold to A. C. Gilbert in 1929.

The No. 1 NORD open wagon for France. (Courtesy Vectis Auctions)

The No. 1 Chemins de Fer de l'État (ETAT) luggage van for France. (Courtesy Vectis Auctions)

The Meccano factory in New Jersey, USA. (Courtesy *Meccano Magazine*)

1928
SOUTHERN RAILWAY AND AUTHENTIC PULLMANS

Southern Railway (SR) liveries arrived at last and were applied to locomotives and rolling stock. Locomotives branded 'Southern' were available in green with white lining, or black with green lining. Green four-wheel coaches started to appear, and many wagons now carried SR transfers and were painted dark brown. This was a change for the better as, until now, almost all company wagons were painted in the same grey. There were several Southern train sets too, and the choice of name for the Southern No. 3 locomotive was pride-of-the-fleet LN Class *Lord Nelson*.

The large Pullman car went through further improvements during the year and a brake end version was added. These improved coaches were, confusingly, referred to as 'No. 2–3' in the catalogue, as they replaced the old No. 2 Pullmans and the new No. 3 ones of the previous year. This was later changed to 'No. 2 Special Pullman'. Now, for the first time, the

The No. 2 SR large tank engine. (Courtesy David Busfield)

The No. 0 SR locomotive. (Courtesy Vectis Auctions)

unsightly screw-fixings had gone from the roofs and they carried authentic names: *Iolanthe* and *Arcadia. Zenobia* and *Alberta* were added later. Name changes in the 1930s would add *Grosvenor, Montana, Loraine* and *Verona.*

In addition to the new French open wagon and brake van used in French export sets, there was now a wine wagon with two bright red barrels. It also sold well in Great Britain and

The No. 1 SR luggage van. (Courtesy Vectis Auctions)

The No. 1 SR tank engine. (Courtesy LSK)

The No. 3 SR 20 V *Lord Nelson*. (Courtesy SAS)

The No. 2 Special Pullman *Iolanthe*. (Courtesy SAS)

the following year a single barrel version with a lookout hut would be available.

Further useful lineside accessories arrived, a favourite among these was the tinplate engine shed, which came in two lengths: 9 in. (No. 1) and 18 in. (No. 2). Also added were a double track signal gantry, double arm signal and a platform crane.

There were also several small items, including a shunter's pole, tarpaulins, an oil can (with a 'K' on the side) and lubricant oil, lineside huts, gradient and mile posts, and a set of notice boards and station name boards. In the budget range a signal cabin, signals and a level crossing were now added.

A particularly important event in 1928 (covered elsewhere) was the launch of the The Hornby Railway Company, which would become a world-wide youth organisation with hundreds of branches.

The No. 1 double wine wagon. (Courtesy LSK)

The No. 2 double engine shed. (Courtesy W&W)

The No. 2 signal gantry. (Courtesy Vectis Auctions)

Railway accessories, No. 7 watchman's hut with brazier. (Courtesy Vectis Auctions)

1929
SPECIAL LOCOMOTIVES

Until now there were growing signs that Meccano Ltd. wanted to move towards greater authenticity with its trains (if we ignore the outburst of brighter colours in 1927). The Metropolitan electric, the Riviera Blue Train, the 1928 new Pullman cars and the more authentic Southern liveries all pointed towards this.

This was finally confirmed in 1929 with the release of four 4-4-0 tender locomotives (known as No. 2 Specials), which were clearly based on real locomotives and intended to be realistically accurate models. The locomotives were: an LMS 'Compound' No. 1185; an LNER 'Shire' Class No. 234 *Yorkshire*; a GWR 'County' Class No. 3821 *County of Bedford*; and an SR Class L1 No. A759. All were excellent value for money. In the mid-1930s, *Yorkshire* would disappear to be replaced by classmate No. 201 *Bramham Moor* and the LMS 'Compound' would see one or two turned out as the similar Class 2P.

The No. 2 Special LMS 'Compound' 4-4-0. (Courtesy Vectis Auctions)

The No. 2 Special LNER 'Shire' Class *Yorkshire*. (Courtesy LSK)

The No. 2 Special SR L1 Class. (Courtesy Vectis Auctions)

The No. 2 Special LNER large tank engine. (Courtesy Vectis Auctions)

EDS1 box of six double-track electric straight rails. (Courtesy LSK)

Both clockwork and 6 V electric versions of the No. 2 Special locomotives were available, the latter having an unsightly large electric bulb protruding from the smokebox door. Later, by special order, you could have this removed and the front end, from the clockwork model, fitted instead. However, judging from surviving models that have passed through auction houses in recent years, this option was not often taken up.

The new No. 2 Special locomotives replaced the original No. 2 4-4-0 tender locomotives of 1921, which were looking rather dated. Likewise, the No. 2 4-4-4T large tank engine of 1923 needed replacing with something more modern and a 4-4-2T with a larger boiler arrived, called in the catalogue a 'No. 2 Special'. Unlike the tender locomotives this did not appear to be based on any real prototype but had just been designed to fit the existing Nord frame, boiler and firebox while retaining the cab of the 4-4-4T. The model was less impressive when compared with the new 4-4-0 locomotives but was available in all four British liveries and sold well.

The original No. 1 0-4-0 tender locomotive of 1920 and the No. 1 0-4-0T (former Zulu 0-4-0T tank engine) remained in the catalogue as less expensive models, but well-detailed, larger boiler tender and tank 0-4-0s were added in 1929 and listed as 'No. 1 Specials'. Again, all four railway companies were represented.

They had outside cylinders with steam pipes above the footplate, low profile cabs, domes and chimneys, embossed boiler backs with detail of firebox doors, more realistic coupling rods and fluted piston rods, lamp irons with detachable lamps and a plate between the bunker and cab on the tank engine. Although not based on any particular prototypes, the detail they carried was another example of the move towards greater realism.

The year 1929 saw the adoption of 6 V motors instead of the 4 V ones and the original 0-4-0 tank engine was now also available fitted with a 6 V DC electric motor, which needed to be run off an accumulator. This was an experiment that was not developed further in 0 gauge. Electric double track was now available.

With so much time put into locomotive development there was little left for anything else. However, one important addition to the rolling stock range was a high-quality tank wagon, which was available in two liveries. In one it was a milk tank wagon carrying United Dairies branding and in the other was a bitumen tar wagon in Colas livery.

The No. 1 Special SR small tank engine. (Courtesy Vectis Auctions)

1920s – A DECADE SUMMARY

This first decade had seen remarkable development of the Hornby Series trains. The first Hornby named train set arrived in 1920 and this was quickly followed by further sets as well as separately sold locomotives, coaches and wagons in various pre-grouping liveries. New track parts and lineside accessories arrived in quick succession so that, by 1925, the public had access to an extensive 0-gauge model railway system, reasonably priced and of a good quality. By 1923 there had been No. 1 0-4-0 tender and tank locomotives as well as larger No. 2 4-4-0 and 4-4-4T engines to choose from. Similarly, coaches and wagons were classified as 'No. 1' or 'No. 2' according to whether they had four or eight wheels.

Following the grouping of the real railways into four companies, LMS and LNER liveries were used in 1923. GWR livery followed in 1926 and SR in 1928. The first electric train set, based on a Metropolitan underground electric locomotive, arrived in 1925. Other electric-powered locomotives and more three-rail track followed. Initially high voltage was used, but this was quickly replaced by 4 V AC in 1926 and by 6 V AC in 1929.

In the second half of the decade we saw the move towards authenticity and greater realism. This was demonstrated with the Metropolitan locomotive, the Riviera Blue Train, 1928 Pullman cars, the No. 1 and No. 2 special locomotives and the 1929 tank wagons.

It should not be forgotten that by now the Great Depression had started to make itself felt, yet the late 1920s and early 1930s saw the peak of Hornby 0-gauge development. The output of the factory was enormous and the choice of locomotives, train sets and assorted railway equipment would never again be repeated in 0 scale.

THE HORNBY RAILWAY COMPANY

In 1928 the formation of the membership scheme 'The Hornby Railway Company' resulted in 12,000 members by the end of the year; this was a major achievement in customer relations. Membership rose to 80,000 over the next ten years and to 120,000 after a further decade. At its peak the scheme had nearly 600 branches around the world. This was a good way to ensure brand loyalty.

OVERSEAS SALES

From the beginning, three French liveries were also used for export and many French-liveried models were produced in Liverpool. Meccano Ltd. opened a factory in France, near Paris, which later developed its own range of French outline trains as well as other products such as Dinky Toys.

For the rest of the world, models for export were manufactured in the Binns Road factory in Liverpool. Many Hornby trains were exported to Argentina, Australia, New Zealand and Scandinavia, and despite the appropriate new liveries they carried the models were still physically the same as those sold in the United Kingdom and were very British-looking.

An attempt was made to break into the American market in 1927 by opening a factory in Elizabeth, New Jersey, and the models made there had a more American look to them. However, that venture failed, probably due to stiff local competition, and was not helped by the Wall Street Crash. The factory was sold to A. C. Gilbert in 1929.

PUBLICITY

The advertising success was down to a highly efficient and imaginative advertising department run by Ellison Hawks between 1921 and 1935. *Meccano Magazine* and 'The Hornby Railway Company' were both successful ways of promoting the Hornby Series trains, but the production of well-illustrated catalogues, which were often personalised for individual toy shops, helped to spread the message.

Between 1925 and 1939, *The Hornby Book of Trains* was published each year and included a catalogue of everything in the Hornby Series range available that year. Unusual for its early date was the use of colour and, of special appeal, was the different express train travelling at speed that illustrated each cover. This was the catalogue to beat all catalogues!

NOVEMBER 1923
MECCANO
MAGAZINE
PRICE 1D
Published in the interests of Boys
THIS CLOCK STANDS 6FT HIGH AND KEEPS PERFECT TIME

MECCANO
MAGAZINE
2D
VOL. IX
Nº 10
OCTOBER 1924

December 1925
MECCANO
MAGAZINE
ERN
Special Christmas Issue
6D

SEPTEMBER 1925.
MECCANO
MAGAZINE
1825
3D
Railway Centenary Number

VOL. XI. No. 5
MAY 1926
MECCANO
MAGAZINE
Cleaning a Giant "Pacific" Loco.
3D

VOL. XII Nº 2
FEBRUARY 1927
MECCANO
MAGAZINE
6D

VOL. XIII. No. 4
APRIL 1928
MECCANO
MAGAZINE

VOL. XIV. No. 12.
DECEMBER 1929.
MECCANO
MAGAZINE
6D

VOL. XIV. No. 2.
FEBRUARY 1929
MECCANO
MAGAZINE
THE TWENTIETH CENTURY LIMITED
6D

1920s MILESTONES

1920 – First Hornby clockwork train sets, 0-4-0 locomotive (No. 1) in three colours, open wagon in GN, MR, LNWR and French liveries, and a copy of a cheap German tinplate train set.

1921 – 4-4-0 tender locomotive (No. 2), first coaches, CR livery, footbridge and new improved track.

1922 – Zulu 0-4-0 and 0-4-0T, new wagons, first bogie wagon, points and buffer stop.

1923 – LMS and LNER liveries, 4-4-4T (No. 2), many new wagons, first private owner van, stations, etc., and presentation sets.

1924 – Hornby Series transfers, private owner vans, new coach and wagon for sets, and many lineside accessories.

1925 – First Hornby electric train set, end of nut and bolt construction, end of Zulu name, cheap tinplate trains now called No. 00 and first issue of *The Hornby Book of Trains.*

1926 – Riviera Blue Train, No. 00 replaced by the M3 range, GWR liveries, 4 V motors and Hornby Control System.

1927 – 4-4-2s (No. 3), brighter colours, reversing rail and start of US production.

1928 – SR liveries, new Pullmans, engine sheds and 'The Hornby Railway Company'.

1929 – No. 1 and No. 2 Special locomotives, greater realism, United Dairies and Colas tanks, 6 V motors and the end of US production.

BOX ARTWORK OF THE 1920s

1921–1925 Standard Train Set.

1925–1929 Metropolitan Train Set.

1925–1926 Standard Train Set.

1926–1929 Standard Train Set.

1927 No.3 Train Set.

1929 No.2 Special Train Set.

1930
EXPORTS TO CANADA AND MO/M1 TRAINS

HORNBY 0 GAUGE

The No. 3 train set, with its 4-4-2 locomotive and two new Pullman cars, was made available on the Canadian market in Canadian Pacific livery. It had maroon cars inscribed with the company name above the windows. The locomotive was the Nord version fitted with a cowcatcher and a light in the centre of the smokebox door and with 'Canadian Pacific' inscribed on the tender. Only an electric set was made and for the first time a 15 V AC motor was used, with a transformer in the set. The set was not available in Great Britain.

Canada also received cheaper clockwork sets made up using remaining stock from the US factory. Waste not, want not! Indeed, finding a use for the residue stock may have been what triggered the idea of paying attention to Canada's markets. The American narrow four-wheel rolling stock was also available in the British catalogue in 1930. These were Pullman cars, *Madison* and *Washington*, and a box car, tanker and caboose. However, they did not sell well and neither did train sets supplied to Canada.

While the US locomotives were not sold in the UK, the new MO locomotives, released here in 1930, had a narrow body made in a single pressing like those of the American locomotives. The MO range was of a smaller scale and yet designed to run on 0-gauge track. The locomotives were tin-printed, in red or green, the red one having the number 6100 (of *Royal Scot*) on its tender, but no company lettering. The green locomotive was the same, but the number was 4472 (of *Flying Scotsman*). They had no outside cylinders or coupling rods, and, after a while, the cab windows would be printed to save having to cut them out and the numbers on the tender changed to 6161 and 2595, respectively.

The green and red colour scheme was also now used on the new M1 locomotives, whichwere very like the MOs of the same

Hornby Lines American train set. (Courtesy Barry Potter)

Hornby Lines American caboose, Union tank car and Pennsylvania stock car. (Courtesy SAS)

Hornby Lines American Pullmans, *Madison* and *Washington*. (Courtesy SAS)

year, but were slightly larger and had more detail, such as outside cylinders and coupling/piston rods. The coaches for both MO and M1 passenger sets were small Pullman cars, those of the MO sets being named *Joan* and *Zena*. New MO rails were also introduced with smaller sleepers

There was further electrification of the system during the year with a 6 V electric version of the large tank engine and among the accessories there were electric versions of the large turntable and double-track level crossing, as well as kits for converting two-rail track into three-rail.

Other new additions were a footbridge with signal attachments, tunnel ends, a platelayer's hut and a tool kit. In the wagon range the company lettering was removed from several items, and the buffer heights on most wagons were altered to bring them to

Electric turntable and level crossing. (Courtesy LSK)

A platelayer's hut. (Courtesy LSK)

the more authentic height of those on the Special locomotives introduced the year before. The old bogie Pullman No. 2 coach returned as a cheaper alternative to the Special Pullmans and it was also sold in LMS maroon and LNER brown, both described as a 'saloon coach'. More authentic non-Pullman bogie coaches were much needed!

The Exchange Scheme was introduced in 1930 and allowed Hornby customers to replace their old and damaged models with new ones. It also encouraged them to transfer to the new systems. If changing from 6 V to 20 V, they could send back their old model and receive a discount on its replacement. Likewise, a change from clockwork to electric could be made.

LMS and LNER saloon coaches. (Courtesy Vectis Auctions)

1931
AUTOMATIC COUPLINGS AND NO. 0 VANS

The new highly detailed No. 1 Special 0-4-0 tender and tank locomotives of 1929 were a lot more expensive than the original No. 1 0-4-0 locomotives and so the old ones had been kept in the catalogue. However, they were looking very dated and in need of updating, and this was done in 1931. These were given a new body with a larger boiler but were smaller and less detailed than the No. 1 Specials.

A new French locomotive, roughly based on those in use on the Paris–Orleans line, was designed at Binns Road for sale in France using the 0-4-0 mechanism. The long central cab carried two pantographs on the roof, and it was fitted with a 20 V motor; a clockwork version was also planned. Until now, France had retained a 4 V AC system, but in 1931 it upgraded to 20 V AC, ahead of the UK. Also new were the Riviera Blue Train coaches produced in Mitropa livery; as before, just a sleeping car and diner.

The most exciting additions to the system during the year were the No. 0 vans, which were tin-printed through use of well-drawn artwork. Although smooth-sided compared with the enamelled wagons, the high quality

The No. 1 (revised) GWR locomotive. (Courtesy LSK)

The No. 1 (revised) LMS locomotive. (Courtesy Vectis Auctions)

The No. 1 (revised) SR locomotive. (Courtesy W&W)

The No. 1E French P. O. overhead electric locomotive. (Courtesy Vectis Auctions)

The No. 2 *Mitropa* sleeping car. (Courtesy Vectis Auctions)

of the artwork made them look more realistic. The vans were all structurally the same as each other, but the printed detail more effectively identified each van type and function.

This method of production allowed for all necessary lettering to be incorporated in the initial artwork and saved the need to apply lettering by hand during assembly; consequently, they were less expensive. Compared with other tin-printed railway models on the market, the careful attention to the artwork ensured that the Hornby vans looked superior. The first three, released in 1931, had sliding doors and grey liveries, and comprised a GWR milk traffic van, an LNER fish van and an LMS meat van.

Other new wagons were the barrel wagon (with four oil barrels in cradles), a fibre wagon

The No. 0 LMS meat van. (Courtesy LSK)

(also nicknamed 'the mouse nest wagon'), a sheet rail open wagon, the coal wagon with 'Meccano' on its sides and the yellow Fyffes banana van. The latter had cupboard doors,

The No. 1 'Fyffes' banana vans, 1931 (left) and 1932 (right). (Courtesy Vectis Auctions)

The No. 1 Meccano coal wagon. (Courtesy LSK)

when launched in 1931, but by the following year they had been replaced by sliding doors.

New patented Hornby couplings were introduced to enable automatic coupling of wagons and coaches, but there was no means of automatically uncoupling them. The coupling on each end of a wagon consisted of a large hook with a sloping edge facing towards the next vehicle. The couplings also had a loose wire hoop. When two wagons were pushed together the hoops rose up over the hooks and engaged. It worked well and allowed a locomotive to back onto a train couple and pull-away with the train without it having to be connected manually.

Towards the end of 1931 a new series of die-cast toys started to appear, called 'Modelled Miniatures'. As the range expanded these included cars, lorries, buses, waterline ships, airplanes, figures and push-along trains. These die-cast toys would later be given the brand name 'Dinky Toys' and the cars and figures provided further accessories for the Hornby 0-gauge trains. For 1931, cast station staff and a field hording were produced to go with the trains.

Other lineside accessories produced during the year were electrically lit lamp standards and a three-rail single-track level crossing. In the M series there was a level crossing, a loading gauge and a taller telegraph pole.

Accessories set No. 1, 'Station Staff'. (Courtesy Vectis Auctions)

1932

20 V LOCOMOTIVES AND ILLUMINATED LINESIDE

In 1931, the UK trains changed to 20 V AC, like the French ones. The first electrically lit lineside accessory had been the station/yard lighting standards, introduced the previous year. In 1932 many more lit accessories followed, allowing you to switch off the room lights in the evening and run night scenes. A 17 V supply was chosen for them so that the 20 V bulbs would last longer. The new items with lighting included both engine sheds, station, island platform, goods depot, signal box, water tank, all the signals, level crossings (red lamps on gates) and buffer stops.

A Swiss 0-4-0 electric locomotive (LE1) was made at Binns Road in 1932 and looked very like the French 0-4-0 pantograph locomotive of the previous year, but with the wheels more visible. This was said to have been based on a locomotive

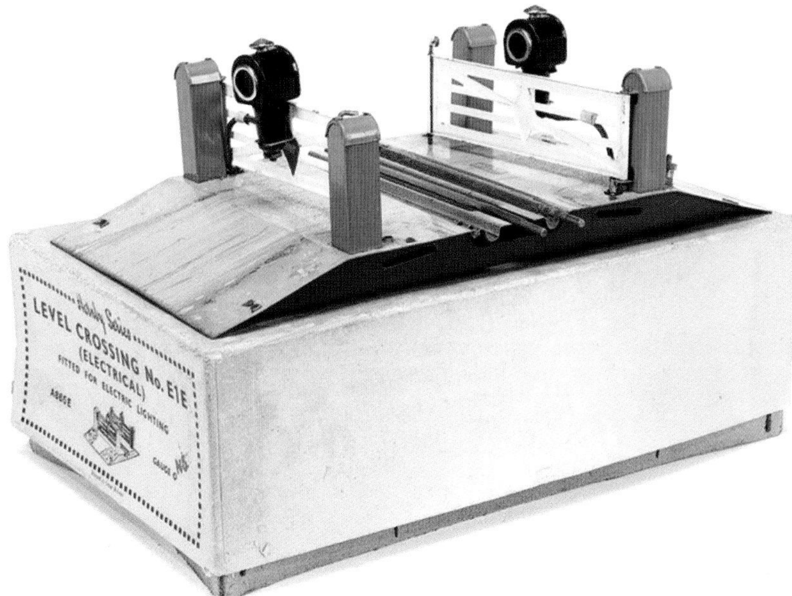

The No. 1E illuminated level crossing. (Courtesy Vectis Auctions)

The No. 2E buffer stop and signals. (Courtesy SAS)

The No. 2E illuminated water tower. (Courtesy Barry Potter)

The No. 2E illuminated Windsor Station. (Courtesy Vectis Auctions)

of the Swiss Federal Railways. Both clockwork and 20 V electric versions were made.

Another new locomotive with pantographs (LE2) also appeared in 1932 and had a body very like that of the Metropolitan electric locomotive of 1925.

A wide range of tunnels, cuttings and countryside sections became available during

The LE1 Swiss pantograph locomotive, 20 V. (Courtesy SAS)

The LE2 pantograph locomotive, 20 V. (Courtesy SAS)

A box of K1 and K2 countryside sections. (Courtesy Vectis Auctions)

the year, the latter being boards on which hedgerows and gates were fitted and to which trees with metal bases could be added.

In the Modelled Miniatures range there was a set of farm animals as well as sets of passengers, railway engineering staff, train and hotel staff, and the model of a real Hall's Distemper advertising sculpture, which was constructed within view of passing trains.

There were also train nameboards to go into clips on coach roofs and a further private owner van – this time Cadbury's Chocolate.

The Dinky Toys GO No. 4, 'Engineering Staff' set. (Courtesy SAS)

The Dinky Toys No. 5, 'Train and Hotel Staff' set. (Courtesy SAS)

Modelled Miniatures No. 2, 'Farmyard Animals' set. (Courtesy Vectis Auctions)

In 1932 Meccano Ltd. produced a cheap train set under the 'British Express' brand. The packaging did not carry the company's name as these sets were for sale through shops which did not hold a Meccano Ltd. franchise. The set contained a red 0-4-0 tender locomotive numbered 3323, a red and yellow coach, a circle of track, a station and station halt, a signal and a signal cabin. These were not items from the M range but were differently printed so that they could not be identified as Hornby.

Tin coach boards. (Courtesy SAS)

Modelled Miniatures No. 13, 'Hall's Distemper Advertisement' set. (Courtesy Vectis Auctions)

The No. 1 'Cadbury's Chocolates' van. (Courtesy Vectis Auctions)

1933
M COMPLETE RAILWAY

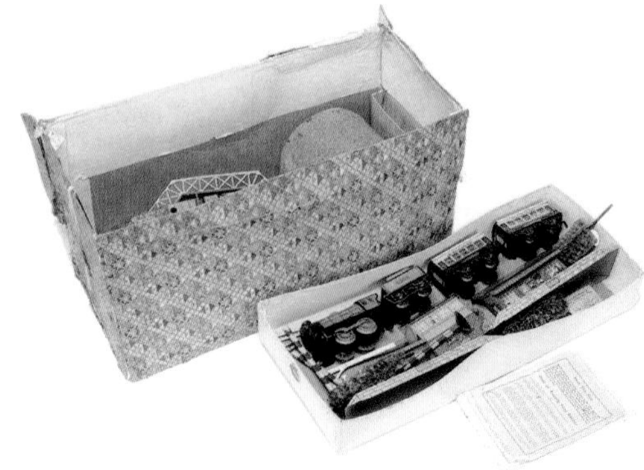

The M10 complete model railway set. (Courtesy Vectis Auctions)

The year 1933 was one of the quietest so far with little in the way of completely new products. As if to compensate for this the factory went mad with the paint brush and paint, so that the wagons and some coaches ended up with brightly coloured roofs and bases, making them even more toy-like. This was a complete contrast to recent attempts to follow a course of authenticity.

More of the smaller locomotives were offered in electric form and existing electric engines re-emerged with 20 V motors.

The budget M range received a footbridge and a complete railway in a box (M10). This contained an 0-4-0 locomotive, Pullman cars,

The No. 2 SR breakdown van and crane. (Courtesy LSK)

The No. 1 (revised) LMS tank engine, 20 V. (Courtesy Vectis Auctions)

track, station and wayside station, signals, telegraph poles, signal cabin, trees, loading gauge, tunnel, six figures, cutting, footbridge, and a level crossing.

Trees of the countryside sections were now available separately, along with the metal stands to hold them and the hedges. Tree types included oak and poplar.

1934
20 V EXPANSION

The range of 20 V electric versions of existing locomotives expanded quickly in 1934 and with them new train sets, of which there were twenty-eight in all, compared with only five the year before. The larger locomotives were fitted with a patented automatic reverse that was triggered by suddenly giving the locomotive full voltage. Smaller locomotives had a modified motor with non-protruding brush caps. This improved the appearance of electric locomotives.

The No. 2 Special SR large tank engine, 20 V. (Courtesy Vectis Auctions)

The No. 1 SR passenger coaches. (Courtesy Vectis Auctions)

As many homes did not yet have mains electricity, the 6 V locomotives continued to be available to run off accumulators. These locomotives now had a permanent magnet motor.

The electric passenger and goods train sets usually carried the same rolling stock as the clockwork sets, but there were now new No. 1 four-wheel passenger coaches, which were far more modern looking. For each company there was a saloon coach and a brake end, but they were non-corridor.

Following the success of the M10 Complete Railway clockwork set of the year before, three more of these sets were released with different selections and at different prices. These were M8, M9 and M11.

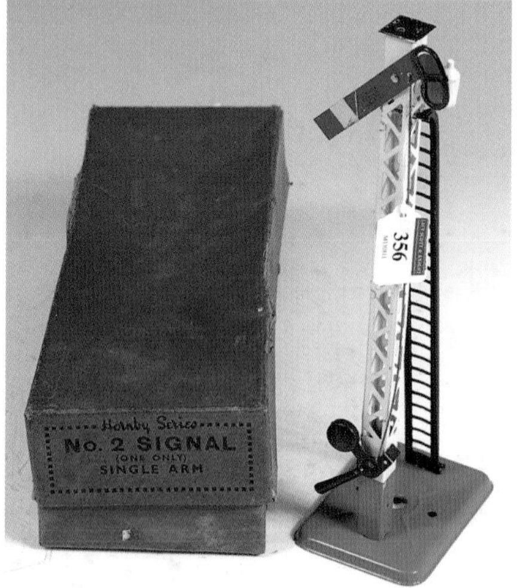

The No. 2 simplified single arm home signal. (Courtesy LSK)

The simplified platelayer's hut. (Courtesy Vectis Auctions)

The No. 1 LMS flat truck with 'Electric Cables' drum. (Courtesy LSK)

The year 1934 also saw a simplification of several of the lineside accessories. The purpose was to reduce the cost of production and therefore their price to increase sales. This simplification affected both single- and double-length engine sheds, the signal gantry and other signals, platelayer's hut, footbridge, water tank and goods platform. An example of this simplification was the replacement of the attractive finials on the top of signals with a flat top.

New products included a flat wagon that was also available with a cable drum load. From the die-casting department came a set containing a shepherd, a sheepdog and four sheep. There were also miniature posters mainly advertising Meccano company products.

1935
REALISTIC COACHES

Surprisingly late in the day, realistic bogie coaches were designed in the same style as the No. 1 coaches of the year before, and these reached the market in 1935. They were non-gangwayed and corridor-less for stopping trains and are sometimes called 'suburban' coaches, although they were not confined to the suburbs. One was a composite coach with two third class compartments at each end and four first class ones in the middle. The other was a brake end coach, containing five third class compartments,

The No. 2 LNER passenger coaches. (Courtesy Vectis Auctions)

The No. 0 LMS banana van. (Courtesy LSK)

The No. 0 LNER fish van. (Courtesy LSK)

The No. 3 LMS *Royal Scot* with smoke deflectors, 20 V. (Courtesy LSK)

The No. 2 Special LNER 'Hunt' Class, *Bramham Moor*, 20 V. (Courtesy Vectis Auctions)

a guards/luggage section and had a detachable tail lamp. These were tin-printed and produced in the liveries of all four railway companies and were the first Hornby bogie coaches available in GWR and SR liveries.

Four more tin-printed No. 0 vans were released, this time without sliding doors. They were a grey LMS banana van, a brown version of the LNER fish van, a dark brown GWR milk traffic wagon, and a new printing of the LMS meat van. A range of new M series wagons arrived in 1935, including a side tipper, a rotary tipper, a petrol tank wagon and a crane truck.

As previously mentioned, this was the year that 'Hunt' Class *Bramham Moor* replaced 'Shire' Class *Yorkshire* in the No. 2 Special locomotive range. The 'Hunts' and 'Shires' were two parts of the same LNER D49 Class and so were basically the same physically. In accordance with prototype practice, new batches of the *Lord Nelson* and *Royal Scot* locomotives were now fitted with smoke deflectors.

Having simplified many of the lineside accessories last year, it was now the turn of the illuminated accessories to be similarly treated.

1936
DEATH OF THE FOUNDER AND PRODUCT RATIONALISATION

In November came news of the death of Frank Hornby – the man who had given the world an unbeatable model engineering construction system with Meccano and, for Great Britain in particular, an affordable quality model railway. It is his legacy of the latter that

The No. 0 LNER A4 *Silver Link* model. (Courtesy David Busfield)

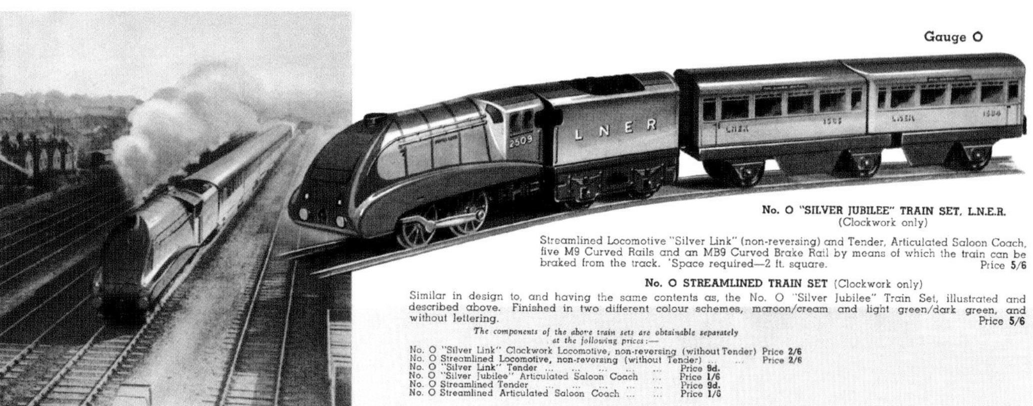

The No. 0 LNER A4 *Silver Link* artwork. (Courtesy David Busfield)

The No. 2 Special GWR large tank engine, 20 V. (Courtesy Vectis Auctions)

this book celebrates. *Meccano Magazine* was another of his lasting successes as too were the youth organisations he created with 'The Meccano Guild' and 'The Hornby Railway Company'. It did not stop there as the factory in Binns Road, Liverpool, turned out more of his ideas, including motor car and airplane constructor kits, Dinky Toys, crystal radio sets, Kemex chemistry and Elektron electrical sets, Dinky Builder and model boats.

As we have seen, Frank's elder son, Roland Hornby, succeeded him as Chairman of the company, but future success really lay in the hands of George Jones, who became Managing Director and Ernest Beardsley as Head of Production.

The previous year had seen the start of the LNER Silver Jubilee service between London King's Cross and Newcastle-on-Tyne. This was hauled by new Class A4 locomotives built for the service. They were painted silver grey, along with their single rake of coaches, and in 1936 a diminutive Class A4 2509 *Silver Link* and articulated coaches were modelled for the Hornby No. 0 'Silver Jubilee' clockwork train set. Great Western locomotives now carried the GWR monogram.

The No. 2 Special GWR *County of Bedford*, 20 V. (Courtesy Vectis Auctions)

The No. 1 Special GWR small tank engine, 20 V. (Courtesy Vectis Auctions)

It seems that the countryside sections were not selling and in 1936 their prices were dramatically reduced. It is assumed that no more were produced. Other items were also disappearing from the catalogue, including the Swiss electric locomotives, and the 6 V locomotives appeared to be on their way out.

New introductions in 1936 included a bogie high-capacity open wagon, a container for the flat truck and the trolley wagon with a cable drum load.

The No. 1 GWR flat truck with insulated container. (Courtesy LSK)

The No. 2 trolley wagon with 'B. I. Cables' drums. (Courtesy LSK)

The No. 2 LMS high-capacity coal wagon. (Courtesy LSK)

1937
THE PEAK OF HORNBY GAUGE 0 DEVELOPMENT

The popularity of the No. 2 Special locomotives had shown the value in investing in more realistic models. The year 1937 saw the arrival of Hornby's most iconic 0-gauge model – the 'Princess Royal' Class 6201 *Princess Elizabeth.* On 16 November 1936 the real locomotive had made a non-stop 401-mile run from London to Glasgow with driver, Tom Clark, at the regulator and fireman, Charles Fleet, with the shovel, doing it again the following day in the opposite direction.

Unlike the Hornby *Flying Scotsman, Royal Scot,* etc., models in the No. 3 locomotive range, *Princess Elizabeth* was a serious attempt at an accurate model of the real express locomotive and, moreover, its price of 105 shillings undercut that of the Bassett-Lowke model of 1935 by a large amount. It was not as accurate as Bassett-Lowke's model, the firebox having too sharp a slope on it and clashing with the reverse slope of the boiler top, but it was still a good model for its time. *Princess Elizabeth* was the only Hornby locomotive to be soldered together. It came in a red or blue wooden presentation box and was available only with a 20 V mechanism.

The other 1937 model, in what became known as the No. 4 Series, was Southern Railway 4-4-0 'Schools' Class No. 900 *Eton.* At the time when the subjects were chosen for the 1929 4-4-0 No. 2 Special range, there was not a suitable named 4-4-0 class of Southern Railway locomotive to choose and so the Class L1 was modelled. The building of the real 'Schools' Class had not started until 1930 and it seems likely

The LMS 'Princess Royal' Class *Princess Elizabeth.* (Courtesy Vectis Auctions)

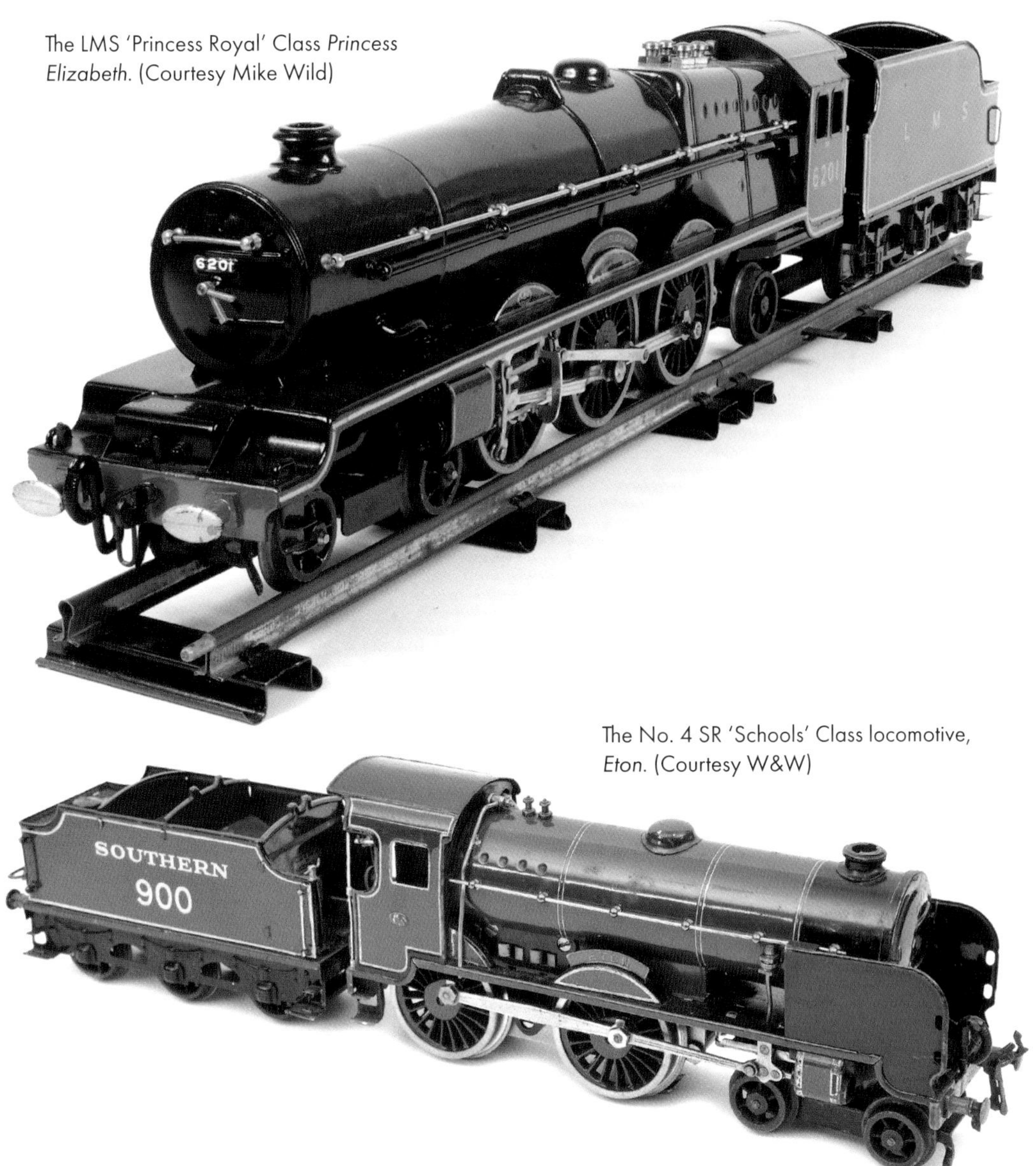

The LMS 'Princess Royal' Class *Princess Elizabeth*. (Courtesy Mike Wild)

The No. 4 SR 'Schools' Class locomotive, *Eton*. (Courtesy W&W)

that the Hornby 'Schools' model of 1937 was viewed as a replacement for the L1, although the latter remained in the catalogue. Years later, when Hornby Hobbies were choosing four 4-4-0 subjects to release in 1981, they also chose an LMS 'Compound', GWR 'County', LNER 'Shire/Hunt' and an SR 'Schools' – a coincidence?

The frames and boiler of *Eton* were very like those of the No. 2 Special *Bramham Moor* and the tender was borrowed from the Class L1, but what turned it into a 'Schools' Class locomotive were the typical 'Schools' cab, the smoke deflectors and several other items of added detail; it was the most accurate Hornby model to date. A clockwork *Eton* was available as well as a 20 V version – this time without that ugly light bulb in the middle of the smokebox door.

The No. 2 Special LMS Class 2P. (Courtesy LSK)

The No. 2 LMS mainline coaches. (Courtesy Vectis Auctions)

The No. 3 'Cornish Riviera Express' passenger train set. (Courtesy SAS)

Both the 'Princess' and 'Schools' had automatic reversing, and neither were sold in sets. Electric versions of the No. 2 Special models could now be ordered without smokebox door lamps. It was about this time that one or two examples of the LMS No. 2 Special 'Compound' 4-4-0 were released as LMS Class 2Ps in black.

The year 1937 also saw the introduction of modern mainline bogie coaches with tin-printed sides and ends. They were designed to take corridor connections and had roof clips to take destination boards (on LMS coaches the clips were on the sides, just below the roofline). For each company there were two vehicles – a first/third and a brake composite. In the case of the Southern green versions the first/third had been replaced with an open third coach. These new mainline coaches replaced older ones in the train sets, which now took on famous names like 'The Bristolian' and 'The Scarborough Flier'. Real train names were also given to cheaper sets such as 'Torbay Express' and 'Queen of Scots'.

The No. 0 A4 locomotive and coaches from the previous year were now available in two alternative colour schemes – maroon and cream and two-tone green. It is sad that the locomotive was never produced in LNER Garter Blue.

There were also eight more tin-printed No. 0 vans consisting of refrigerator, meat or fish vans for the four companies. There was also now available an LNER bogie brick wagon with a brick load as well as a 3-ft radius electric track. The station platforms now took on a speckled finish.

The delightful *Princess Elizabeth* and *Eton* for 1937 suggested a great future for the Hornby 0-gauge system – but things were about to change.

The No. 0 SR refrigerator van. (Courtesy Vectis Auctions)

The No. 0 streamlined train in maroon and cream. (Courtesy Vectis Auctions)

The No. 2 LNER brick wagon. (Courtesy LSK)

1938
A TABLE RAILWAY

HORNBY DUBLO

The arrival of the 00-scale Hornby Dublo system was announced in the September 1938 issue of *Meccano Magazine* and, although not realised at the time, it would prove to be a nail in the coffin of the 0-gauge system, but death would be slow. The name 'Dublo' was suggested by George Jones, who almost certainly was the man who had persuaded the Meccano New Products Committee to move into 00 production.

At the time consideration was given to making a two-rail electric system, but it was decided instead to copy the Märklin three-rail track. That decision would come back to haunt the company in future years. Also, the Leeds Model Company was already successfully moulding rolling stock bodies in plastic, but Meccano Ltd. decided to stick to processes with which they were familiar: in hindsight, another mistake. The first drawings were completed late in 1937 and the year ahead saw immense progress made in tooling the new system and producing the first batch of stock.

It is easy to ignore the difficulty of deciding to branch out into a major new product line. There are numerous considerations that must be discussed as so many things will be affected. These considerations are listed by Richard Lines in his book *The Art of Hornby* and, rather than repeat them here, I refer those interested to page 40 of that book.

Announcement of Hornby Dublo in September 1938. (Courtesy *Meccano Magazine*)

The Bing 00 electric No. 1 LNER passenger set. (Courtesy Vectis Auctions)

The pre-war Trix Twin Railway H0 locomotive. (Courtesy LSK)

The idea of trains that were small enough to operate on the living room table was not a new one. In 1914, model manufacturer Bassett-Lowke came up with the idea of a table model railway system, half the size of his 0-gauge models. Model engineer, Henry Greenly, designed the range of tinplate trains, track and lineside accessories and the

German manufacturer Bing produced them in 4-mm scale, initially for sale in Great Britain. With the First World War intervening, the system was not available in the shops until late in 1922. However, it set the standard track gauge for 00 or H0 at 16.5 mm for all time. The scale of the Bing Table Railway was 3.5 mm to 1 ft, which would become known as H0 (half-0) and electric sets and equipment followed.

The next small-scale system to arrive in Great Britain was the electric German Trix Express with its 16.5-mm track on Bakelite bases, freelance die-cast locomotive bodies and 3.5-mm scale tinplate rolling stock. With increasing political problems in Germany, a separate British company – Trix Ltd. – was formed to build a British version known as the 'Trix Twin Railway'. This was an electric system from the start and was marketed by Bassett-Lowke, who was one of the company's directors.

HORNBY DUBLO

Trix had arrived early in 1935 and it is likely that this influenced the decision by Meccano Ltd. to produce their own table-top system. It was found that the 3.5-mm scale was too restricting when designing models to run on

The Dublo SR three-rail 0-6-2T. (Courtesy Vectis Auctions)

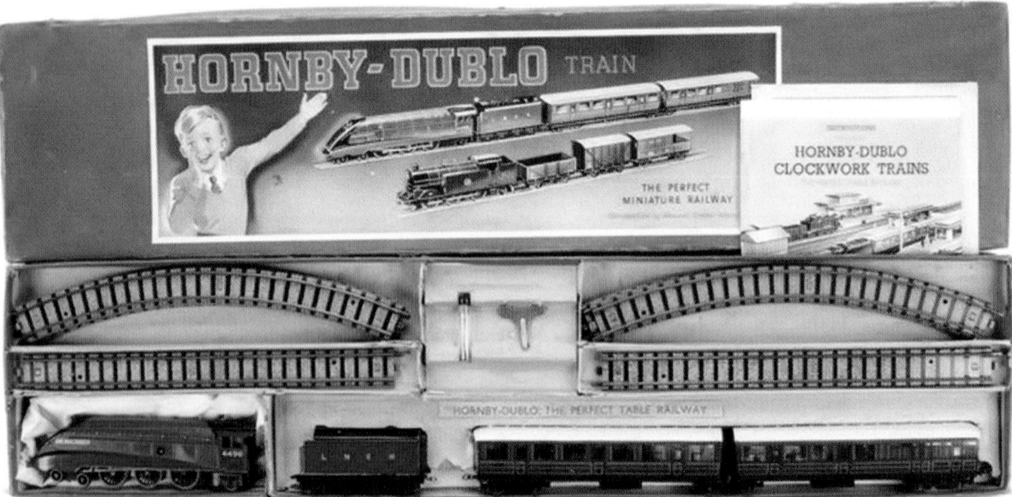

The Dublo pre-war clockwork train set with *Sir Nigel Gresley*. (Courtesy Vectis Auctions)

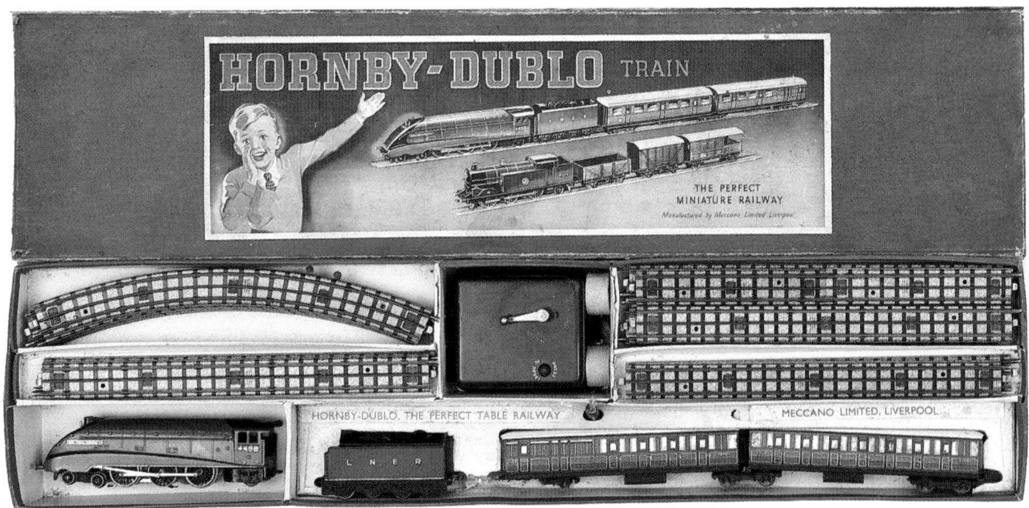

The Dublo pre-war electric train set with *Sir Nigel Gresley*. (Courtesy W&W)

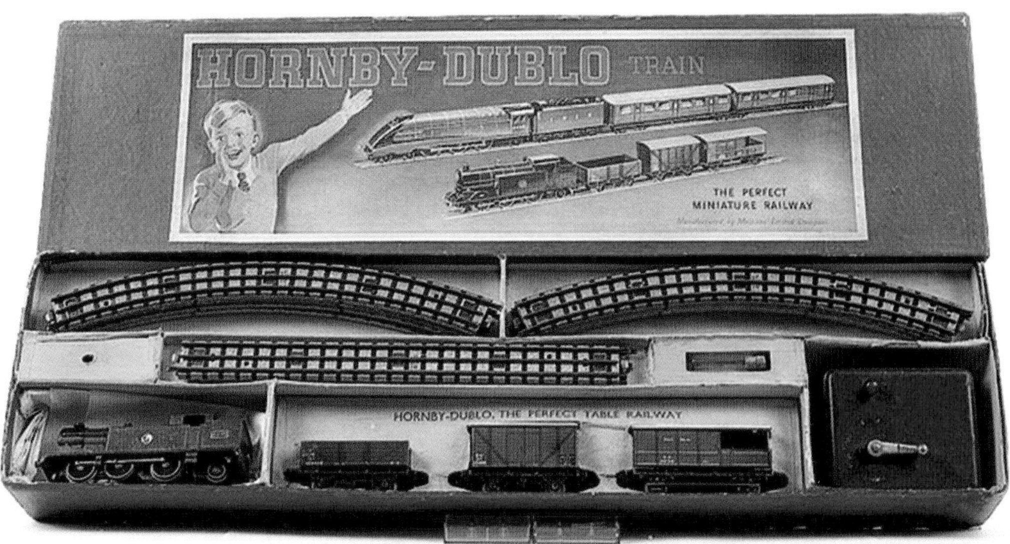

The Dublo pre-war GWR goods train set. (Courtesy Vectis Auctions)

16.5 mm track, especially if you wanted moving valve gear between the wheels and the body of the locomotive. Also, British locomotives were smaller than those on the Continent due to the tighter loading gauge on Britain's network and a scale of 3.5 mm to 1 ft left too little room for the motors available at that time.

To provide extra room, the scale of the new Hornby system was increased to 4 mm to 1 ft. This made the models out of scale with the track, but able to run without problems. Looked at in reverse, 00 scale makes the standard British track gauge of 4 ft 8½ in. look like 4 ft 1½ in. So successful was Hornby Dublo, that after the war the hybrid gauge/scale ratio was adopted by new manufacturers and it became the British standard. While most of the rest of the world has adopted the correct H0 ratio, to this day Great

Britain has been out of step (how very British!) and it was mostly due to Hornby Dublo.

Like Trix, the Dublo locomotives had die-cast bodies. However, Trix had 14 V AC motors, but 12 V DC was adopted for Dublo. This was easier to control and would become the international standard. Initially, Dublo also had a two-rail clockwork alternative. The rolling stock was tinplate and looked very like the new Hornby 0-gauge No. 0 vans. The electric track was like Märklin's with a live centre rail. The rails themselves were initially brass on a tinplate base, but later steel rails were used.

The most significant difference between Dublo and its rivals was the greater realism in its locomotives and the superior artwork of the tin-printed rolling stock. The locomotives were based on real prototypes: an LNER Class A4 4-6-2 and LNER Class N2 0-6-2T. The A4 was in LNER blue livery, with valances, and named *Sir Nigel Gresley* and the N2 tank engine was available in LNER black, but also in LMS, SR and GWR (with a GWR safety valve cover).

With this attention to detail, it could not fail to be an instant success, helped by the fact that it hit the market as a complete model railway system with a choice of five electric train sets and five clockwork ones (with two-rail track). There were Gresley-style coaches, including an articulated pair, track points, buffer stops, open wagons, vans and brake vans, as well as transformers and controllers. There were also wooden accessories, including a through station, an island platform, a goods depot, tunnels, signals and a signal box; all in the shops in time for Christmas.

HORNBY 0 GAUGE

With the concentration on the new Dublo system, work on developing the Hornby Series 0 gauge slowed down. A Palethorpe's sausage van was added to the private owner vans.

The choice of train name boards was extended in 1938 and the Metropolitan electric locomotive was upgraded with a 20 V mechanism.

Hornby Dublo wooden station buildings. (Courtesy Vectis Auctions)

The Hornby 0 gauge 'Palethorpes' van. (Courtesy SAS)

1939
THE REST OF THE RANGE

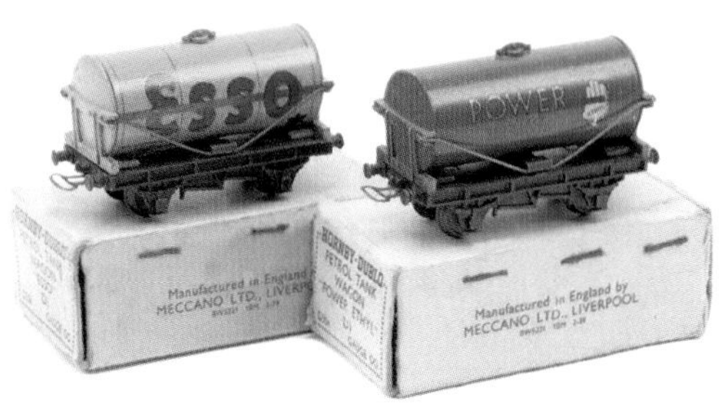

HORNBY DUBLO

The pre-war Dublo range was planned as a complete package, but, arriving late in 1938, it was not possible to get the entire range into the shops before the end of the year.

The remaining items arrived in 1939. These included three tank wagons, four coal wagons, two high-sided open wagons, a horsebox, two cattle trucks as well as two meat vans, a fish van and an LNER bogie brick wagon, which was a miniature version of the 0-gauge model released in 1937. There were also electrically operated points, signals and an isolating rail.

1938-1939

HORNBY-DUBLO TRAINS

THE PERFECT TABLE RAILWAY

Gauge OO

Hornby Dublo reproduction of the first catalogue. (Courtesy M. Wild Collection)

A Dublo clockwork pre-war GWR 0-6-2T. (Courtesy Vectis Auctions)

A Dublo pre-war LMS open goods wagon. (Courtesy Tony Cooper)

A Dublo pre-war LNER high-sided coal wagon. (Courtesy Darren Cooper)

The Dublo pre-war clockwork LNER *Sir Nigel Gresley*. (Courtesy Tony Penn)

The three tank wagons were in the liveries of Esso (buff), Power Ethyl (green) and Royal Daylight (red). For the train sets the open wagon was a five-plank and produced in the liveries of the four companies (as were the vans), but the coal wagons were the LNER and LMS versions with a black plastic moulding dropped inside. The high-sided wagons were seven-planks and were also available in LNER and LMS liveries and there were coal versions of them. The cattle trucks were LMS and GWR, with different side cut-outs, and the horsebox was in LNER teak livery to go with the Gresley coaches. The fish van was also LNER, but the meat vans were LMS and SR. Four different goods brake vans were tooled up so that each set could have the correct design. All the models in the sets were also available separately.

The range of station buildings now included a large city station and engine shed; today these are the hardest to find of the pre-war buildings. They were made for such a short period of time and did not return after the war. The city station came as a kit of parts which included the main building, a train shed with a printed clear roof sheet, standard width central platforms,

The Dublo pre-war city station. (Courtesy Vectis Auctions)

The Dublo pre-war engine shed. (Courtesy Vectis Auctions)

The Dublo pre-war long tunnel. (Courtesy LSK)

half-width side platforms with walls, buffer stops, ramps and advertising panels that plugged into the side openings if required. Its appearance was similar to that of the Trix Many-Ways station and it could be assembled as a terminus or through station. The pre-war buildings were all wooden and painted a cream colour and the roofs were either orange-red or green. With so much going on in the factory in 1938, it seems likely that the job of producing the wooden buildings was given to an outside contractor.

The Hornby Book of Trains for 1939 included a picture of a hand-built *Duchess of Atholl* in the Dublo section.

HORNBY 0 GAUGE

In 1939, there were no new products for the Hornby Series 0-gauge system. Instead there were further deletions.

1930s – A DECADE SUMMARY

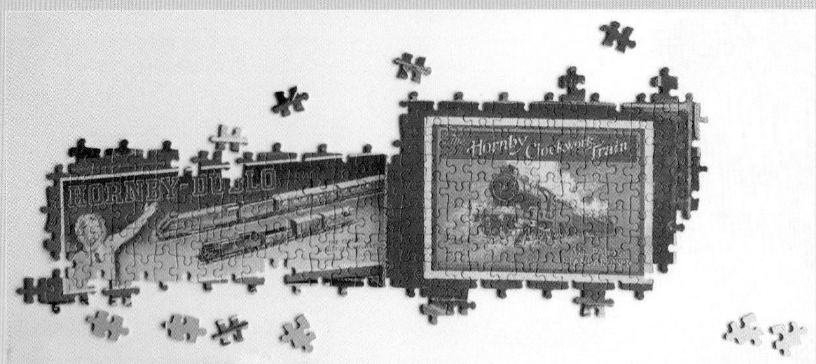

After an explosion of colour in 1933 there was a gradual return to more authentic liveries as the decade progressed. This partly resulted from the success of the No. 2 Special locomotives and the realisation that growing youngsters now wanted realism. The new suburban and mainline bogie coaches of the late 1930s, and the printed tinplate wagons of the same period, quickly changed the appearance of the Hornby Series trains and at the same time indicated the standard the public would expect in the new Hornby Dublo models when they came.

The first Hornby electric train set had arrived in 1925 and the 1930s saw a changeover to 20 V AC and ended with the excellent Dublo 12 V DC system. By the end of the decade Hornby Series was predominantly an electric 0-gauge system with an extensive range of track parts and lineside accessories, many of which had electric lighting. Nearly all the houses in Great Britain now had mains electricity and for those that did not there was still the 6 V system, which could be run off an accumulator, and a clockwork alternative as well. The introduction of the 'Princess Royal' locomotive *Princess Elizabeth* marked the end of the growth of the 0-gauge system and one cannot help but wonder what might have happened if the Second World War had not occurred when it did.

The introduction of an entire table-top railway over a two-year period (1938–39) was a masterpiece of organisation, good design and high quality of engineering. Not only did it take the company into the changing world, but it set a standard that none of Hornby's rivals could attain.

THE HORNBY BOOK OF TRAINS

At its peak, about 100,000 of the books were printed each year and there were also overseas editions. The 1935–36 edition was replaced by a large catalogue that included other products from the factory, but no articles. Hornby Series coverage was reduced to thirty-one pages and the price rose from threepence to ninepence. Sales of the book

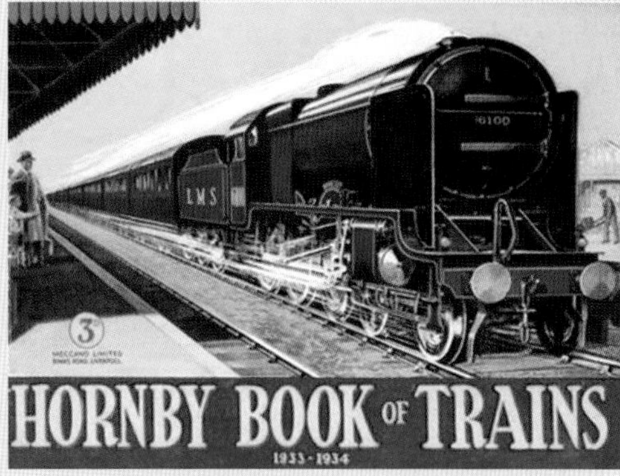

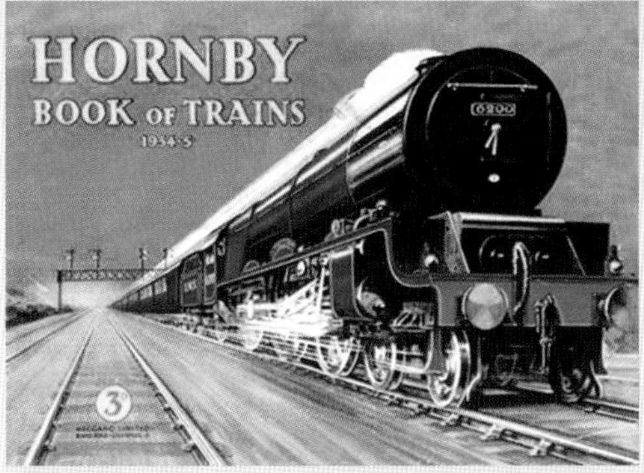

slumped, and one might think that all of this was connected to Ellison Hawks leaving that year.

RIVALS

We should remember that there had always been a gulf between toys for children and models built or bought by engineering enthusiasts. During the inter-war period, in the toy camp in Britain were Chad Valley (established in 1860), Whitanco (since 1912), Wells (1919), Brimtoy (1923), Mettoy (1934), Betal (1938) and others, producing cheap tinplate trains for children. For the adult O-gauge market, on the other hand, there were Bonds (1887), Bassett-Lowke (1898), Leeds Model Company (1912), Mills Brothers (1919), and Exley (1922), for example. Hornby fell between these two groups – originally very much leaning towards the toy market and maintaining a budget range throughout, but gradually taking the top part of its range in the other direction until the Second World War. The move by the public into smaller scales would change the whole picture dramatically.

MODELLED MINIATURES TRAIN SETS

Hornby 0 gauge and Hornby Dublo were not the only trains to come out of the Liverpool factory during the 1930s. There was a series of lead die-cast miniature trains originally sold under the 'Hornby Series' brand. These were intended for children too small to play with Hornby 0 gauge, but who were – it must be hoped – immune to lead poisoning! They were part of the 'Model Miniatures' range and were later sold as 'Dinky Toys'.

The first set (No. 21 Hornby Train Set) arrived in 1932 but was withdrawn in 1934 and replaced by set No. 19 'Mixed Tank Goods Train', probably because the crane wagon was difficult to make. There was the No. 20 'Tank Passenger Train Set', which also arrived in 1934. There were other sets produced, including the well-known No. 16 'Streamlined Train Set' (A4 and coaches) of 1937, which remained in the Dinky Toys range until 1959.

1930s MILESTONES

1930 – Train sets for Canada, new MO and M1 locomotives and sets, further electrification, altered buffer heights and removal of company letters from many wagons.

1931 – Automatic couplings, first No. 0 tinplate vans, new French locomotive, new bodies for 0-4-0 locomotives, Mitropa livery and first 'Modelled Miniatures'.

1932 – First 20 V locomotives, illuminated accessories, countryside sections and British Express set.

1933 – Gaudy wagon colours and M10 complete railway.

1934 – Expansion of 20 V range, simplified lineside accessories and Modelled Miniatures becomes 'Dinky Toys'.

1935 – Suburban bogie coaches, M-series wagons and *Bramham Moor* replaces *Yorkshire*.

1936 – Death of Frank Hornby; Roland Hornby becomes Chairman and No. 0 *Silver Link* released.

1937 – *Princess Elizabeth* and *Eton*, new mainline bogie coaches and Hornby Series now mainly an electric system.

1938 – Launch of Hornby Dublo; Hornby 0-gauge expansion slows.

1939 – Delivery of the rest of the planned Dublo range; last edition of *The Hornby Book of Trains*.

NO. 2 SPECIAL LOCOMOTIVES OF THE 1930s

GWR black 'County Class' *County of Bedford* 20v. (Vectis)

GWR green 'County Class' *County of Bedford* 20v. (Vectis)

LMS Class 2P No. 700 20v. (Vectis)

LMS 'Compound' No. 1185 20V. (Vectis)

LMS 'Compound' No. 1185 Clockwork. (Vectis)

LNER 'Hunt Class' *Bramham Moor* 20v. (LSK)

LNER 'Shire Class' *Yorkshire* clockwork locomotive. (LSK)

SR Class L1 No. 1759 20v. (Vectis)

SR Class L1 No. A759 clockwork locomotive. (Vectis)

1940–44
WAR WORK

Great Britain and France entered the Second World War at 11 am on 3 September 1939. The cost of materials went up, the government imposed a purchase tax and skilled workers moved on to war work. Production of toys finally ceased in 1941. Products remained on sale and price lists were produced until November 1941. In July the same year the repairs department had closed and in January 1942 the exchange service ended. Sales of stock continued, and prices climbed upwards. After September 1943 the sale of metal products was banned by the 'Misc. Goods (Prohibition of Manufacture and Supply) (No. 4) Order' (SRO966). *Meccano Magazine* continued to be published but was a shadow of its former self.

HORNBY DUBLO

In the January 1941 issue of *Meccano Magazine* was an advert for the Hornby Dublo model of an LMS 'Princess Coronation' Class, 6231 *Duchess of Atholl*, but it was later withdrawn, and the model would not be released until after the war.

HORNBY 0 GAUGE

The year 1940 had seen the appropriate introduction of the Pool tank wagon in the Hornby Series, marking the government's requisition of privately owned wagons for the war effort. Throughout the year more and more of the 0-gauge trains were withdrawn from sale as production of them ceased. It seems that during the Second World War some French-made Meccano and Hornby products were released from the French factory with Märklin transfers.

Dublo 'Duchess' advertisement, October 1941. (Courtesy *Meccano Magazine*)

1945

DUSTING OFF THE COBWEBS

The Meccano Ltd. factory at Binns Road, Liverpool. (Source unknown)

Meccano Magazine, December 1945, toy production re-started.

THE MECCANO MAGAZINE

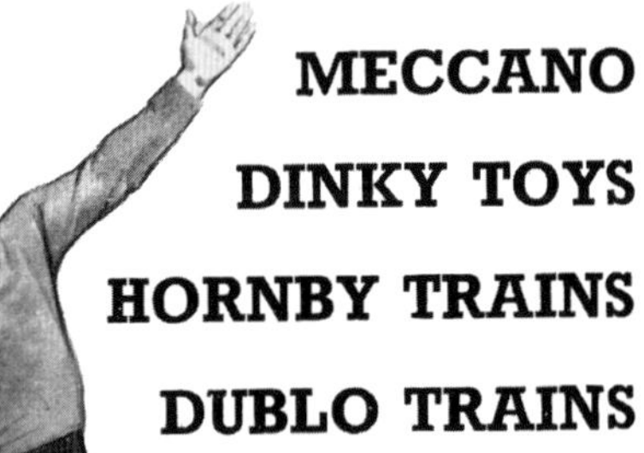

MECCANO

DINKY TOYS

HORNBY TRAINS

DUBLO TRAINS

Here is what you are looking for—
THE FIRST GOOD NEWS.

A limited supply of the smaller Meccano Outfits and a first instalment of Dinky Toys will be ready during December.

Obtainable ONLY from Meccano dealers.

MECCANO LIMITED - BINNS ROAD - LIVERPOOL 13

PUBLISHED BY MECCANO LTD., BINNS ROAD, LIVERPOOL 13, ENGLAND.
Printed by John Waddington Ltd., Leeds and London.

HORNBY TRAINS

Victory in Europe Day (VE Day) was celebrated on Wednesday 8 May 1945 to mark the formal acceptance by the Allies of Nazi Germany's unconditional surrender of its armed forces. The war in the Pacific continued until 2 September 1945 when Japan surrendered.

The return of peace was one thing, but the return of factories to peacetime production was quite another. Installed machinery was for the manufacture of the government's requirements and there were still contracts to complete. Workers in the armed forces needed to be repatriated and new sources of raw materials needed to be found.

The restriction on toy production was lifted and staff at Meccano Ltd. sorted through their tools. Toys were needed for the government's post-war export drive and this was a priority. Also, the company's own priorities were, first, Meccano sets then Dinky Toys and finally trains.

HORNBY 0 GAUGE

It seems that Meccano Ltd. were still thinking that their Hornby Trains were what people wanted most, and that the smaller Hornby Dublo could follow once they had got the 0-gauge back on the market. In late 1945 work was done on drawings to update the Hornby 0-gauge system, which was now referred to as 'Hornby Trains'.

1946
0 GAUGE RETURNS

HORNBY 0 GAUGE

The priority for new Hornby Trains 0-gauge production was the M series, and these became the mainstay of the post-war 0-gauge range. MO goods and passenger sets were the first to arrive in March, with their red or green locomotives. The M1 sets were also produced, with their more detailed red or green locomotives, the Pullman cars carrying the names *Aurelia, Marjorie* or *Viking.* Later in the year, two tank engine sets, No. 101 'Passenger' and No. 201 'Goods', arrived and were available in four different company liveries.

It is said that some pre-war 0-gauge items came out of the Binns Road factory in December 1946 carrying the liveries of all four companies. They may well have been stock left over from before the ban on sales was imposed in 1943.

Finding out which retailers had survived the Second World War was an early task undertaken by the company's only remaining travelling salesman. As early supplies were going to be restricted, pre-war orders were looked at to determine the level of stock allocation that should be made to each retailer when stocks were available. Some retailers, such as Gresham Models in London, had been destroyed during the bombing.

HORNBY DUBLO

A small batch of Dublo models was also available in December 1946, again probably

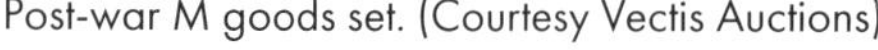
Post-war M goods set. (Courtesy Vectis Auctions)

cobbled together from parts left over when production ceased in 1941.

Sadly, the problem of impurities in alloys was not fully understood before the Second World War and the Mazak used for the castings often contained these. Subsequently it led to the metal expanding on some models, which resulted in twisting, cracking and crumbling of the casting in later years. Consequently, pre-war castings in good condition are hard to find and expensive to buy. By the time production resumed after the war the problem seems to have been dealt with.

ROVEX

In 1946 a company called Rovex Manufacturing was wound up by the Venetzian brothers and a new company, called Rovex Plastics Ltd., was formed by former racing driver Alexander Venetzian. By this act, an acorn had been planted.

THE MECCANO MAGAZINE 29

Club and Branch News

WITH THE SECRETARY

A NEW YEAR TASK

This month I have the pleasure of wishing members of the Guild and the H.R.C. a happy and prosperous New Year. We are making a better start than in any year since 1939, and the prospects are bright as far as the Guild and H.R.C. are concerned. For Clubs and Branches too 1946 should be a year of progress. Old established organisations that have been suspended during the war have begun operations, and efforts are being made in various parts of the country to form new ones.

In this revival the best results will only be attained if all Guild and H.R.C. members do their utmost. Those who are not already members of one of these organisations should look round to see if there is one that they can join, and if not they should get their friends together with the idea of starting one themselves. This is not difficult. All that is wanted is that two or three enthusiasts should begin to meet for model-building or for train operations. Others will soon join them and all will begin to get more and more pleasure from their hobbies. Those who do this have no need to be discouraged if they cannot straightaway form a large Club or Branch, with a well appointed room and an imposing list of meetings. Small Clubs of the friendly type are doing splendid work and I am just as much interested in their activities as I am in the larger organisations.

Whether they join or form a Club or Branch or not, members should remember to write to me often. I am always delighted to hear from them, even if they have nothing particular to say, and I am here to give advice and information to all who are in need of it.

MERIT MEDALLIONS

I want to draw the attention of Leaders of Meccano Clubs to the Merit Medallion, the premier award of the Meccano Guild. This is presented on the recommendation of Leaders to members who show outstanding zeal and merit in Club work. Two Merit Medallions are available in each Session in every Club, and I want Leaders to let me have immediately the names of those whom they think deserving of the award in respect of the first Winter Session, just ended.

PROPOSED CLUBS

TROWELL—Mr. W. Haynes, Moor Farm, Trowell, Notts.

BEXHILL-ON-SEA—Mr. J. Collins, Police Station, Barrack Road, Bexhill-on-Sea.

MORECAMBE—Mr. H. Penberthy, 37, Acre Moss Lane, Morecambe W.E., Lancs.

PUDSEY—Mr. K. Hargreaves, 79, Waterloo Grove, Pudsey, Nr. Leeds.

HAMPTON HILL—Mr. J. E. Brown, 20, St. James's Road, Hampton Hill, Middlesex.

PROPOSED BRANCHES

HOVE—Masters Skelton and Bernardi, 64, St. Aubyns, Hove 3.

BLYTH—Mr. J. Morgan, 12, Maughan Street, Blyth, Northumberland.

The committee of the Perse School, Cambridge, Branch No. 485, Chairman: Mr. D. Smith; G. P. Walker, Vice-Chairman, is in the middle of the back row; and H. Rishbeth, also Vice-Chairman, and D. M. Mann, Secretary, are in the second row. The Branch was incorporated in October 1945. An excellent layout is operated, and Film Shows, Lectures and Visits make up a very attractive programme.

Club Notes

WHITGIFT SCHOOL (CROYDON) M.C.—Owing to war conditions the activities of this Club have been suspended, but a beginning has now been made under the Leadership of Mr. F. Broadbent, B.A., LL.B., with G. E. H. Ellis, Esq., B.A., Headmaster, as President. Officials have been elected at a general meeting and there are so many members that two sections have been formed. Great interest is taken in the "*Meccano Magazine*" and similar literature in the Club Library. A Hornby Train layout is used regularly by each section in turn, the other section meanwhile taking part in competitions. Club roll: 53. *Secretary:* P. Perryman, 10, Buckingham Way, Wallington, Surrey.

WORCESTER COLLEGE FOR THE BLIND M.C.—Keen Model-building activity continues. A Swivelling Crane with a 4 ft. 6 in. jib and a locomotive and tender over 3 ft. in length have been constructed, and competitions in which each member is allowed only a limited number of parts have also been successful. A gratifying feature is that those who joined two or three years ago and are now Seniors are taking part in general Club work, helping and encouraging younger members. Club roll: 21. *Leader:* Mr. R. D. Follett, Worcester College for the Blind, Worcester.

BRANCH NEWS

STUART ROAD (EAST BARNET)—A new start has been made with the election of officials. A shed serves as Branch room, and discussions are being held on the track to be laid down in it. Games meetings also have been held. *Secretary:* T. Loader, 12, Stuart Road, East Barnet, Herts.

SHAWE HALL (FLIXTON)—An excellent Branch room has been secured and the track has been designed and constructed. Ample engine power is available and good operations are carried out at meetings, which are held three times weekly. An excellent Library is available and a Magazine is to be run. Football is played regularly. *Secretary:* C. Chatburn, 11, Porlock Road, Flixton.

This January 1946 MM extract shows the activities of 'The Hornby Railway Company' and the photograph features the author's school branch, which had disbanded by the time he attended the school in the early 1950s.

1947

A NEW DUBLO LOCOMOTIVE

The LMS No. 101 passenger set. (Courtesy LSK)

In March 1946 the first Meccano sets had appeared, and it seems that the first Dinky Toys also arrived in April that year. Supplies were very limited, and I can recall the first Dinky Toy to arrive in our local shop was the Riley saloon car and there was only one colour, dark blue. My brother and I were each bought one before they disappeared. The *Meccano Magazine* advert tells me that it was the new model for July 1947 and so I must have been just four years old – and yet I still remember the excitement of that occasion.

The LNER No. 101 tank passenger set. (Courtesy LSK)

The *Duchess of Atholl*. (Courtesy Vectis Auctions)

HORNBY 0 GAUGE

The 0-gauge train sets released the previous year continued to be available, but only in small quantities. There were no lineside accessories, but there were a few No. 1 wagons used in the sets available separately, including the open wagon with one of the four companies' initials, a timber wagon and a petrol tanker (grey Pool or grey Royal Daylight).

The first post-war Dublo advertisement, December 1947.

HORNBY DUBLO

It was in December 1947 that Hornby Dublo train sets were being advertised again and the advert included a new LMS set containing a model of 'Princess Coronation' Class 6231 *Duchess of Atholl* and two LMS Stanier coaches.

The 'Princess Coronation' (or 'Duchess' as it is more commonly known) was the locomotive model designed before the Second World War and its release was held up when toy production was closed-down. In September 1947 it featured on the cover of *Meccano Magazine*. The LMS Stanier coaches were tin-printed and, unlike the Gresley ones, had the windows cut out and glazed.

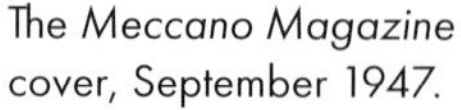

The *Meccano Magazine* cover, September 1947.

A Stanier LMS composite coach.

1948

BACK TO FULL PRODUCTION AND A 00 NEW RIVAL

HORNBY 0 GAUGE

During the year, production returned almost to full capacity and the flow of products progressively increased throughout the year. By October two more Hornby Train sets were being advertised, these being the No. 501 'Passenger Set' and the No. 601 'Goods Set'. The locomotives in these sets were similar to the pre-war No. 1 locomotive. Electric versions of these sets were also made, but it is thought that most went to Australia, along with extra three-rail track, as part of the post-war export drive.

The No. 601 LNER goods set. (Courtesy SAS)

The No. 501 LMS passenger train set. (Courtesy SAS)

The No. 1 post-war GWR goods brake van. (Courtesy SAS)

Wagons and track used in the Hornby sets were now listed as solo items in the pricelists. In fact, nineteen wagons were now listed, and these included the bogie goods van. Some of the enamelled vans now had lamp brackets fitted and two-aspect lamps were available. Examples were the brake vans, a milk traffic van, cattle truck, refrigerator and both goods vans (four-wheel and eight-wheel). Lettering on the vans was to the post-war style with small letters in the lower left-hand corner.

Liveries were also corrected for authenticity, as brown with grey roofs for LMS and bauxite with white roofs for LNER. Southern wagons

The No. 1 post-war GWR flat truck with 'Liverpool Cables' cable drum. (Courtesy Vectis Auctions)

The No. 1 post-war LNER refrigerator van. (Courtesy LSK)

The No. 1 post-war SR flat truck with SR meat container. (Courtesy Vectis Auctions)

were dark brown and GWR ones were dark grey, both with white roofs. The refrigerator vans carried white or cream livery and the body paintwork for most of these wagons now extended to include the solebars. The tipping and hopper wagons were back, as was the flat wagon in company liveries. The latter was also used as the basis for cable drum and container wagons, the containers being in company liveries. A red Shell tank wagon replaced the grey Pool one.

The new pre-war non-corridor bogie and four-wheel coaches in all four liveries were also now available. A post-Second World War Hornby M1 locomotive would feature on a British postage stamp in 2003.

HORNBY DUBLO

The Dublo advert in *Meccano Magazine* throughout the year showed only the train sets with a message that supplies would be limited as the priority was exports.

It is likely that the Hornby Dublo tank engine sets were released first, followed by the new 'Duchess' set. If so, the *Sir Nigel Gresley* Class A4 set would have come out last, due to a need to redesign the body. During the war the real A4 locomotives had the side valances removed to make it easier to maintain them and, to keep the model up to date, a new body without valences was tooled up. The model was also given its new post-war number – '7'. The shortage of packing materials meant that some early Dublo sets were sold in MO series boxes from the 0-gauge range.

The clockwork train sets, locomotives and track were not re-introduced after the Second World War. Another casualty of the war was the LNER articulated coach pair that later would be replaced by an all-third coach. Also not returning were the wooden buildings and the sprung metal couplings.

The Dublo EDG7 goods train set in a Hornby 0 gauge box. (Courtesy Vectis)

ROVEX

Venetzian had borrowed money from Marks and Spencer (M&S) to set up his Rovex toy manufacturing business. M&S were keen to market a battery-powered 00 plastic train set and had asked Venetzian to produce one based on the 4-6-2 locomotive *Princess Elizabeth*. The set was to be 00 gauge using two-rail track and mainly plastic mouldings.

1949
DUBLO IMPROVEMENTS

HORNBY DUBLO

Dublo train set adverts on the back cover of *Meccano Magazine* continued throughout the year – but were for just the six train sets.

An improvement in locomotive design after the war was the introduction of the more powerful new split Alnico magnets. Use of these

A post-war LMS goods van.

A post-war LMS high-sided coal wagon.

A post-war LMS low-sided coal wagon.

in Hornby Dublo locomotives is believed to have started in the summer of 1949, replacing the previously used horseshoe magnets.

It had been decided that all Dublo locomotives and rolling stock manufactured after the war would be fitted with an automatic Simplex coupling designed by Peco and, by 1949, work had already started on an uncoupling rail for the new couplings. In the December issue of *Meccano Magazine* there was a demonstration on how useful they could be during shunting operations.

Sydney Pritchard, Managing Director of Pritchard Engineering Co. (Peco), had himself invented a new coupling that was unobtrusive and allowed stock to couple on contact, and to be separated remotely. The coupling had been patented and was offered to manufacturers. Both Trix Ltd. and Hornby chose to use the design, and, in Hornby's case, it was fitted to all post-war Dublo locomotives and rolling stock. Hornby were happy to pay the fee without question and demonstrated it at the first British Industries Fair after the war. Trix chose not to pay and lost a court case over it.

HORNBY 0 GAUGE

Nationalisation of the railways had taken effect at the start of 1948, but it would be another

The No. 1 post-war GWR cattle wagon. (Courtesy Vectis Auctions)

five years before Hornby caught up with the livery changes. Despite this, the 0-gauge LMS 'Compound' 4-4-0 was seen on the Hornby stand at the 1949 British Industries Fair with 'British Railways' on its tender. The drawings for the No. 2 Special 4-4-0s and 4-4-2T of 1929 were prepared for their re-introduction, but it never

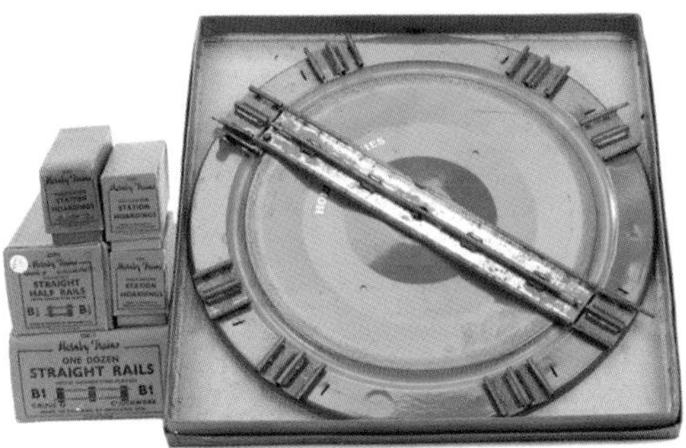

Post-war accessories. (Courtesy Vectis Auctions)

The post-war No. 1 footbridge. (Courtesy LSK)

happened and 1949 marked the highpoint of post-war Hornby 0-gauge development.

A new base for the four-wheel 0-gauge wagons was introduced; this was similar to the 1930 base, but with different embossed detail. Further 0-gauge wagons were added to the lists of products once again available and these included the following bogie wagons: a cattle truck, a trolley wagon, a high capacity wagon, a lumber wagon and a breakdown wagon with crane.

In 1949 the 0-gauge lineside accessories started to appear again, including the single-track level crossing, the footbridge, a water tank, the island platform, a signal box, the platform

The post-war No. 1 Wembley island platform. (Courtesy LSK)

The post-war No. 1 goods depot. (Courtesy Vectis Auctions)

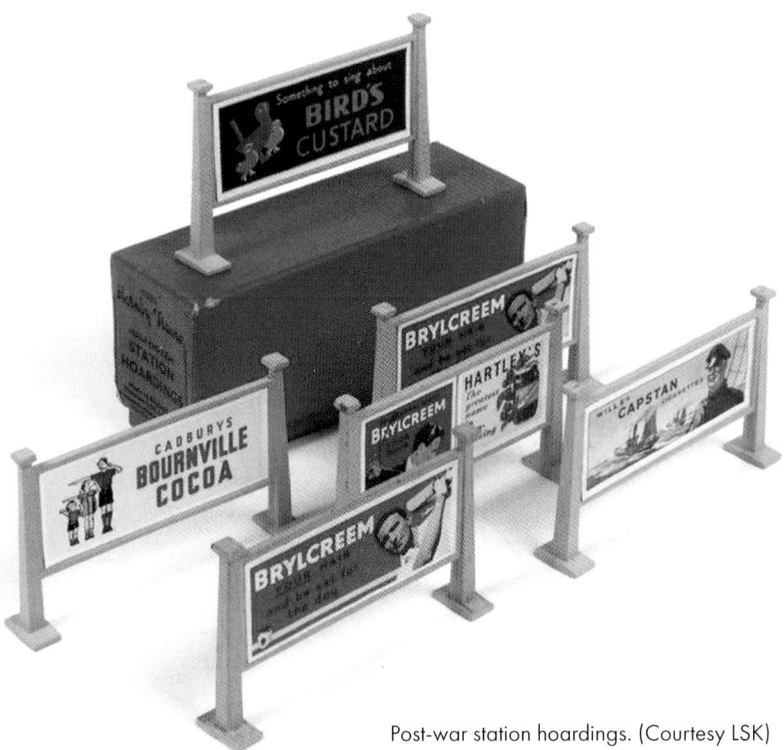

Post-war station hoardings. (Courtesy LSK)

crane, double and single arm signals, a turntable, goods depot and station. Also available were the posters and station hoardings.

The Trackmaster boxed train set. (Courtesy Vectis Auctions)

However, it seemed that 0 gauge was not selling as well as it did before the war and one of the reasons for this was that the market was awash with second-hand 0 gauge being sold by people who had changed to Hornby Dublo before the war. Hornby Trains and Meccano were not advertised at all in *Meccano Magazine* in 1949. The company was now under pressure from the public to develop the Dublo system and yet adverts did not suggest that this was happening.

ROVEX

Needing more space in which to produce the new train set, Rovex Plastics Ltd. had moved to a former brewery in Richmond, Surrey and, during the year, John Doyle joined as works manager. During 1949, Pyramid Toys also launched a train set, but theirs was a clockwork goods train called 'Trackmaster' and this had well proportioned wagon and van bodies moulded in cellulose acetate, which looked realistic.

1940s – A DECADE SUMMARY

Production of most lines continued in 1940 despite the Second World War and was not halted until 1941 when government work required the company's full attention. Lists of goods for sale continued to be published and it was not until September 1943 that sales of metal toys ended by government order.

What would have happened to the 0 gauge if peace had continued in 1940? We will never know, but we can assume from the releases in the late 1940s that Meccano Ltd. thought that Hornby 0 gauge was expected to retain its popularity despite the rise of the smaller scales. On the other hand, why were there no adverts for 0-gauge Hornby Trains in the *Meccano Magazine* throughout 1949? The only products from Meccano Ltd. that were advertised that year were a growing range of Dinky Toys (and the new Supertoys), Dinky Builder sets and Hornby Dublo, with an unchanged advert on the back cover. The only progress reflected in the advertising was with Dinky Toys.

Judging by the order in which the company's products returned to production after VJ Day on 15 August 1945, it is assumed that Hornby Dublo was low down on the list of priorities and certainly behind the 0-gauge Hornby Trains, but was this because Dublo was at the forefront of the company's export drive? For 1948 and 1949, the Hornby Dublo advert on the back cover of *Meccano Magazine* offered only train sets.

By the end of the decade it seems to have been clear to the management that the public were not clamouring for more 0 gauge but were demanding more Hornby Dublo. The 0-gauge No. 2 Special locomotives had been prepared for re-release and some 0-gauge bogie stock appeared briefly, but this quickly disappeared from the catalogue and the locomotives did not materialise. Ironically, in *Meccano Magazine*, Bassett-Lowke were advertising their own red and cream Stanier-style bogie 0-gauge coaches and, judging by the numbers around today, they must have sold a lot of them.

POST-WAR FRENCH PRODUCTION

Unlike the British-made Hornby 0 gauge, it is difficult to distinguish between French sets made before and after the Second World War. Immediately after the war, a list of planned re-introductions was released, but the first proper catalogue for French-made products did not arrive until 1949. The French post-war range continued to expand through the 1950s, more so than the British range, as there was no second smaller gauge system like Dublo produced in the French factory at that time. However, when French Hornby Acho (H0) was introduced in 1960 the French

Hornby 0 gauge was quickly run down. It is worth mentioning that the French Hornby range had a much smaller share of the French model railway market than British Hornby had in the UK.

RIVALS

The chosen priorities which delayed getting Hornby Dublo back on the British market left the way open for rival companies. Like Meccano Ltd., Trix had given preference to getting its construction sets back in the shops, but despite this Trix Twin Railway was back in spasmodic production again in the spring of 1947. Expansion of the range increased quickly, but most went for export. By 1949 a full Trix Twin catalogue was in the shops in Great Britain and some of the first locomotives were in the early British Railways (BR) Express Blue livery – the railways having been nationalised in January 1948. With a hunger for model railways after the war, many customers bought the early post-war Trix train sets just because they were available, along with the accessories with which to expand them.

Meanwhile, a company called Graham Farish Ltd. was looking for ways to put to good use all the new machinery the government had installed in their factory – and chose to produce model railways. The result was the first two-rail 00-scale electric train set in Britain. Pyramid Toys launched a clockwork train set in 1949, but, more important to our story, Rovex Plastics Ltd. was formed in 1946 and in 1950 the company released the Rovex train set. Once the giant Lines Bros. toy group acquired and developed the Rovex system, it would become Hornby Dublo's biggest rival.

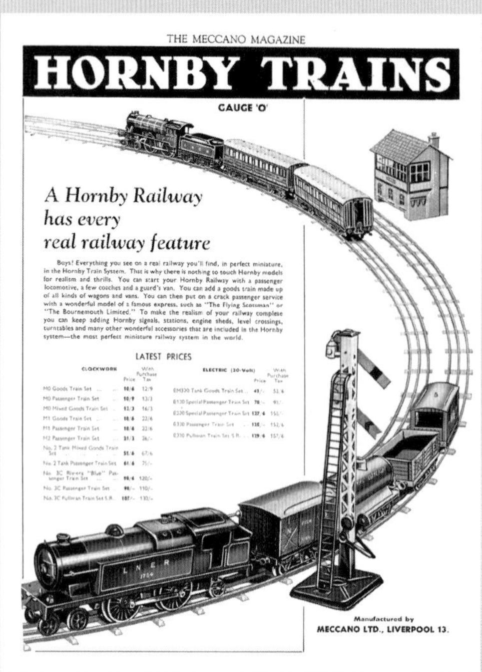

	List Price	Price with Tax
M8 Complete Model Railway	17/3	21/-
M9 Complete Model Railway	21/9	26/6
M10 Complete Model Railway	34/6	42/-
M11 Complete Model Railway	47/-	57/6

MECCANO LTD. - BINNS ROAD - LIVERPOOL 13

THE MECCANO MAGAZINE

VE Day has brought us nearer the time when we shall be able to supply these famous toys.

Our Works, which are still on war production, will change over to our own goods as rapidly as conditions permit—soon, we hope!

So keep looking out for our announcements

MECCANO LIMITED - BINNS ROAD - LIVERPOOL 13

PUBLISHED BY MECCANO LTD., BINNS ROAD, LIVERPOOL 13, ENGLAND
Printed by John Waddington Ltd., Leeds and London

NEW DINKY TOYS
Now ready!
Lagonda Sports Coupe - No. 38c
Jeep - No. 153a
Here are the first of the new Dinky Toys for which you have waited so long. Others are coming soon. Watch our announcements.
LAGONDA SPORTS COUPÉ, No. 38c. This is a fine model of one of the outstanding cars that will soon be familiar on our roads. You will be proud to own this model.
Price 2/9 each (including Tax
JEEP, No. 153a. A wonderfully realistic miniature of the most famous car of the war. On all fronts, in all countries, the Jeep was ready to go anywhere and do anything.
Price 2/6 each (including Tax
Obtainable ONLY from Meccano Dealers
MADE IN ENGLAND BY MECCANO LIMITED

THE MECCANO MAGAZINE
MECCANO
DINKY TOYS
HORNBY TRAINS
DUBLO TRAINS
Meccano Outfits and Dinky Toys are once again in the shops. To prevent disappointment, an early visit to your Meccano dealer is recommended. A further limited quantity of Hornby Trains will be ready before Christmas
Obtainable ONLY from Meccano Dealers
MADE IN ENGLAND BY MECCANO LIMITED LIVERPOOL

THE MECCANO MAGAZINE
NEW DINKY TOYS
Now available!
"Viking" Air Liner
"VIKING" AIR LINER, No. 70c. The new British twin-engined "Vikings" are being used extensively by British European Airways.
Price 2/3 each (including Tax)
"Meteor" Twin Jet Fighter
"METEOR" TWIN JET FIGHTER, No. 70e. This is the first jet aircraft to be included in the Dinky Toys range. The "Meteor" holds the World Absolute Air Speed Record.
Price 1/3 each (including Tax)
"Tempest" II Fighter
"TEMPEST" II FIGHTER, No. 70b. The original of this Hawker fighter is one of the fastest piston-engined machines in service.
Price 1/- each (including Tax)
Avro "York" Air Liner
AVRO "YORK" AIR LINER, No. 70a. A striking model of one of the latest British transport aircraft. "Yorks" are in service with the B.O.A.C.
Price 3/9 each (including Tax)
Lagonda Sports Coupé
LAGONDA SPORTS COUPÉ, No. 38c. This is a fine model of one of the outstanding cars that will soon be familiar on our roads.
Price 2/9 each (including Tax)
JAGUAR SPORTS CAR, No. 38f. Here is a model that will make a special appeal to all sports car enthusiasts.
Price 2/9 each (including Tax)
JEEP, No. 153a. A wonderfully realistic miniature of the most famous car of the war. On all fronts, in all countries, the Jeep was ready to do anything.
Price 2/6 each (including Tax)
ARMSTRONG SIDDELEY COUPE, No. 38e. A handsome model that reproduces splendidly the fine lines and modern style of an attractive post-war car.
Price 2/6 each (including Tax)
MADE IN ENGLAND BY MECCANO LIMITED
Jaguar Sports Car
Jeep
Armstrong Siddeley Coupé

THE MECCANO MAGAZINE

Dinky SUPERTOYS

A Fine New Series of Models

THIS month we announce the arrival of the first of our new products—the Dinky SUPERTOYS. These fine models have been given this name because they are die-cast miniatures similar in general style to our famous Dinky Toys, but much larger.

Take for instance the Foden Wagon shown on the right. The overall measurements of the actual wagon are 29 ft. 7½ in. long and 7 ft. 10 in. high; the corresponding measurements of the SUPERTOY model are 7½ in. and 1⅞ in. The same dimensions of the Guy Lorry are 20 ft. 1½ in. and 7 ft. ¾ in.; those of the SUPERTOY are 5¼ in. and 1¼ in.

These big SUPERTOYS are very striking in appearance. Their size alone is impressive, and the great amount of accurate detail that has been included in them makes them wonderfully realistic. The Foden Wagon and the Guy Lorry illustrate these features well. They have the same distinctive appearance as their prototypes, to which the roomy cab in a forward position contributes greatly. The front is faithfully reproduced, with the chromium-plated radiator grille flanked by the two headlights. On the near side of the chassis, tucked under the body, is a miniature of the tank, and there is even the spare wheel, bolted in its correct place under the body at the rear. The bodywork is equally realistic. Two types are available, one with head, side and tail boards, the other a flat truck.

Equally attractive is the fine model of the famous Short "Shetland" Flying Boat illustrated at the foot of this page. This will be welcomed by all who are interested in aircraft. The "Shetland" is the largest British flying boat ever built, and its general appearance, with its stepped hull, large wing span and four engines, is admirably reproduced in this striking model.

Dinky Supertoys No. 501 Foden Diesel 8-wheel Wagon.

Dinky Supertoys No. 502 Foden Flat Truck.

Dinky Supertoys No. 511 Guy 4-ton Lorry.

Dinky Supertoys No. 512 Guy Flat Truck

Dinky Supertoys No. 701 "Shetland" Flying Boat.

1940s MILESTONES

1940 – Production reduced; 0-gauge 'Pool' tank wagon released.

1941 – Production ceased for the rest of the war.

1943 – Sale of metal toys stopped by government order.

1945 – End of the war and work on drawings started.

1946 – First post-war Dinky Toys, first post-war 0-gauge train sets and Meccano sets.

1947 – Dublo sets advertised with new coupling and new locomotive, but initially went for export.

1948 – Dublo sets on sale; more 0-gauge train sets and more authentic liveries on re-issued 0-gauge wagons.

1949 – Much more of the 0-gauge wagon range and several lineside accessories available.

OVERSEAS WAGONS OF THE 1940s

Argentine FCCA wagon. (Vectis)

Argentine FCCA hopper wagon. (Vectis)

Argentine FCO wagon. (Vectis)

Argentine FCS wagon. (Vectis)

Danish DSB wagon. (Vectis)

Danish DSB pair. (Vectis)

French ECO Essence wagon. (Vectis)

French ETAT wagon. (Vectis)

French EST wagon. (LSK)

French ETAT Citerne. (Vectis)

French Fyffes wagon. (Vectis)

French Nord wagon. (Vectis)

French PLM wagon. (LSK)

French PLM wagon. (Vectis)

South African SAR pair. (Vectis)

1950
DUBLO ALUMINIUM BUILDINGS

The outbreak of the Korean War in June 1950 was about to bring renewed restrictions on the use of non-ferrous metals (as used in electric motors) and other materials.

HORNBY DUBLO

At the start of 1950 there were no Dublo adverts at all in *Meccano Magazine,* suggesting that there

The D1 signal cabin and the D1 footbridge. (Courtesy Darren Cooper)

The D1 through station and the D1 island platform. (Courtesy Darren Cooper)

were no stocks available. Despite this, in the February issue, the Dublo article concerned the use of the isolating rail and the March article featured a water crane. The June article showed us the footbridge for the first time, but still no advert.

It was in September that things began to move again with the release of three aluminium buildings: the through station, the island platform and the signal box. These were painted cream with orange roofs. Before the war the buildings were made of wood and they had featured in the Dublo articles right up to the month before. From the September issue of *Meccano Magazine,* the new buildings were advertised on the back cover.

HORNBY 0 GAUGE

There was a sharp rise in prices and a reduction in the list of items available in the 0-gauge range. Already the bogie coaches and several of

D1 water crane. (Darren Cooper)

the lineside accessories were no longer listed, but a silver Esso tank wagon replaced the red Shell one.

ROVEX

The first Rovex train sets were delivered to Marks & Spencer in time for Christmas. The motor used in the locomotive had been developed by Zenith, a company recently set up by ex-RAF engineer, John Hefford. To secure the source, Rovex bought Zenith and Hefford was put in charge of the motor department.

The Rovex *Princess Elizabeth* train set. (Courtesy SAS)

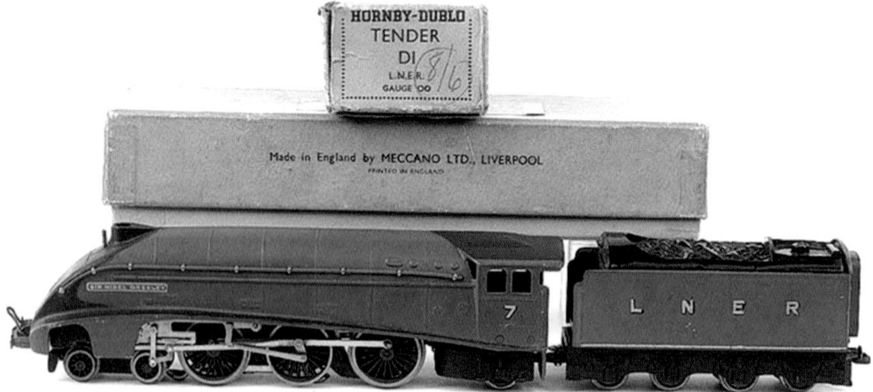

The Dublo EDL1 post-war LNER 4-6-2 A4 Class No. *7 Sir Nigel Gresley*.

The Dublo EDG7 post-war LNER goods train set.

1951

METAL RESTRICTIONS BITE

The material shortages caused by the Korean War continued to get worse. Nickel, brass and Mazac were the most affected and a factory Meccano Ltd. had at Speke was closed until October 1953. Lead, instead of Mazac, was used for some castings to get around the problem. Parts with a black 'Brunofix' finish instead of nickel date from this period.

HORNBY DUBLO

Owing to metal shortages there were no new products for Hornby Dublo.

HORNBY 0 GAUGE

The metal shortages also resulted in the change to plastic for 0-gauge rolling stock wheels instead of tinplate; plastic continued to be used from then on as it was cheaper. At some stage, plastic wheels were being bought in from Lines Bros. and these are clearly marked with 'Tri-ang' on the back of each wheel.

ROVEX

A large Rovex layout was displayed at the 1951 British Industries Fair to try and attract export business. Lines Bros. Ltd. wanted to get into the model railways business and were looking for a company to buy. They found Rovex with a train set that had problems and needed money to sort them out. Lines Bros. bought Rovex in October 1951, promoted Doyle to Managing Director and installed Richard Lines to represent the interests of Lines Bros. In need of a goods train, Rovex also bought the tools of the Trackmaster set and the plastic-bodied wagons gave birth to a whole range of new wagons, which would one day carry the Hornby name.

The Rovex *Princess Elizabeth.* (Courtesy Bob Leggett)

1952
MORE SHORTAGES

HORNBY DUBLO

The year 1952 was another poor year for Hornby Dublo due to the Korean War. In February, insulating tabs to isolate sections of track were available and, in April, 00-scale painted metal figures returned. The goods yard loading gauge became available and, in September, the electric points were again in the shops. October brought the steel re-railer and November the electrically operated signals.

With the government pressing industry to export during those early post-war years and with some surplus *Duchess of Atholl* bodies left over when the tooling was being adapted ready for the launch of *Duchess of Montrose*, a black Pacific locomotive in Canadian Pacific livery was designed with a lamp in the centre of the smokebox door and a cowcatcher attached to the front. However, it would not be until five years later that two Canadian train sets would be released. One was a passenger set and the other a freight set, but both contained the locomotive designed in 1952. The coaches and wagons were standard British ones, excepting the caboose on the freight train, which was a black LMS guards van with an observation box on the roof. This was to have been followed up with a full range of Canadian vehicles, for which research was done, but sales of the sets were poor and the project was dropped.

The Dublo Canadian Pacific loco made from the 'Duchess' tooling. (Courtesy Tony Cooper)

Dinky Toys 053 passengers. (Courtesy LSK)

The Dublo D1 Canadian Pacific caboose. (Courtesy Tony Cooper)

HORNBY 0 GAUGE

The situation with shortages and rising prices continued into 1952. Mazac became more plentiful and the Dinky 0-scale railway figures returned, but with two of the staff sets reduced in size with one figure missing. The finish was also not as good as on pre-war sets. The four M series wagons also reappeared but, apart from the GWR milk traffic van, the GWR- and SR-liveried wagons disappeared.

ROVEX

The design problems were overcome and the Rovex train set was re-launched as 'Tri-ang Railways' in May 1952, at the British Industries Fair. Work immediately started on expanding the system. The red and yellow packaging and an 'R' prefix for catalogue numbers, found on Hornby models today, date from this time.

Early Tri-ang Railways dark red and yellow packaging and 'R' number.

1953
DUBLO BR LIVERIES

HORNBY DUBLO

The change to BR liveries for the Dublo system had arrived at last and was advertised in the April issue of *Meccano Magazine*. Although welcomed at the time, because these were the changes boys were seeing on the real railways, actually it reduced choice. This was an advantage to the factory, but not necessarily to the public. Instead of wagons in four different liveries, now there would be only one. Likewise, the four goods train sets were replaced by a single one in BR livery, the locomotive being the Class N2 tank in gloss

The BR goods train set. (Courtesy LSK)

The BR 0-6-2T Class N2. (Courtesy LSK)

black with early BR decals and numbered 69657. However, the goods sets had an addition in the form of a tank wagon, most likely the attractive red Esso Royal Daylight.

The LMS 6231 *Duchess of Atholl* was replaced by a gloss green 46232 *Duchess of Montrose*, and LNER 7 *Sir Nigel Gresley* was replaced by gloss green 60016 *Silver King*. As the BR livery was late in arriving, we missed out on the BR Express blue, which looked so good with the early red and cream coaches. The two glazed LMS Stanier coaches were now in BR red and cream, as too were the LNER Gresley composite and brake third coaches, still with printed windows.

It was for Christmas 1953 that I received my first Hornby Dublo set. This was the LMS goods set and, as obsolete stock, it was probably bought at a reduced price. Father Christmas could not afford to waste money! It would have been bought at Eden Lilly's in Cambridge, as they were the local Meccano agent. Our odd mix of second-hand Hornby 0 gauge had been

The D11 BR Gresley coaches. (Courtesy Darren Cooper)

The EDL11 BR *Silver King*. (Courtesy Darren Cooper)

The EDP12 BR 'Duchess' passenger train set. (Courtesy Vectis Auctions)

The EDL12 BR *Duchess of Montrose*. (Courtesy Darren Cooper)

boxed up and sold through the local paper. Father Christmas pocketed the money and some lucky person got a blue Caledonian 0-4-0.

In the Dublo goods wagon range, the five-plank and seven-plank wagons were BR grey, and the goods van and ex-LMS and ex-LNER brake vans were brown. The Esso tank wagon was now coloured silver and the red Royal Daylight tank wagon now carried additional Esso branding. The change to the post-war brick wagon was barely noticeable, but it gained an 'E' in front of its number and the chassis mostly turned black.

From mid-summer 1953 there was a string of new Dublo introductions, including the first of the die-cast bodied wagons consisting of the bogie bolster wagon, which had been planned before the war, and the steel mineral wagon. Also new were the isolating switch points, the junction signal (including the electric version), large radius curves and the level crossing.

A D2 BR high-sided coal wagon.

A D2 16-ton BR mineral wagon.

HORNBY 0 GAUGE

A revised version of the 0-gauge junction signal appeared. The posts were shorter and were plain instead of latticed; this had also previously applied to other signals re-introduced. The tank wagon livery changed again, this time to National Benzole.

A D1 BR bogie bolster wagon. (Courtesy Hattons)

ROVEX

Rovex Plastics Ltd. was renamed 'Rovex Scale Models Ltd.' An ex-LMS 'Jinty' 0-6-0T was the first new Tri-ang locomotive, but more importantly its chassis was used to develop three more 0-6-0 locomotives plus a 2-6-2 tank engine, thus quickly expanding choice at low cost. Five electric and two clockwork sets were already available.

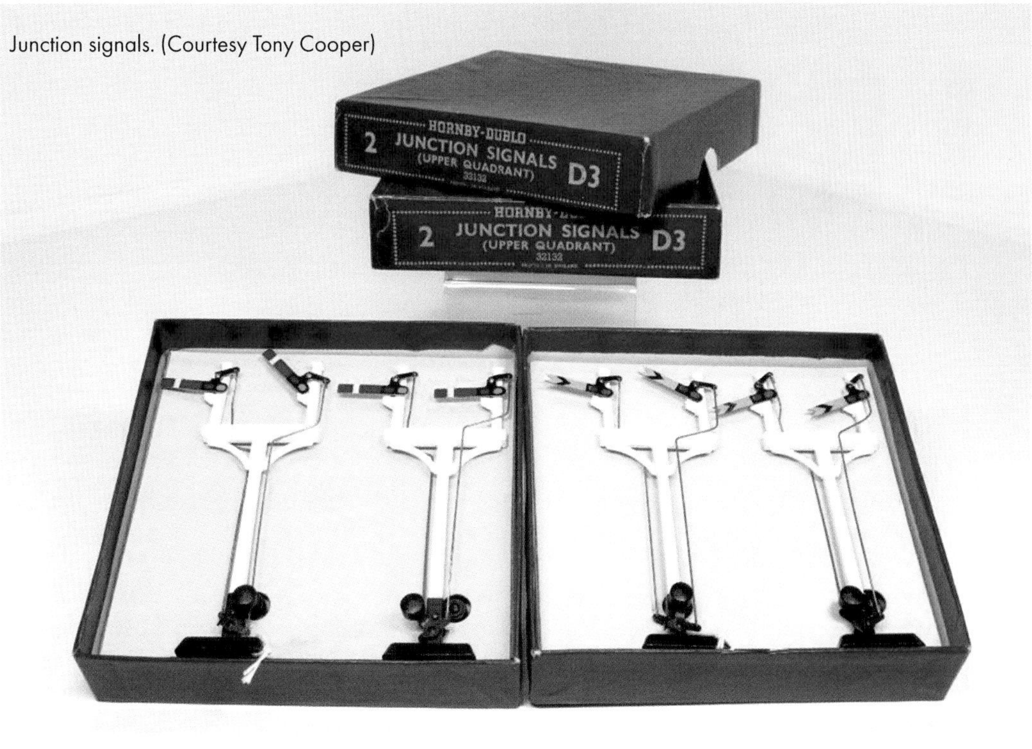

Junction signals. (Courtesy Tony Cooper)

1954

DUBLO 2-6-4T AND 0 GAUGE BR LIVERIES

A BR horsebox.

A BR meat van.

HORNBY DUBLO

More of the Dublo wagons appeared in BR livery during the year and these included the fish van in brown; both meat vans were replaced by a white one. The BR horsebox was maroon, and the green Power Ethyl wagon was re-issued as just 'Power'. It is thought that the replacement for the GWR and LMS cattle trucks was later in arriving and when it did it was brown.

The big news of 1954 was the arrival in October of the first completely new post-war locomotive and, with the change to BR liveries, appropriately the choice was the BR standard Class 4MT large tank engine. The design, by Robert Riddles, was based on the LMS Stanier and Fairburn 2-6-4Ts. They were built at Derby and Doncaster works, but most were built at Brighton and first made their appearance in 1951. Having owned several examples of this model over the years, I found it to be the best runner in the Dublo fleet and I understand that the company only ever had six returned with serious defects.

A BR fish van.

A particular value of the subject chosen was its mixed traffic classification, which led the company to release a pair of non-corridor ('suburban') coaches to go with it as well. These were tin-printed

The BR 2-6-4T 'Standard' Class 4MT. (Courtesy LSK)

The D13 BR suburban coaches. (Courtesy LSK)

The D1 BR cable drum wagon. (Courtesy Hattons)

and initially had printed windows. They consisted of a first/third composite and a brake third.

Other new arrivals were the die-cast low-sided wagon in BR brown, which was also available as a grey wagon with a cable drum load. Also included this year were the left-hand and right-hand diamond crossings.

HORNBY 0 GAUGE

BR liveries began to appear in the Hornby Trains range, starting with the MO locomotive being replaced by the No. 20 locomotive in BR lined green livery, with early decals on the tender. The wagon in the set was now in

Hornby 0 Gauge No. 20 BR 0-4-0 clockwork loco. (Courtesy LSK)

Hornby 0 Gauge No. 20 goods train set. (Courtesy LSK)

BR grey and the coach in BR red and cream. At this time 1-ft radius curves replaced the 9-in. radius ones in the cheap sets.

Next came the more up-market No. 40 tank goods set and the No. 41 tank passenger set which replaced the No. 101 and No. 201 sets – the locomotives both being in BR lined black livery. The No. 41 set coaches were a four-wheeled suburban coach and a full brake in BR red, and the wagon in the goods set was now BR grey.

Last to come were the replacements for the No. 501 and No. 601 train sets and these were No. 50 and No. 51. The No. 50 locomotive was in enamelled BR lined black and the No. 51 in enamelled BR lined green.

Hornby 0 Gauge No. 41 BR passenger train set. (Courtesy Vectis)

Hornby 0 Gauge No. 50 BR goods train set. (Courtesy Vectis)

The new Rovex factory, Margate, first phase. (Courtesy Lines)

The No. 51 four-wheeled coaches were a main line composite and a full brake both in red and cream.

Many wagons were now in BR livery, with a mixture of number prefixes, including some with 'B', indicating that they had been built after nationalisation.

ROVEX

The building of a modern highly efficient factory was completed for Rovex at Margate and the company moved in during the summer. A range of models called 'Transcontinental', mainly for export to North America, was released. The first model made at the Margate factory was a girder bridge.

1955
CHANGES ON THE REAL RAILWAYS

The British Railways 1955 Modernisation Plan proposed a major shake-up of BR with the move away from steam traction towards diesel and electric power. This would influence the choice of subjects modelled in the years ahead, but at the time few railway enthusiasts showed much interest in anything other than steam traction. Steam outline locomotives would dominate Hornby's locomotive stable for many more years and it would be rail enthusiasts born into the diesel age who would have the greatest influence in the years to come.

It was around 1955 that Meccano Ltd. were considering introducing an S-gauge system.

A buffer stop.

A 'Vacuum' tank wagon.

The BR well wagon.

Hornby 0 Gauge No. 3 station with orange roof. (Courtesy LSK)

The gauge would have been 22 mm, half-way between 0 and 00 in scale, but wisely the idea was abandoned. Palitoy had produced an S-gauge set as early as 1950 and, although it sold quite well, the scale did not catch on in the UK. It was, however, more successful in America.

HORNBY DUBLO

New Dublo products referred to or advertised in 1955 were an electric uncoupling rail, a book of Hornby Dublo layouts, the buffer stop, and two new tank wagons. The latter were the red Vacuum and yellow Shell Lubricating Oil. In November the advert for the die-cast-bodied 40-ton bogie well wagon appeared in *Meccano Magazine*.

HORNBY 0 GAUGE

The National Benzole tanker was replaced by a yellow Shell Lubricating Oil and a green Manchester Oil Refinery. A flat wagon with a white insulated meat container was also added (the furniture container wagon already existed in the range of BR wagons). There was a change in the colour of the roofs of station buildings, which had orange tiles from 1955 onwards, and the name on the island platform changed to 'Trent'.

ROVEX

Rovex released their first retail catalogue and Lines Bros. started manufacturing Tri-ang Railways train sets in South Africa.

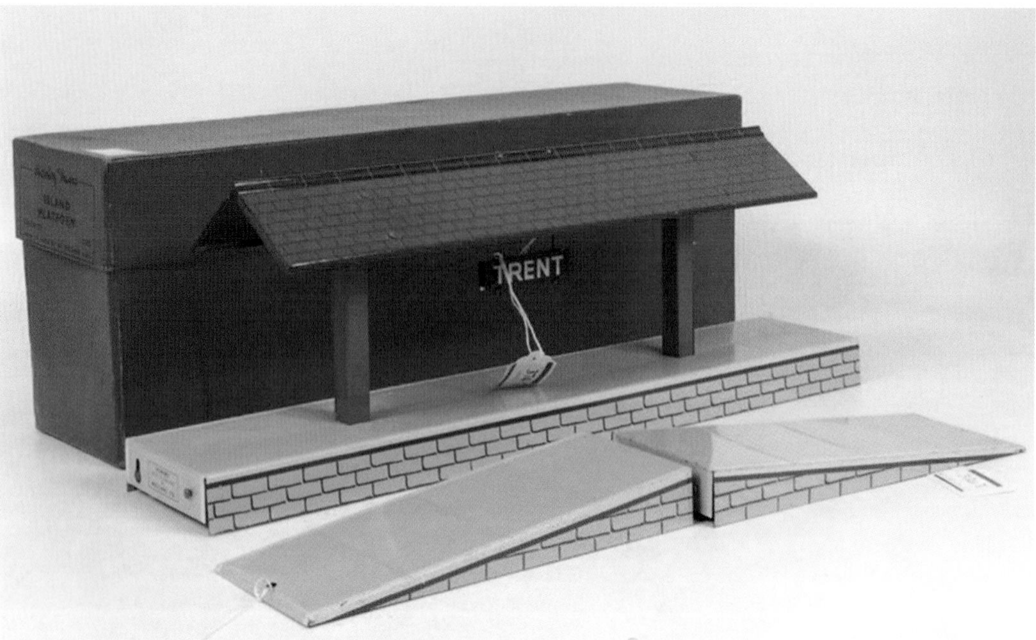

Hornby 0 Gauge 'Trent' island platform. (Courtesy LSK)

The Tri-ang Lines factory in South Africa. (Courtesy Lines)

1956
DUBLO LONG WHEELBASE WAGONS

In June BR started using a new logo on its locomotives. The old logo had a lion riding astride a wheel while the new one showed a lion holding a wheel. It has been said that this symbolised the change from the railways carrying the British public to the British public carrying the railways. This change was picked up by Meccano Ltd. and applied to its locomotives. BR originally had the lion facing forwards on both sides of the locomotive or tender, but that meant that on one side of the locomotive the logo was incorrect. Under pressure from the College of Heralds, BR corrected this around 1960 and Meccano Ltd. followed suit with their models.

A D1 13-ton low-sided wagon with 'Insul-meat' container.

A D1 BR (ex-GWR) goods brake van.

The D1 through station platform extension. (Courtesy Darren Cooper)

HORNBY DUBLO

This year saw the arrival of the Dublo platform extensions for both the through station and the island platform, and two containers for the low-sided wagon. These containers were blocks of wood covered with printed paper. One was the maroon furniture type and the other was the white insulated container. It also saw the return of the former GWR brake van, now in BR grey livery.

The Gresley type coaches were deleted during the year and in the *Silver King* sets they were replaced by the red and cream Stanier

The D14 BR suburban coaches with glazed windows. (Courtesy Tony Cooper)

ones. Having released the new non-corridor coaches with printed windows two years earlier, the company had second thoughts and in September 1956 released them with cut-out glazed windows. Neither early nor late types had coach numbers.

Two new Dublo tinplate wagons arrived in November, both of which used a longer five-inch wheelbase. They were the open 'Tube' wagon and the ex-GWR long wheelbase van,

Dublo D1 BR long van.

Dublo D1 BR 'Tube' wagon.

Dublo BR double bolster wagon. (Courtesy Hattons)

both in brown. A third long wheelbase wagon was added in December and that was the grey die-cast double bolster wagon.

HORNBY 0 GAUGE

In 1956 the M series train sets were replaced by No. 30 (goods) and No. 31 (passenger) sets and both had a new style of locomotive. Gone was the American-style single body pressing and instead it had a proper cab and a redesigned tender. The M1 mechanism was retained, but with cast rods. The train set's tin-printed open wagon and goods van were new and smaller than the main range of wagons, while the red and cream four-wheeled No. 31 coach came in composite and brake third versions. The cable drum and both containers could now be bought on their own.

ROVEX

Tri-ang Railways production started up in New Zealand and Rovex changed from moulding in cellulose acetate to using polystyrene. The catalogue went full-colour and showed a cattle wagon which would still be in production in the twenty-first century. However, the black

The Hornby 0 Gauge No. 31 BR passenger train set. (Courtesy LSK)

Tri-ang Railways R44 passing contact lever switch, also introduced in 1956, is still made by Hornby Hobbies today as the R044 switch!

The Tri-ang Lines factory in New Zealand. (Courtesy Lines)

1957
BRISTOL CASTLE AND NO. 50 WAGONS

HORNBY DUBLO

The next locomotive to arrive is probably the one which created the most excitement and praise of any Dublo model and the one which seems to create the most nostalgia. It was the GWR 'Castle' Class 7013 *Bristol Castle*. A hand-made model of the subject had been exhibited at a trade fair early in the year. Particularly praised were the rivet detail on the tender and the copper-capped chimney. It was the first Dublo locomotive to carry the new BR decals from the date of its introduction. The real engines had been designed by Charles Collett as a development of the 'Star' Class and were built between 1923 and 1950.

Also arriving in 1957 were the turntable (an electric version did not get beyond the drawing office), the girder bridge and the travelling post office (TPO) set.

The D1 girder bridge. (Courtesy Darren Cooper)

The *Bristol Castle* locomotive. (Courtesy Vectis Auctions)

The D1 travelling post office ('TPO') boxed set. (Courtesy LSK)

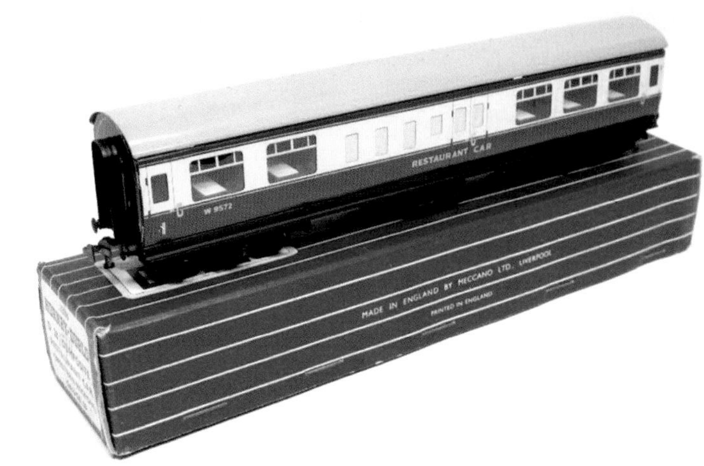

A D20 Stanier coach in Western Region (WR) brown and cream livery. (Courtesy Tony Cooper)

Dublo Dinky Toys. (Courtesy SAS)

With the livery changes taking place at the time on British Railways, in July the Stanier coaches were released in maroon livery and these replaced the red and cream ones in the *Duchess of Montrose* train set. It was announced that the earlier livery would be dropped. The need only to produce models reflecting the current practice seems strange to us today when we can buy models in almost any livery, including those of the pre-grouping companies. The coaches were also released in brown and cream for *Bristol Castle,* which had arrived in September. The coach bonanza did not end there as a restaurant car was added in brown and cream as well as red and cream – both fitted with plastic wheels!

The first three Dublo Dinky Toys arrived in December, these being the Austin lorry, the Morris pickup and the Bedford flat truck that could also carry the Dublo container.

One introduction in 1957, which may have been an indicator that Dublo was feeling the effects of competition, was the EDG16 train set. This was cheaper than any of the others, although still using standard parts. The magazine referred to its '*favourable price*' and declared that this was an attempt at attracting more beginners to the Hornby Dublo system. The Canadian CPR set was now at last ready for release.

Dublo Dinky Toy production.

The EDG16 goods train set. (Courtesy LSK)

The Canadian Pacific Railway (CPR) set. (Courtesy Barry Potter)

Hornby 0 Gauge No. 50 wagons. (Courtesy LSK)

HORNBY 0 GAUGE

Meccano Ltd. completely retooled most of the 0-gauge wagon range in 1957 and these were listed as the No. 50 wagons. They were attractively tin-printed and, for the first time, had dummy brake hand-levers, a feature which makes them easy to identify. Many have questioned why money was spent on a system that was on its way out. Sales of 0 gauge were falling and there were other financial pressures on the company. From then on, the only news of Hornby Trains was about deletions.

Following the death of George Jones, Ernest Beardsley had stepped up to the position of Managing Director and, although an excellent engineer, he was not necessarily the right person to be leading the company. It is thought that Jones would have put all his energy into a two-rail 00 system and given Tri-ang Railways a run for its money.

When I was researching my first book, I discovered that things were already going wrong at Binns Road by the mid-1950s. The factory had not been modernised and was overstaffed. I understand that salesmen at shows seemed complacent, trusting in the company's reputation to protect it from market forces. In contrast, the Tri-ang Railways models were produced in a modern semi-automated factory, with lower overheads and producing a cheaper two-rail system with plastic mouldings providing finer detail. When Meccano Ltd. made the much-needed changes it was too little and far too late.

ROVEX

Rovex, expanding fast, added an electric turntable and operating hopper wagon set to increase play value; also, a Southern 4-SUB EMU. Under pressure from Lines Bros., Tri-ang Railways TT was launched. Lines Bros. opened their third overseas Tri-ang Railways production line at Moldex Ltd. in Australia.

The Tri-ang Moldex factory in Australia. (Courtesy Lines)

1958
DUBLO PLASTIC WAGONS

HORNBY DUBLO

The arrival of first Hornby Dublo plastic wagons was an exciting time for railway modellers in 1958. The first subject was the grain wagon, an excellent choice and this is still in production today in the Dapol range. I recall seeing it in the local model shop window on my way back from school and knew I had to have one. Changing from the limitations of tin-printed wagons, the Hornby Dublo grain wagon really showed what could be done with polystyrene.

Meccano Ltd. were determined that their plastic range would be better than any others on the market, but this came at a price. They employed one of the best tool-making companies in Great Britain to make the moulds and they were expensive. The grain wagon was certainly more accurate than the Tri-ang version, which came out the same year, and the Dublo one instantly became a best seller. However, the Tri-ang one would appeal to a younger market as it had opening top hatches and a gravity unloading mechanism.

This does raise a question: 'If Meccano Ltd. had abandoned its 0 gauge and its Dublo three-rail tinplate trains and concentrated on a quality two-rail 00 system for enthusiasts, could it have survived?' Perhaps not, as it was not just the railways which were under attack. Corgi, Spot-on

The SD6 grain wagon.

and Matchbox die-cast ranges were competing with Dinky Toys while Lego and other plastic constructor systems were taking business away from Meccano. Before the Second World War, Meccano Ltd. had been reasonably free of competitors but by the 1950s things were very different. People had more money to spend on toys for their children and many new toy firms had sprung up to help them spend it. Once the UK joined the European Economic Community (EEC) in January 1973 it exposed itself even more to the toy manufacturers in continental Europe.

Dublo SD6 'Mica B' refrigerator van. (Courtesy Hattons)

Dublo SD6 16-ton mineral wagon.

Dublo SD6 ex-LMS brake van. (Courtesy Hattons)

The SD6 'Saxa Salt' van.

Dublo SD6 five-plank orange open wagon.

The new plastic-bodied wagons were released at the rate of approximately one per month and in 1958 we received an 8-ton cattle wagon, steel goods wagon, ventilated van, 13-ton five-plank open wagon, ex-GWR brake van, 16-ton steel mineral wagon, 'Mica B' refrigerator van, ex-LMS brake van, UGB sand wagon, five-plank coal wagon and the Saxa Salt van. There were also new train sets incorporating the new wagons.

With a growing range of much-improved wagons a freight locomotive was needed, and the subject chosen was the former LMS Stanier 8F 2-8-0. This was a heavy freight locomotive and adopted by the government during the war as a standard locomotive, producing many of them for the war effort. The model was advertised in August and, by December, a second new locomotive had arrived. This was the first Dublo diesel and the first

Dublo SD6 BR 5-plank wagon.

The L30 Bo-Bo Class 20 diesel. (Courtesy Vectis Auctions)

Coloured light signals. (Courtesy Ebay)

Dublo SD6 ex-LNER steel open wagon.

The LMS 8F. (Courtesy Vectis Auctions)

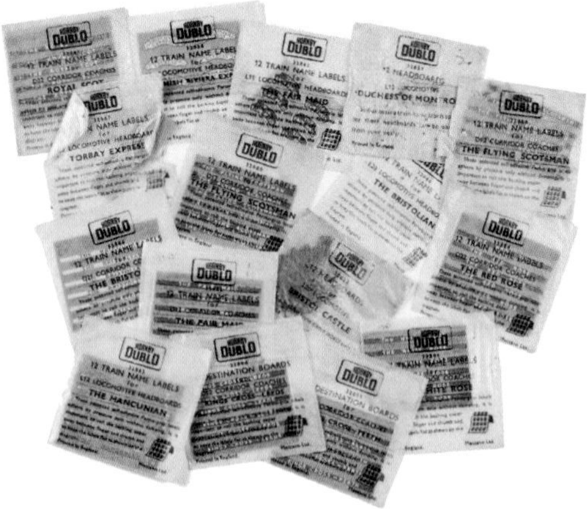

Headboards and train labels. (Courtesy SAS)

Dublo locomotive to have a polystyrene moulded body. It was an English Electric 1000 bhp Bo-Bo Type 1, which would later become the Class 20.

Other additions during the year were colour light signals, three more Dublo Dinkies – a van, Singer Roadster and Ford Prefect – and headboards and coach boards, the former being featured in the catalogue cover illustration. During the year the exchange scheme was re-introduced for the first time since the war, possibly in readiness for an announcement the following year.

ROVEX

Rovex now offered a choice of fourteen locomotives and multiple units, plus twenty-three coaches and thirty-two wagons as well as a large range of lineside accessories. Very popular was a new Met-Cam DMU. Open-base Series 3 track was launched during the year and Rovex started fitting tension-lock couplings. These would become the British standard 00 coupling.

1959
DUBLO 2-RAIL

HORNBY DUBLO

Far too late, Meccano Ltd. introduced a two-rail Hornby Dublo system, but it had an Achilles heel – the track. Pursuing the policy that Hornby Dublo had to be better than its rivals, the track was designed with two unforeseen problems: it was complicated, and it was not sufficiently tough.

With three-rail track you could alter the direction of a train by running it diagonally across the centre of the layout, but this was not easily possible with two-rail layouts because the two rails were of different polarity. To overcome this limitation, the design team at Liverpool developed a series of single and double isolating rails and points, which were fine for an intelligent enthusiast, but too complicated for children and anyone else. In trying to ensure that the track was as accurate as possible the chairs, which held the rails in place, were too small to withstand rough handling by children and rails often broke away. Plus-points were that the rails were nickel silver, ensuring better running, and it was

Hornby Dublo Book of Trains, 1959.

The BR low-sided wagon was now released with a Dublo Dinky Toy tractor load.

During the year the BR double bolster wagon received a timber load. (Courtesy David Busfield)

The SD6 standard brake van. (Courtesy Hattons)

The two-rail 'Castle' Class *Denbigh Castle*. (Courtesy Vectis)

The two-rail A4 *Golden Fleece*. (Courtesy LSK)

The two-rail 'Duchess' Class *City of London*. (Courtesy Vectis)

cheaper to produce than the metal three-rail track. Because of these difficulties, a number of modellers switched to the easier Tri-ang system, thus reducing further Hornby's customer base.

The introduction of a two-rail system brought new versions of existing locomotives. The BR green Class A4 in two-rail was 60030 *Golden Fleece* and the 'Castle' Class was 7032 *Denbigh Castle*. However, the green *Duchess of Montrose*

The two-rail Class 8F No. 48109. (Courtesy LSK)

would remain in the three-rail system and, in addition, there was a re-bodied modified front end 'Duchess' in the new BR maroon livery and a new plastic tender for it. For three-rail it was released as 46247 *City of Liverpool* and for two-rail it was 46245 *City of London*.

The 4MT tank engine, Class 8F and Type 1 diesel were all re-numbered for the two-rail versions and the Class N2 was not offered in two-rail at that time. Instead, a completely new tank engine was introduced – the ex-SR Class R1 0-6-0T.

The Class R1 locomotives were rebuilds, by Harry Wainwright, of the Class R 0-6-0 tanks built to a design by James Stirling, of the South Eastern Railway, as shunting engines for the London, Chatham & Dover Railway and dated from 1888. The model had a plastic body and was available in two two-rail versions. One was in plain black and the other was a plain bright green.

A pair of bright green suburban coaches were released at the same time. The new locomotives had nickel-plated driving wheels. All the above

The BR 0-6-0T Class R1 tank engine. (Courtesy LSK)

BR green suburban coaches.

appeared in the excellent enlarged full-colour catalogue, named *Dublo Book of Trains,* which carried additional articles.

To introduce the two-rail system, twelve layouts were built at Liverpool for display in principal Hornby dealer's shops. The baseboard was made from pegboard, in a solid wooden frame, painted light green. It carried a double track three-rail layout with turntable and station in the centre and a two-rail circuit on

A shop layout being built in a factory. (Courtesy Michael Foster)

a nicely built raised track. Many years later I answered an advertisement in the local paper from someone selling an ex-shop layout. The story, the lady told me, was that she had bought it after Christmas from a shop in London for her nephews, but the locomotives and rolling stock had been stolen from her London flat. When she moved to Yorkshire, she brought the layout with her and it had been stored for years in her shed. I bought it from her, restored it and ran it at exhibitions for several years. It was sometime later, reading Michael Foster's wonderful book *Hornby Dublo Trains*, that I came across a picture (p. 118) showing one of these layouts being tested at the factory, by the man who built it, and it was exactly the same as mine, except that the one in the picture has a three-rail circuit on the upper level.

As if a new two-rail system was not enough for one year, a whole new range of plastic buildings also arrived in 1959. These included a through station, island platform, goods depot and an engine shed with an extension kit also available. There were also a set of gradient posts, telegraph poles and lineside huts.

Further introductions included more Dublo Dinky Toys (Royal Mail van, tractor, articulated lorry and AEC tanker), a single-track tunnel, BR standard brake van and the popular breakdown crane. Also, the restaurant car was now available in red livery; it should have been maroon to match the existing coaches, but sadly it was too bright.

The policy of keeping faith with its existing three-rail users, by keeping it in production alongside the new two-rail system, was a mistake and it bled the company of money it needed. While all the newer plastic-wheeled rolling stock was compatible with either system, the locomotives and track were not, and required duplication. Had the three-rail system been dropped, three-rail enthusiasts would not have been left in the lurch as a three-rail second-hand market resulted from those switching to the two-rail sytem. Second-hand Hornby Dublo three-rail was readily available for many years and was much

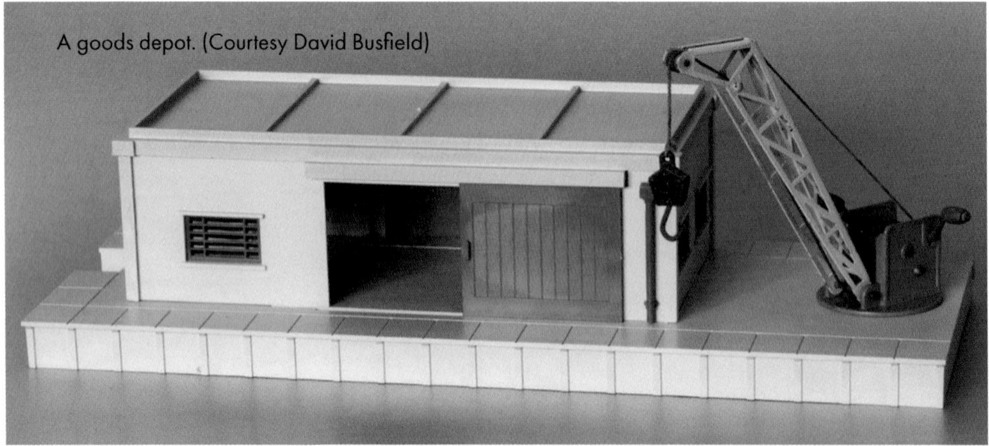
A goods depot. (Courtesy David Busfield)

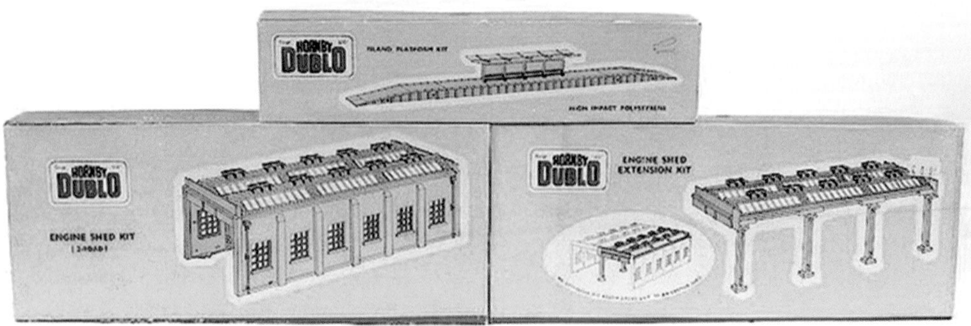

An engine shed, extension kit and island platform. (Courtesy Vectis Auctions)

Telegraph poles, lineside posts and platelayer's huts. (Courtesy Vectis Auctions)

The breakdown crane for export. (Courtesy Vectis Auctions)

cheaper to buy than new. It is still available today. Furthermore, a trade in locomotive conversions also developed, ensuring that future two-rail locomotives could be converted to three-rail.

ROVEX

An overhead electric locomotive and complete catenary system were introduced by Rovex and a Primary series of sets for beginners started to arrive.

1950s – A DECADE SUMMARY

The decade started badly for Meccano Ltd. with metal shortages due to the Korean War. Little could be made, but the Dublo aluminium buildings were the exception. In 1953 the Dublo system was relaunched in British Railways liveries and the 0-gauge system followed a year later. The latter was now reduced to 0-4-0 locomotives and four-wheel rolling stock and remained so, slowly losing its customers to smaller gauges.

In 1954 Dublo received its first completely new post-war locomotive, the standard 2-6-4T, along with suburban coaches and a growing range of new wagons. In 1957 a 'Castle' Class locomotive arrived, along with the first of the Dublo Dinky series. There were new coach liveries and a restaurant car. A large range of plastic wagons was launched in 1958, along with two more locomotives – an 8F 2-8-0 and a Type 1 Bo-Bo diesel. The following year saw the launch of two-rail Hornby Dublo with new track, two-rail versions of the existing locomotives, plus an 0-6-0T and a modified 'Duchess'.

For Rovex Plastics Ltd. the decade started with the launch of their first train set, followed by joining the large Lines Bros. group of toy manufacturers. The company was re-named Rovex Scale Models Ltd. and the train set became the start of Tri-ang Railways. Expansion was fast and Rovex was rehoused in a new purpose-built factory at Margate. A Transcontinental export range was launched, followed by a new system in TT gauge. During the decade, new Tri-ang Railways production lines were started up in Lines Group factories in

South Africa, New Zealand and Australia. By the end of the decade, Rovex were in a strong position with a large range of products and a commanding share of the market.

LINES BROS. LTD.

The involvement in the toy industry by the Lines family goes back to the Victorian era, long before Frank Hornby invented Meccano. George and Joseph Lines formed their company, G&J Lines, around 1866 and over the years became famous for their rocking horses and wooden toys. Returning from the First World War, three of Joseph's sons formed their own company which they called Lines Bros. As there were three brothers named Lines, and three lines make a triangle, a triangle was adopted as their trademark and Tri-ang as their brand name. The brothers were William, Walter and Arthur Lines.

Like their father and uncle, the brothers made toys and baby carriages in wood. They bought their first factory in the Old Kent Road in 1919 for £28,000, complete with machinery. As their business grew, they acquired other nearby premises as factories. In 1924, having bought twenty acres at Merton in South London to build on, they moved into the new factory which one day would be claimed to be the largest toy factory in the world with a floor area of over 1,000,000 square feet.

Over the years Lines Bros. bought several companies that had a product they felt had potential to be profitable. Examples are Frog model aircraft, Rovex trains and Scalex slot-cars. At one time they owned a string of toy shops as well as Hamley's in London's Regent Street. They eventually had about forty companies within the group and included businesses in the Australia, Canada, France, Germany, Ireland, New Zealand, South Africa and the USA. Besides Merton, they had factories in Basildon, Belfast, Birmingham, Lavant, Merthyr Tydfil, Plymouth and Richmond. They built four similar new factories at Calais, Canterbury, Havant and Margate.

In 1958, a limited-circulation book called *'Looking Backwards and Looking Forwards'* was published by the company. In it the chairman, Walter Lines, told the story of the company from its earliest days through to 1958. It contained many photographs of the various factories and showrooms around the world.

The year 1957.

The year 1959.

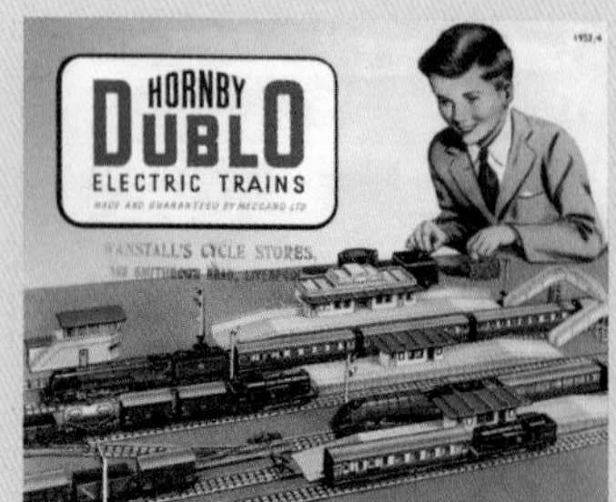

From 1953 to 1954.

From 1954 to 1955.

From 1954 to 1955.

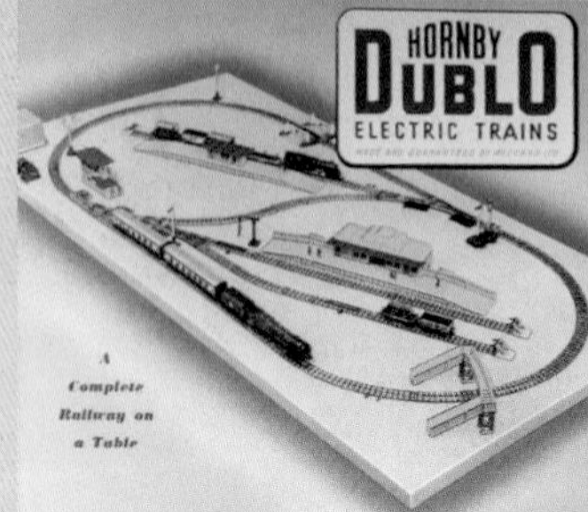

From 1955 to 1956.

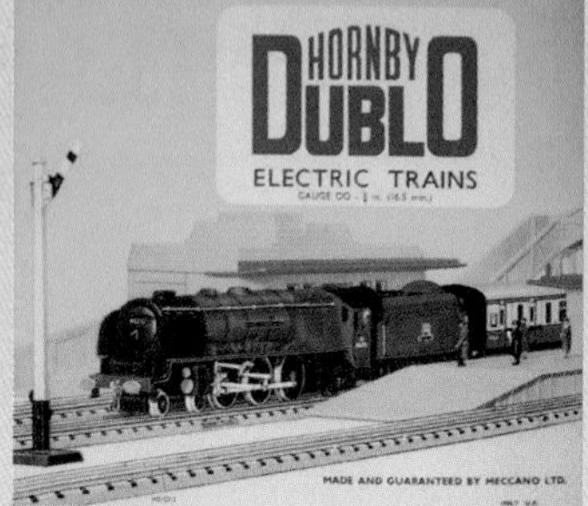

From 1956 to 1957.

The year 1958.

The year 1959.

1950s MILESTONES

1950 – Dublo aluminium buildings; 0-gauge deletions and price rises; first Rovex train set.

1951 – Metal shortages due to the Korean War and plastic wheels on 0-gauge wagons; Lines Bros. buy Rovex and Trackmaster tools.

1952 – A few Dublo small accessories; Canadian train sets, 0-gauge M wagons and SR and GWR identity removed; Tri-ang Railways launched; first red and yellow packaging and start of 'R' numbers.

1953 – Dublo in BR liveries and first die-cast wagons; Rovex Scale Models Ltd. and first Rovex 0-6-0 locomotive.

1954 – Dublo 2-6-4T and suburban coaches; 0-gauge BR liveries; Rovex moves to Margate and first of Transcontinental series.

1955 – More Dublo wagons; first Tri-ang retail catalogue and Tri-ang production starts in South Africa.

1956 – Dublo Gresley coaches deleted and first long wheelbase wagons; Tri-ang production starts in New Zealand.

1957 – Dublo *Bristol Castle*, new coach liveries and first Dublo Dinky Toys; 0-gauge No. 50 wagon range; Tri-ang production in Australia and Tri-ang TT launched.

1958 – First plastic Dublo wagons, 8F 2-8-0 and Type 1 Bo-Bo; Rovex tension-lock coupling and Series 3 track.

1959 – Dublo two-rail locomotives and track, plastic buildings, 0-6-0T and modified 'Duchess'; Rovex catenary system and Primary Series sets.

DUBLO LOCOS OF THE 1950s

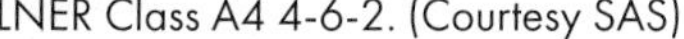
LNER Class A4 4-6-2. (Courtesy SAS)

LMS 'Princess Coronation' Class 4-6-2. (Courtesy LSK)

GWR 'Castle' Class 4-6-0. (Courtesy LSK)

SE&CR Class R1 0-6-0T. (Courtesy Tony Cooper)

BR Class 4MT 2-6-4T. (Courtesy LSK)

LNER Class N2 0-6-2T. (Courtesy Vectis)

BR Class 20 Bo-Bo. (Courtesy Tony Cooper)

LMS Class 8F 2-8-0. (Courtesy Vectis)

1960
RINGFIELD MOTOR AND SD COACHES

The SD6 passenger fruit van. (Courtesy Hattons)

HORNBY DUBLO

More, new Dublo wagons arrived in 1960, including some impressive tank wagons – the white ICI chlorine tank and the silver Traffic Services ferry tank. These were better than any we had seen before. There was also the long wheelbase ex-GWR fruit van and the BR standard Mk 1 horsebox, with opening doors and a horse. The horsebox was made in both BR maroon and Southern Region green. A criticism of the new wagons had been that they still had the die-cast chassis of 1938, which badly lacked detail. The chlorine tank wagon was the first to have a detailed chassis. This and the other three wagons released in 1960 were all longer than the standard chassis and so each had their own specially designed one. There was an additional livery for the metal tank wagon, this time in black with Esso branding.

The SD6 horsebox in Southern Region green.

With such attractive wagons there was a new heavy-duty freight set with the 8F as motive power. Called the 'Express Goods' set it contained three of the new SD6 wagons, a metal tank wagon and the bogie well wagon.

Other additions in the Dublo Dinky Toys series during the year included the Volkswagan van, Lansing Bagnall tractor with platform trailers and the Landrover with a horsebox trailer.

The two-rail version of the Type 1 Bo-Bo arrived during the year and was the first to be fitted with traction tyres, but problems with its supposedly unsolvable poor performance led to it being withdrawn from sale two years later. At the end of the year two more diesel locomotives were launched through *Meccano Magazine* and these were the Co-Co mainline diesel and the 0-6-0 diesel shunter. The latter was the standard diesel shunter built by BR in their hundreds and used throughout the country, many still in use today. It was the standard BR 350 hp 0-6-0 diesel shunter

The two-rail 'Express Goods Train' set. (Courtesy Vectis Auctions)

Dublo Dinky Land Rover and horsebox with horse. (Courtesy UK T&M)

Dublo Dinky Lansing Bagnall tractor and trailer.

The two-rail Co-Co diesel. (Courtesy LSK)

The three-rail Class 08 diesel shunter. (Courtesy Vectis Auctions)

(later to become the Class 08) and the Dublo model had the benefit of a moulded plastic body, which showed-off the rugged detail of the prototype.

The Co-Co diesel had a die-cast body which did it no favours. Most mainline diesels have little detail on their bodies and what little there is needs to be brought out when modelled or they look featureless – which is why polystyrene is a better material than the alloy that was used by Meccano Ltd. for the Co-Co. It looked class-less when it first appeared, having no number, as though it was intended to be a generic-type diesel. It was not until 1962 that it would be identified as an English Electric 'Deltic' (later Class 55) and be given appropriate livery, numbers and names. A 'Deltic' was an excellent choice. It became the thoroughbred that pulled the East Coast expresses and earned its status as an icon with railway enthusiasts, but this was a poor model of one and a lost opportunity. Both new diesels were available in two- and three-rail format.

The three-rail *Ludlow Castle*. (Courtesy Vectis Auctions)

The two-rail *Cardiff Castle*. (Courtesy Vectis Auctions)

The SD BR (WR) brake third.

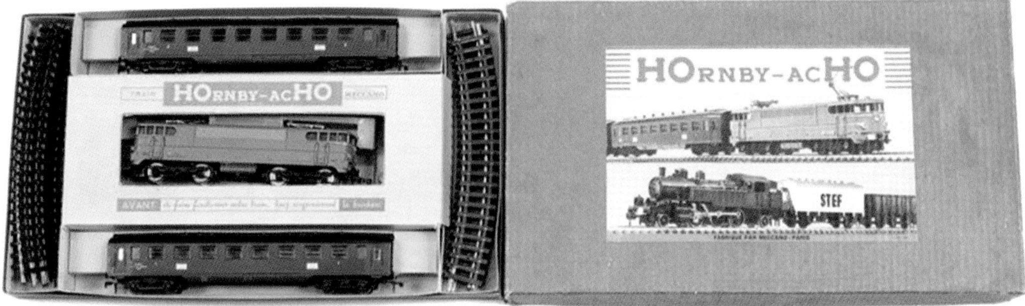

The 'HOrnby-AcHO' passenger train set. (Courtesy Vectis Auctions)

It was in 1960 that the revolutionary new Ringfield motor was fitted into the Class 8F and 'Castle' Class models as well as the two new diesels. It was smoother running and a more powerful unit, capable of pulling longer trains. It was, unfortunately, over-large and protruded into the cab area on both steam locomotives. The latter were available in both two- and three-rail formats, with two new identities in each case. For the 'Castle' this meant two new names – 4075 *Cardiff Castle* in two-rail and 5002 *Ludlow Castle* in three-rail. This in turn led to further new train sets. One of the *Cardiff Castle* models was used in a promotion to demonstrate the new motor and it ran 153 real miles, earning a place in the *Guiness Book of Records.*

Just before the end of the year the first super-detail coaches arrived. These were the first of what was planned to be an extensive range covering different BR Mk 1 types and liveries. To keep the sleek look of a clean and shining Mk 1 coach, the sides were tin-printed, while the roof and ends were moulded in plastic. The first two released were a CK and a BSK and they were available in both maroon livery and brown and cream. Also available now was the two-rail version of the Class N2 0-6-2T.

Lastly, the French Meccano company launched its own smaller-scale model railway system in 1960, but in H0 scale (3.5 mm: 1 ft) and so took the name 'Hornby Acho'. It was first seen at the Nuremberg Toy Fair in January. From September 1961 its products were sold in Great Britain and it remained in production in France until the end of 1973.

ROVEX

The year 1960 saw the release of the model of 'Britannia', which set new modelling standards for Rovex. Lines Bros. purchased French VB train manufacturer as part of its plan to manufacture trains inside the EEC (later the European Union).

1961
FOUR NEW LOCOMOTIVES AND PULLMAN CARS

The two-rail re-built 'West Country' Class, *Barnstaple*. (Courtesy Vectis Auctions)

HORNBY DUBLO

Two more locomotives arrived in 1961. The best of these was the Southern Region 4-6-2 rebuilt 'West Country' (BB/WC) Class, which was 34005 *Barnstaple* as a two-rail locomotive and 34042 *Dorchester* as a three-rail model. It had a die-cast body and was a very attractive addition to the range. The BB/WCs were Oliver Bulleid's light Pacifics for the Southern Railway for mixed traffic duties and many were rebuilt by British Railways. It was the most expensive Dublo model produced, but seems to have been a poorer seller, largely due to there being less interest in the Southern Region at that time.

The other new locomotive was another mainline diesel, but again with a die-cast body and available as two-rail and three-rail. Many felt

The three-rail re-built 'West Country' Class, *Dorchester*. (Courtesy Vectis Auctions)

The two-rail Metropolitan Vickers Co-Bo. (Courtesy Vectis Auctions)

that the Metropolitan Vickers Type 2 Co-Bo (later Class 28) was a strange choice as the real locomotives won no accolades. The class was unique in the BR fleet in having a six-wheel bogie at one end and a four-wheel one at the other and twenty were introduced during 1958–59. They were built at Stockton-on-Tees and based at Derby, but were poor performers and withdrawals started as early as 1967. I suspect that it was

The Pullman first, *Aries*.

The SD passenger full brake.

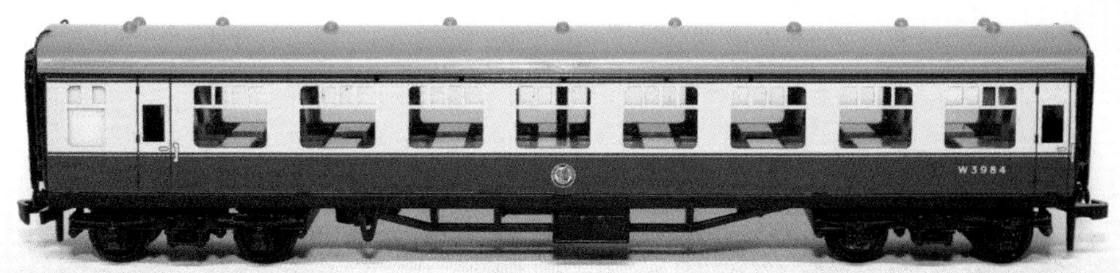
The SD open second in BR brown and cream livery.

The SD6 Southern Region covered carriage truck (CCT).

The SD6 'Lowmac' machine wagon.

The SD6 'Presflo' wagons.

chosen as it looked different and for that reason it appealed to me. The Dublo stable now consisted of four diesels and nine steam locomotives. This was a vast improvement in a relatively short time.

The Pullman cars and more of the super-detail coaches were released in 1961. There were three types of Pullman based on the 1928 design for the LNER's East Coast mainline. These were parlour first, *Aries*, parlour third, *Car 74* and brake third *Car 79*. The models originally had Gresley bogies, but by 1963 BR-type bogies were being fitted by Meccano Ltd. A BR maroon sleeping car (SLE), full brake (BG), open first (FO) and open second (TSO) were added to the SD range.

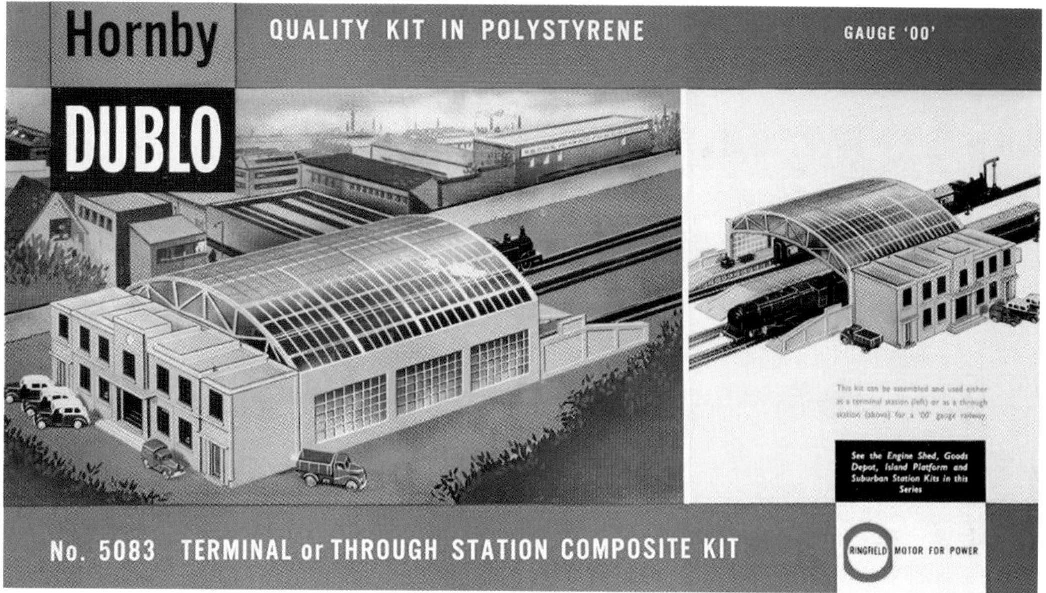

The terminal or through station.

The TSO and FO were also released in BR brown and cream livery.

New wagons included the 'Lowmac' machine wagon, 'Presflo' cement and salt bulk carriers, the SR green long wheelbase CCT van, 'Blue Spot' fish van and the sand open wagon now carried the name 'United Glass'.

Added to the plastic buildings was the large station kit, which could be built as a covered through station or a terminus station. The kit was in the same cream colour as the rest of the buildings.

HORNBY 0 GAUGE

The Hornby Trains No. 50/51 locomotives and sets were dropped this year.

ROVEX

Lines Bros. opened a purpose-built factory in France at Calais, where Tri-ang Railways TT and other Tri-ang products were to be built within the EEC. In 1961 Walter Lines retired as Chairman of Lines Bros. Ltd., and his eldest son Walter Moray Lines became Chairman.

The first Tri-ang scale length Mk 1 coach, a sleeping car, arrived in 1961 as well as the Countryside Series of moulded rubber buildings made by Young & Fogg. There were also the first classic locomotive *Lord of the Isles* and clerestory coaches.

The arrival of very cheap Playcraft train sets, sold through F. W. Woolworth, provided a new threat to Hornby Dublo.

1962
GREEN MK 1 COACHES AND EMU

HORNBY DUBLO

The Dublo range received its first multiple unit in the form of a BR Ashford/Eastleigh Class 416 Southern 2-EPB EMU. It was a two-car unit and was available in both two- and three-rail format, with the same running numbers. The subject was possibly chosen because a very similar design was built for South Tyneside on the Eastern Region and this would have allowed a Tyneside version to be released later on. This may explain why a later Wrenn catalogue showed the model in maroon livery, even though Wrenn did not get around to re-introducing the model.

The Co-Co diesel was now also in two-tone green and named as members of the 'Deltic' Class. The two-rail version was D9012 *Crepello* and for three-rail it was D9001 *St Paddy*.

Southern green was now very evident amongst the super-detail coaches, with green livery on the Mk 1 CK and BSK and on a new pair of SD non-corridor coaches (C and BS). The green non-corridor composite coach (C) could provide trailers to extend the EMU.

The two-rail 'Deltic', *Crepello*. (Courtesy Vectis Auctions)

The Class 501 EMU. (Courtesy Vectis Auctions)

The three-rail Co-Co 'Deltic' Diesel, *St Paddy*. (Courtesy Vectis Auctions)

There were also maroon versions of the non-corridor coaches.

At last an attempt was made to improve the standard wagon chassis and from now several wagons had a die-cast chassis with open brake gear. New wagons during the year included the 'Prestwin' silo wagon, UD six-wheel milk tank wagon, a gunpowder van, 'Yellow Spot' banana van, brown steel mineral wagon, red packing van (to go with the breakdown crane) and the ICI bogie caustic liquor tank wagon.

The two-rail level crossing as well as left- and right-hand diamond crossings were released.

The SD BR green corridor composite.

The SD BR green suburban brake second.

The SD6 'Prestwin' silo wagon for export. (Courtesy Tony Cooper)

The SD6 16-ton mineral wagon in BR brown. (Courtesy LSK)

The SD6 banana van.

HORNBY 0 GAUGE

This is thought to have been the last year that any 0 gauge was produced.

ROVEX

The year 1962 was the peak year for the expansion of Tri-ang Railways and saw the introduction of Super 4 track, an extensive modern station system, Magnadhesion, smoking locomotives, pinpoint axles, a new elevated track system and much more. It also saw the start of the high play-value military wagons. There is little doubt that the 1962 modernisation of Tri-ang Railways helped it to survive the market depression, which was beginning to take hold of the toy industry.

The excellent Class B12 model was designed in 1962 and went on to be the second longest surviving Hornby locomotive; it would not be re-tooled until 2016 – over fifty years later! The 'Achilles' Class 4-2-2 holds the record. The original B12 tools were sent out to China in 1996 and it became the first Hornby locomotive to be made there from original Tri-ang Railways tooling.

A well-illustrated 116-page book called *Tri-ang Railways – the First 10 Years* was published in 1962. It is full of facts and figures, hints and ideas about the railway system and how the models were made.

The Tri-ang Class B12.

1963
FALLING SALES AND RISING STOCK

HORNBY DUBLO

The serious financial trouble the company was in, and the growing level of unsold stocks building up in the Meccano factory, resulted in a reduction in the number of new models introduced during 1963. More of the planned SD coach range were released, including the restaurant car in both maroon and in brown and cream, but the green version was not to appear. The much loved six-wheel 'Stove' passenger

The SD six-wheel 'Stove' brake van. (Courtesy Vectis Auctions)

The SD restaurant car in brown and cream livery. (Courtesy Vectis Auctions)

The SD6 21-ton hopper wagon. (Courtesy Vectis Auctions)

brake van, in maroon livery, did make it and, in the wagon range, the hopper wagon arrived.

At the Meccano Trade Fair in 1963 there was displayed a pre-production model of an AEI/ Birmingham RC&W Class AL1 (later Class 81) West Coast Main Line 25 kV AC electric locomotive. This was in production, but it would be too late to save the company. There were also bumper boxes of Dublo two-rail track assortments to be bought.

Hornby Dublo artwork for the AL1 Class 81 electric locomotive.

The Class AL1 (Class 81) electric locomotive. (Courtesy Vectis Auctions)

Dublo 2001 'Ready to Run' starter set with black 0-4-0T locomotive. (Courtesy Darren Cooper)

As a last-ditch attempt to attract new custom, a cheap beginner set was launched which contained a power unit all for 89/6. It contained a small freelance 0-4-0 tank engine and three cheap wagons made from existing plastic wagon bodies mounted on a new plastic chassis. In the same year Tri-ang were offering twelve of their sets at a lower price than this, and there were also cheaper Playcraft sets on the market. Although the Dublo starter sets sold quite well, the competition was far too strong.

ROVEX

Rovex took over the manufacture of Real Estate building kits from IMA, another member of the Lines Group, as well as the Lionel science sets. Other introductions were the tiny Rocket locomotive, the grand Victorian suspension bridge, CKD locomotive and coach kits, and a joint train and Minic Motorway set.

1964

THE END OF HORNBY DUBLO

HORNBY DUBLO

Another last-minute starter set had the body of the diesel shunter in yellow, mounted on a four-wheel mechanism, and another release was the track cleaning wagon, which was made of the old mineral wagon sprayed black. Very few were sold, and today genuine ones are highly prized. There are many fake ones around as well as tales of disposal of unsold stock as landfill, prompting suggestions of treasure hunting expeditions!

In order to avoid the need to call in the Receiver, the Board of Meccano Ltd. invited Lines Bros. Ltd. to buy them out, and Meccano Ltd. became a member of the Lines Group. All Hornby train production had already stopped by then, leaving a large amount of unsold stock which needed disposal.

ROVEX

Meccano Ltd. was purchased by Lines Bros. Ltd. on 14 February 1964. The same year, Lines Bros. turned down an invitation to buy the Lone Star 000 (N gauge) electric trains. During the same year the 00-scale Model-Land building kits and Minix cars were launched and a model of a West Coast mainline electric locomotive was announced. Lines Bros. also bought a controlling interest in model designer and manufacturer, G&R Wrenn.

The Dublo rail cleaning wagon. (Courtesy Vectis Auctions)

Dublo 'ready-to-run' starter set. (Courtesy Vectis Auctions)

1965
NEW OWNER, NEW NAME, NEW ERA

TRI-ANG HORNBY

Tri-ang Railways became Tri-ang Hornby and, except for some slight name changes in 1972 and 1997, this is the Hornby system which is in the shops today. Indeed, it has carried the Hornby name for ten years longer than the Hornby products made in Liverpool. As we have seen, the current system was launched with that first Rovex train set back in 1950. Not only did the Hornby brand become one hundred years old in 2020, but the model railway system, which currently carries its name, became seventy years old as well.

In May 1965 an eight-page 'Amalgamation' leaflet was released, showing several Hornby Dublo models still available but now with 'R' prefixed catalogue numbers. These included the terminus station, goods depot, island platform, platform extension, footbridge, engine shed, double tunnel, girder bridge and seven two-rail locomotives. The latter were *Barnstaple*, Co-Bo, N2 0-6-2T, R1 0-6-0T, diesel shunter 0-6-0DS, AL1 electric locomotive and the Class 416/2 EMU. The first five locomotives would be sold with a converter wagon as Dublo and Tri-ang couplings were not compatible. The models were sold in their original boxes with a 'Tri-ang Hornby' sticker stuck over the Hornby Dublo

The 1965 'Amalgamation' leaflet.

Tri-ang HORNBY

The re-labelled Dublo Co-Bo diesel. (Courtesy Darren Cooper)

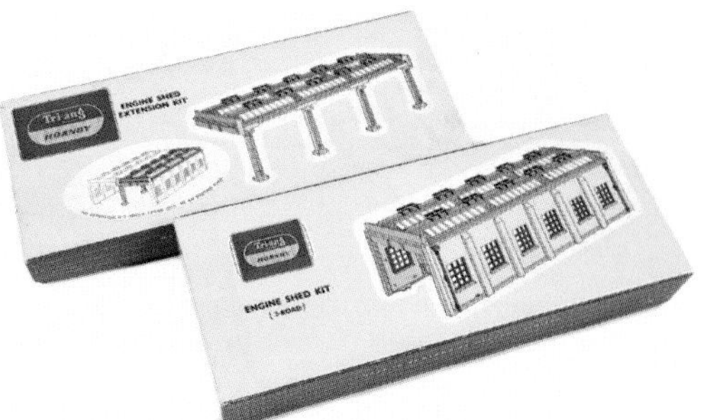

The re-labelled Dublo engine shed kits. (Courtesy Vectis Auctions)

The re-labelled Dublo plastic girder bridge.

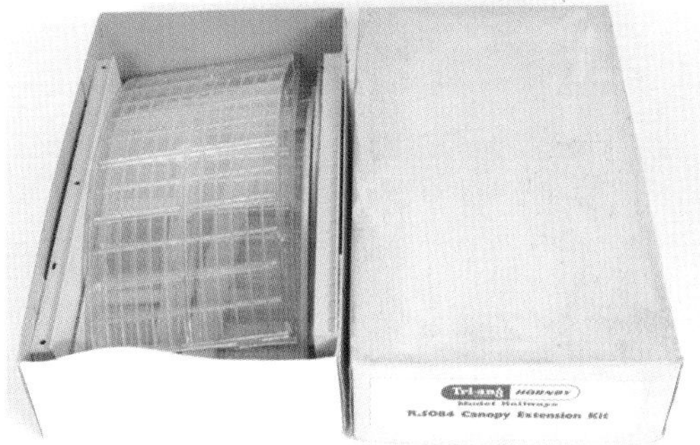

The white box for the Dublo 5084 station canopy extension. (Courtesy LSK)

logo and some not yet boxed Dublo buildings were sold in plain white Tri-ang Hornby boxes.

The converter wagon was the Tri-ang seven-plank open wagon (ex-Trackmaster) with a Dublo coupling at one end and a tension-lock coupling at the other. A suitable converter wagon for passenger trains would be produced when the stock of Dublo coaches sold out. The leaflet also revealed that a converter rail was to be released, which would join Hornby two-rail track to any Tri-ang track.

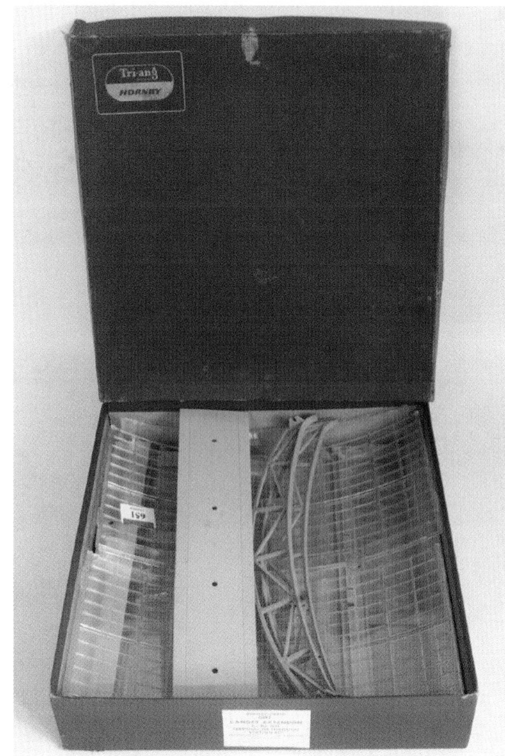

The re-labelled Dublo station canopy extension. (Courtesy LSK)

A goods train converter wagon.

The picture on the cover of the leaflet was a painting by Terrance Cuneo of a night scene featuring a 'Jinty' tank engine alongside a blue Class AL1 electric locomotive. The same picture appeared on the cover of the first Tri-ang Hornby catalogue in 1966.

What proved to be a very popular wagon was added during the year. It was the 'Tierwag' car transporter (or Car-a-belle) which carried six Minix cars. The 'Tierwags' used by British Railways were built by Newton Chambers in 1959 and the batch amounted to just six wagons.

The Tierwag 'Car-a-belle' car carrier.

The Class 37.

Meccano Ltd 0-gauge *Percy* and wagons. (Courtesy Vectis)

A Canadian bubble pack.

A new locomotive in the catalogue this year was an English Electric Type 3 diesel (later to be the Class 37) in BR green as D6830. A comparison between this model and the former Dublo 'Deltic' shows how much better polystyrene is for body detail when modelling the smooth lines of diesels. A total of 309 Class 37s were built between 1960 and 1964. Intended mainly for freight, the class also did sterling service on passenger trains as well.

At Lines Bros. (Canada) Ltd., plans were underway to start assembling sets for the Canadian market with six sets planned for the Christmas period. The Transcontinental models were supplied by the Margate factory.

An important year in terms of railway liveries was 1965, as that year saw the standardisation on a colour that became known as 'Rail Blue'. The colour was defined by British Standards BR28/6001 (Airless spray finish) and BR28/5321 (Brush finish), and was a dark, greyish blue tone that hid the effects of dirt well. The first Hornby models to carry this subdued blue livery were released three years later in 1968.

HORNBY 0 GAUGE

Although not a Hornby item, Meccano Ltd. released a clockwork 0-gauge plastic train set in 1965 called 'The Percy Play Train'. Based on 'Percy the Small Engine' in the Rev. W. Awdry's *Thomas the Tank Engine* books, it contained no Hornby parts and ran on plastic track.

1966
DISPOSING OF STOCK

TRI-ANG HORNBY

Back in 1960 Terence Cuneo had been commissioned to paint a picture for the cover of the 1962 Tri-ang Railways catalogue, and so pleasing was the result it had been decided to ask him to paint more of them in the future. As we have seen, the subject requested for the 1966 catalogue was the BR Class AL1 electric locomotive. As he was unimpressed with the subject, Cuneo chose to do a night scene in which an electrical spark provided the lighting and a 'Jinty' tank engine the smoky atmosphere, which he loved. The result was a superb picture that was not only used on the catalogue but, as previously mentioned, also on the cover of the amalgamation leaflet of the year before.

Rovex had also been working on their own model of a West Coast electric locomotive and the surviving incomplete model in a private collection suggests that it would have been an AEI/MV Beyer Peacock 25 kV AL2. This was abandoned and the Dublo AL1 would be added to the fleet in its place in 1966. It had first undergone various modifications and had live pantographs, which could run under the Tri-ang catenary. However, this revised model was a poor performer and was dropped from the catalogue in 1971.

Until now, Rovex had not released any Western Region locomotives, but that was about to change with the arrival of two. From the former GWR came a model of the BR 'Hall' 49xx Class 4-6-0 4983 *Albert Hall* and, for

The Dublo AL1 (Class 81) E3002. (Courtesy Vectis Auctions)

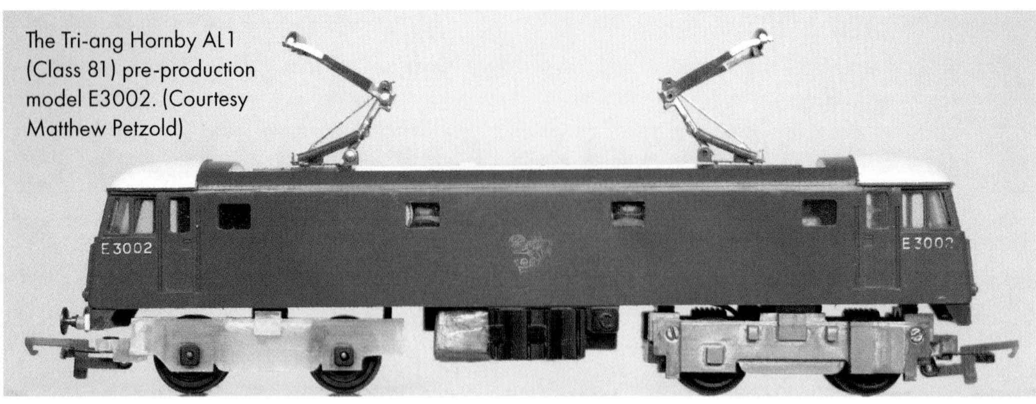

The Tri-ang Hornby AL1 (Class 81) pre-production model E3002. (Courtesy Matthew Petzold)

The Tri-ang Hornby AL1 (Class 81) E3001.

Pre-production sample of the 4-6-0, *Albert Hall*.

The Class 35 'Hymek' in BR green.

A 'Blue Circle' Cemflo wagon.

Western Region modern image modellers, the Type 3 Beyer Peacock 'Hymek' B-B diesel-hydraulic (later Class 35) in BR green as D7063. Designed in 1928, the GWR 'Hall' Class was one of Charles Collett's mixed-traffic locomotives, of which 259 were built based on the earlier 'Saint' Class.

The 'Hymek' was also a mixed-traffic locomotive which started to appear on

The Battle Space! 'Strike Force 10' set. (Courtesy LSK)

The Class EM2, *Electra*, now in electric blue livery. (Courtesy LSK)

The Mk 1 corridor composite in blue and grey livery.

20 Tri-ang HORNBY **Ultra Modern and**

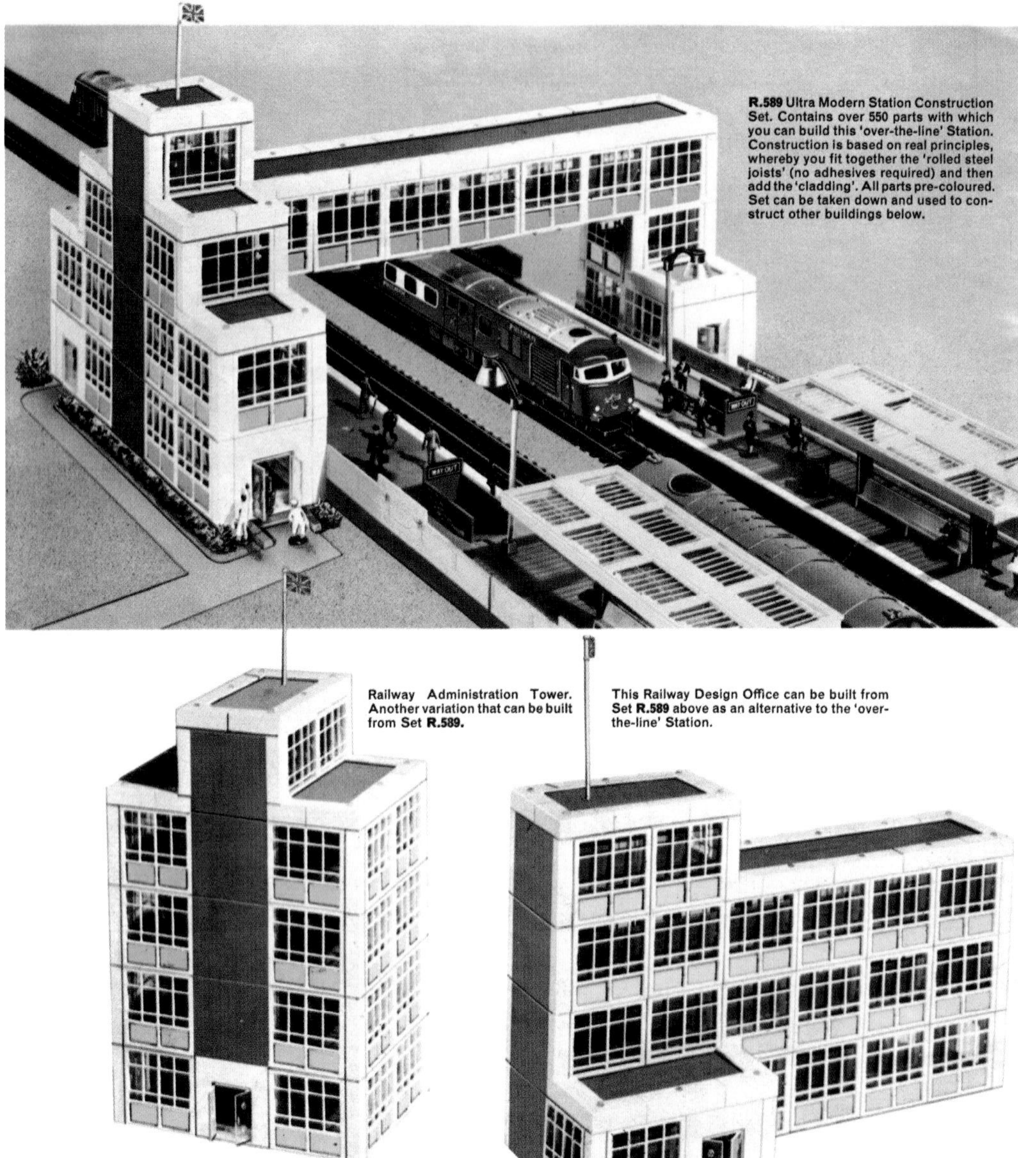

The Arkitex 'Ultra Modern' station kit.

the Western Region in 1961. A total of 101 were built by Beyer Peacock and the last was withdrawn in 1973. The model probably did not reach the shops until the following year.

A 'Cemflo' cement wagon was also in preparation and would be the first true Tri-ang Hornby wagon.

To the military range, now re-launched in a new livery as 'Battle Space' with the 'Strike Force

10' train set, were added the plane launching car, satellite launcher, radar tracking car and the assault tank transporter.

The first blue and grey Mk 1 coaches arrived during the year and the former Tri-ang BR/Metro-Vickers EM2 Co-Co electric locomotive (later Class 77) and Brush Type 2 A1A-A1A diesel (later Class 31) were now both in electric blue.

The catalogue also showed, for the first time, the Arkitex Ultra Modern Station, Arkitex being a construction system that had been developed at the Tri-ang Spot-On factory in Belfast. It would be dropped in 1968 and the sets are much sought after today. Tri-ang Big Big 0-gauge trains were made at Margate and launched during the year, and Frog plastic kit manufacturing was moved to Margate, from the Merton factory. Also, in 1966, Lines Bros. was invited to buy British Trix electric trains, but after consideration turned down the offer.

In hindsight, it was sad that Rovex did not see a future for the four Dublo super-detailed tank wagons in the Tri-ang Hornby range. They would have spruced up the wagons no end, as too would some of the other SD6 wagon bodies if given new plastic chassis. Unfortunately, the model railways were still seen as toys and the potential of the enthusiasts' market, with accurate detail and ever-changing liveries, was a long way off. The lost opportunity by Rovex was G&R Wrenn's gain, and later that of Dapol.

HORNBY DUBLO

Some unsold stock and former Hornby Dublo tooling was sold by Meccano Ltd. to G&R Wrenn (now a member of the Lines Group) to be marketed as 'Tri-ang Wrenn'. The former Hornby Dublo *Cardiff Castle* was the first to be advertised by Wrenn.

1967
INTERNAL MERGERS

TRI-ANG HORNBY

Internal mergers within the Lines Group resulted in the formation of Rovex Industries Ltd. as the 'models' wing of Lines Bros. At the same time the production of Minic Motorway (from Minic Ltd. in Canterbury) and Scalex Boats (from Minimodels Ltd. at Havant) were moved to Margate. The idea was to market the Minic Motorways alongside Tri-ang Hornby. This left space at the Minic factory at Canterbury to take over Pedigree doll production from the main factory at Merton. All these moves over the last two years were attributed to shrinkage in some product lines and rationalisation owing to a recession in the toy industry.

The catalogue cover picture was again specially painted by Terrance Cuneo and featured a Class M7 0-4-4T on shed, the subject being chosen to welcome the Tri-ang Hornby

The M7 Class tank engine.

The horsebox converter wagon for passenger trains.

model released that year. This had two brand new features – an opening smokebox door and firebox glow coming from the cab. Designed by Dugald Drummond for the LSWR in 1897, more than a hundred of the M7 tank engines were built. Rovex wanted a large tank without the expense of outside cylinders and valve gear, in order to keep its price down, and the M7 filled the bill. The model was in BR lined black as 30027.

As promised in the amalgamation leaflet, a converter wagon for passenger trains was released during the year, this was the Tri-ang Hornby horsebox with both a Dublo and a tension-lock coupling.

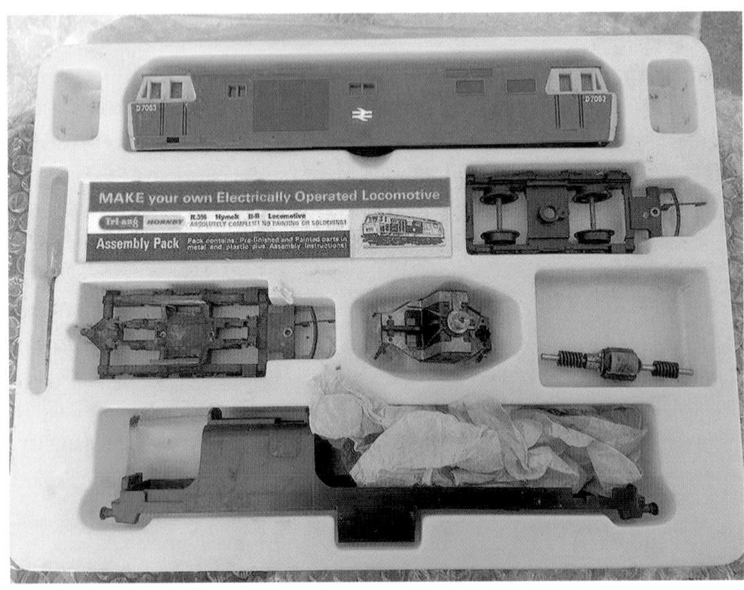

The Class 35 'Asssembly Pack'. (Courtesy Dave Clark)

During the year the former Tri-ang CKD kits were replaced by 'Assembly Packs', which were in flat trays with clear film covers showing you all the parts to be assembled. A new addition to the range of kits was the 'Hymek' Bo-Bo diesel model, which arrived in 1968.

Additions in the Battle Space! range were the POW car, tank recovery car, both twin and multiple missile sites, the Honest John missile

The Battle Space! multiple missile site.

The 'Honest John' missile pad.

Boys' World Annual 1967, featuring Battle Space! on the cover.

The POW car.

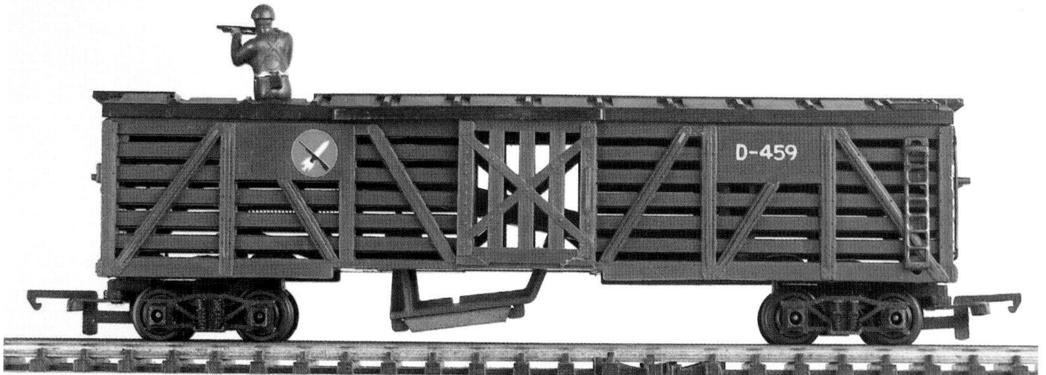

The sniper car.

The tank recovery car.

The bogie bolster wagon with Minix Ford Thames vans.

The 'Freightliner' container wagon.

A BR standard brake van.

launch pad and the sniper car, which was based on the Tri-ang giraffe car. Battle Space! featured on the cover of the *Boys' World Annual 1967*.

Three new wagons released during the year were the standard BR brake van, a bogie flat wagon with three Freightliner 20-ft containers and the bogie bolster wagon carrying three Minix Ford Thames vans.

During the year, the Tri-ang Big Big 0-gauge concept was sold to Lima who launched their 'Jumbo' 0-gauge trains, with better 0-gauge models following.

HORNBY DUBLO

The former Hornby Dublo tooling was back in production at G&R Wrenn and the first locomotive models were on the market, fitted with tension-lock couplings. Included were the 4MT standard tank, 'Castle' and 8F.

1968
FLYING SCOTSMAN

TRI-ANG HORNBY

This year's catalogue was the first of four which included the Minic-Motorway range, now made at Margate. It included a new emphasis on motor racing and while the two systems were marketed together as complementing each other, it was conveniently forgotten that they were in different scales. Minix cars were near enough the correct scale for the railways, while Minic cars were twice as large! The Minic lorries and buses were much closer to 00 scale. Road and rail sets were already available.

The big news in 1968 was the planned model of an ex-LNER BR Class A3 60103 *Flying Scotsman*. Both Rovex and British Trix had announced they were developing this model, and both were too advanced in the work to pull out when they realised that they would not have the market to themselves. Consequently, there was a race to see who would get theirs on the market first. The race was a close-run thing, but Rovex were first with their BR-liveried model. However, the BR model did not sell well.

It seems strange that such a popular subject had been left so late in the day, but it had become newsworthy thanks to the end of steam on Britain's railways in 1968 and the arrangement which owner, Alan Pegler, had with BR to continue to run *Flying Scotsman* after the steam ban. As an afterthought, Rovex decided to also produce the model

A BR vent van with sliding doors.

The *Flying Scotsman* of 1968.

The Tri-ang Hornby 'Haig' bulk grain wagon.

in LNER apple green livery as 4472, like the real locomotive restored by Pegler. The management at Rovex were taken by surprise at the huge demand for the LNER version and this led to a new era of pre-nationalisation liveries that swept through the model railway industry and helped to create a revised interest in model railways. The Tri-ang Hornby model in both liveries had firebox glow.

New additions in the wagon range in 1968 were a ventilated van with sliding doors and a BRT bulk grain wagon, which Trix had developed and suggested Rovex could sell fitted with tension-lock couplings. The new BR corporate blue livery was expanded within the Tri-ang Hornby range and with it came the first

The Rovex 'Miniville' train set.

pair of BR Mk 2 coaches, which had interior lighting powered from the track.

It was also about this time that Rovex produced the Miniville series. These were very cheap unbranded sets for sale in small shops and 'budget' stores; a similar idea to the British Express set produced by Meccano Ltd. in 1932. The last of the Battle Space! models was launched and today it is the rarest of the series. This was the Q car, which was based on the

The Mk 2 TSO in BR blue and grey.

The rare Battle Space! Q car.

The Tri-ang Hornby *Book of Trains.*

exploding car, but revealed a working rocket launcher within.

During the year the *Tri-ang Hornby Book of Trains* was published by Ian Allan Ltd., and was an attempt at reviving the pre-war publications. It consisted of illustrations of the current range of models and accessories with detailed captions, the whole supported by articles about the real railways. The editor was the famous railway expert and writer, O. S. Nock, and it sold for five shillings.

HORNBY DUBLO

The first Tri-ang Wrenn wagons were released, all made from the former Hornby Dublo tooling.

1969
BLUE LIVERIES

TRI-ANG HORNBY

The company name was changed again, this time to Rovex Tri-ang Ltd.

Until now the blue of the plastic used to represent the new BR livery had been too bright as it was the same as that used on early electric locomotives and called 'Electric Blue'. In 1969 this was corrected by Rovex and a more accurate 'Rail Blue' colour was used from now on. The 'Blue Pullman' DMU had changed colour to grey and blue, and there was a new range of inexpensive starter sets. Another new colour scheme was that applied to the 'Battle of Britain' Class locomotive, which was now in Southern bright green as 21C151 *Winston Churchill* – although it was not in the catalogue, being a late decision.

The year saw the release of several new wagons, including the light blue Bowaters china clay slurry tank wagon and a large hopper wagon in BR grey livery. The Car-a-belle car transporter had been a very popular model and, riding on its success, Rovex introduced the articulated 'Cartic' transporter with sixteen Minix cars as its load.

The 'Blue Pullman' in new grey and blue livery.

The Class 31 in 'Rail Blue'.

The Motorail 'Cartic' car carrier.

The large hopper wagon.

The most important addition was a range of six liner train container flat wagons with different loads. The loads included 20-ft and 30-ft box containers as well as 20-ft open and tank containers. The model represented a 60-ft long flat wagon that could take two 30-ft containers or three 20-ft ones. There was also a manually operated container depot with a cross-track crane with which you could pick up containers and transfer them to an articulated lorry, which was also provided in the pack, along with a 20-ft Tartan Arrow container.

The former Hornby Dublo terminus station was now illustrated in the catalogue in the red-brown plastic used for the former Tri-ang buildings. This was an indication that it was now

Container flat with 30-ft containers.

Container flat with 'Harold Wood' containers.

The Dublo covered station, made in the Margate factory.

The Freightliner depot crane.

being manufactured at Margate. The engine shed and extension were the only Dublo old stock still listed as available from Rovex. There were also rumours of a fifth track system based on an advert for a new third radius curve, but this was in Super 4 track.

HORNBY DUBLO

The former Dublo locomotives built by G&R Wrenn were now included in the Tri-ang Hornby catalogue and the revised 'Duchess' and 'West Country' had been added.

The year saw the founding of the Hornby Railway Collectors' Association, which caters for those interested in the history of, and in the collection of, Hornby 0-gauge and Hornby Dublo.

HORNBY 0 GAUGE

The last year in which the Meccano Ltd. list included Hornby Trains was 1969. All that was left was track, a few accessories and a few wagons. What was left would be sold off to retailers, with Hatton's of Liverpool being a principal purchaser. They listed it for a few years, and it would mostly have been bought by collectors.

1960s – A DECADE SUMMARY

By 1961 a new threat had emerged in the form of Playcraft, which was sold in F. W. Woolworth stores up and down the country, as well as in model shops. It was made in France by Jouef, but marketed by the British company, Mettoy Ltd. Train sets could be purchased for a fraction of the price of any Hornby Dublo ones. Meccano Ltd. decided to hit back in 1963 with a cheap train set of their own. However, Rovex was also responding to the Playcraft threat and offered a range of cheaper sets, with a target price of just £1.00.

At Liverpool there was no further development of Hornby 0 gauge, but the Hornby Dublo system was still expanding, with a revolutionary new motor and a full range of super-detail coaches to go with the still growing selection of super-detail wagons. New locomotives included a 'West Country' Class 4-6-2, a diesel shunter and two mainline diesels. There was also an EMU and a West Coast electric locomotive. However, all this activity hid financial problems for Meccano Ltd. With falling sales, unsold stock built up in the factory. To avoid going into receivership, the Meccano board approached Lines Bros. Ltd., seeking a take-over.

The growth in the popularity of slot-car racing was now being felt throughout the model railway industry, but one would not have thought so from the catalogue which Rovex had released in 1962. There is little doubt that the 1962 modernisation of the Tri-ang Railways system did much to ensure the survival of Rovex in the years ahead.

In 1964, Meccano Ltd. became a member of the Lines Group. While Dinky Toys and Meccano were useful additions to the Lines Group's large range of products, it was difficult to justify their making two rival model railway systems. In May 1965, it was announced that the two systems were to merge under the name Tri-ang Hornby. As we now know, the Tri-ang Railways system effectively carried on under the new name, but with some former Hornby Dublo models sold in re-labelled boxes until the stock had cleared. The Hornby Dublo terminus station was made at Margate for a short time, but the only locomotive to be absorbed was the Hornby Dublo Class AL1, after a rebuild.

Production of the Hornby Acho range had been started in Paris by Meccano (France) in 1960. With the purchase of Meccano Ltd. by Lines Bros., Hornby Acho production was moved to the modern Lines Bros. Calais factory, which had been built in 1962, and its production continued there until it came to an end in 1973.

By 1965, Tri-ang Hornby was left with a weak market, but little local competition. There was competition from abroad, but – as yet – the models made there were rarely of British prototypes and were in the slightly smaller H0 scale. It would be the 1970s before foreign manufacturers would take the bold step of manufacturing models exclusively for the British market and the respite helped Tri-ang Hornby. Despite the recession and lack of competition, eighteen new locomotives were designed, developed and released by Rovex during the 1960s.

The recession had brought spare capacity at Rovex, which led to the transfer of other Tri-ang product ranges to the Margate factory. These included the Real Estate

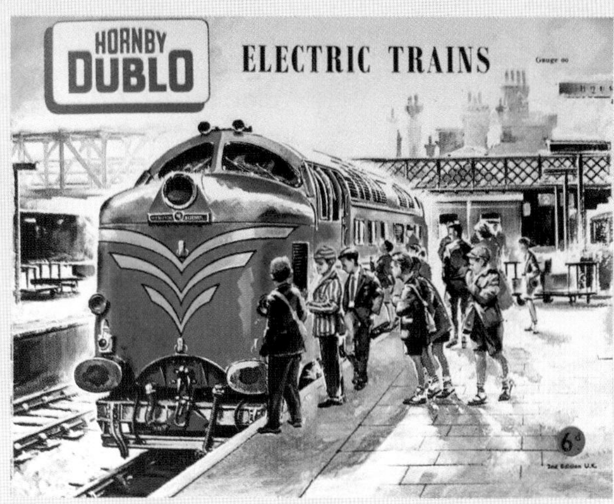

The year 1960.

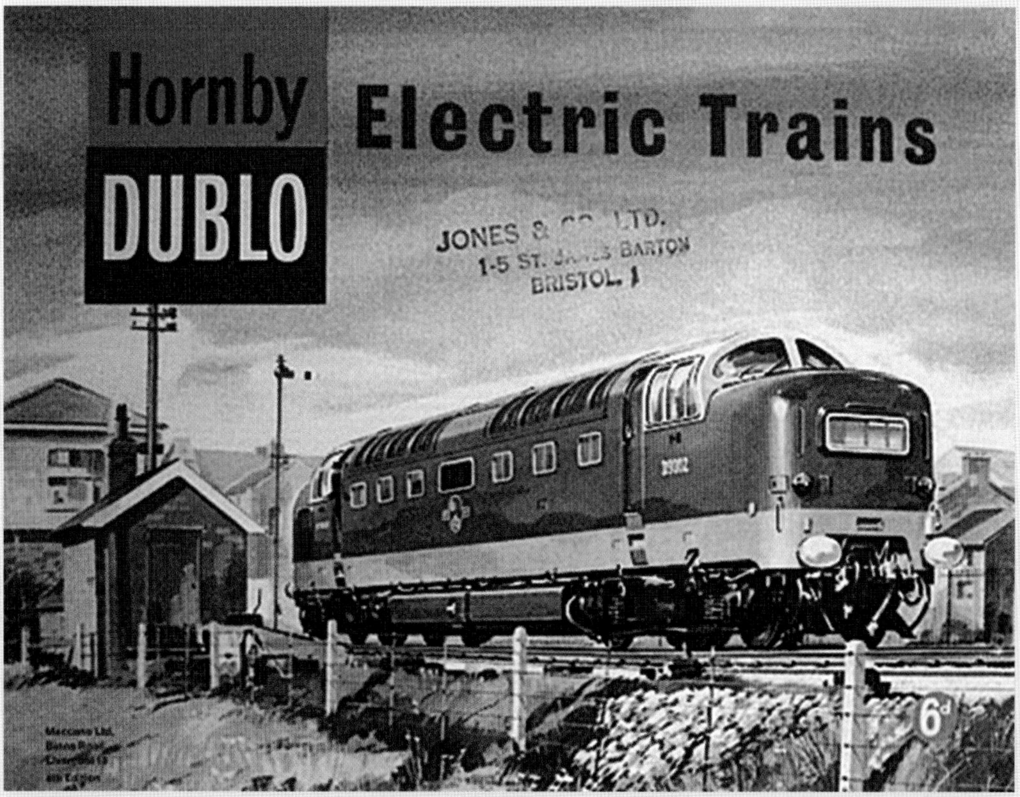

The year 1962.

The year 1963.

(Model-Land) building kits, Frog aircraft kits, Minic Motorway and some products from the Spot-On factory in Belfast. Later, Scalextric would also move to Margate. Battle Space! and Tri-ang Big Big were both launched at Margate during the decade, but production of the TT range ceased as not sufficiently profitable.

In 1967, Rovex Industries Ltd. was formed as an umbrella company for the Lines Bros. model-making companies. As production in the Group's overseas factories reduced due to their poor profitability, the Margate factory took on more production for the overseas markets. Trains made for the Canadian, American and Australian markets saw many strange liveries passing down Margate's production lines. In 1969, Rovex Industries Ltd. became Rovex Tri-ang Ltd. and was now centred on the twin factories at Margate and Canterbury. By the late 1960s, the British toy industry was in a spiral of decline and Lines Bros. was pulling in its horns.

The year 1965.

The year 1966.

13th Edition · 1/6

NEW THIS YEAR
M-7 Tank Locomotive!
with Fire box Glow!
Liner Trains!

Tri-ang HORNBY

MODEL RAILWAYS

The year 1967.

The year 1968.

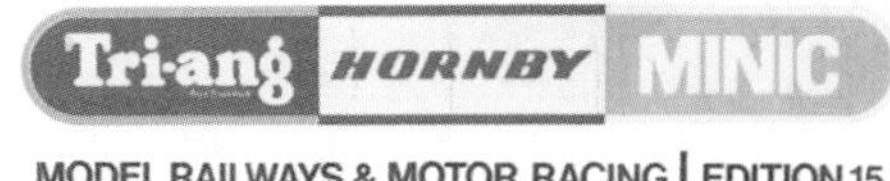

The year 1969.

1960s MILESTONES

1960 – Dublo Ringfield motor; first SD coaches and Hornby Acho launched; Lines Bros. buy VB in France.

1961 – Dublo rebuilt WC 4-6-2, 0-6-0DS, Co-Co, Co-Bo, Pullmans, Mk 1 sleepers and terminus station; Lines Bros. Calais factory opens; arrival of cheap Playcraft sets.

1962 – Co-Co becomes 'Deltic'; Dublo EMU and open brake gear on wagons; end of Hornby 0 gauge; Rovex major expansion and *'The First Ten Years'* published.

1963 – Dublo starter set; Rovex take over building kits.

1964 – Dublo AL1; end of Dublo production and Meccano Ltd. joins Lines Group; Lines buys G&R Wrenn.

1965 – Tri-ang Hornby launched; Rovex Type 3 diesel and train set assembly starts up in Canada; Meccano France moves to Calais factory.

1966 – Tri-ang Big Big, Battle Space! Frog kits move to Rovex; 'Hall', 'Hymek', Arkitex Ultra Modern Station and first blue liveries; ex-Dublo models in Tri-ang Hornby catalogue.

1967 – Rovex Industries Ltd.; Minic Motorway and Scalex Boats move to Rovex; Class M7 and first firebox glow; more Battle Space! wagons; first ex-Dublo locos by Wrenn.

1968 – *Flying Scotsman*; BR Mk 2 coaches; Trix BRT grain wagon; first models in Rail Blue and Q Car; ex-Dublo wagons by Wrenn.

1969 – Rovex Tri-ang Ltd, 'Cartic', container wagons and depot, and Rovex made ex-Dublo terminus station.

BATTLE SPACE! FROM THE 1960s

Four-rocket launcher.

Aircraft searchlight.

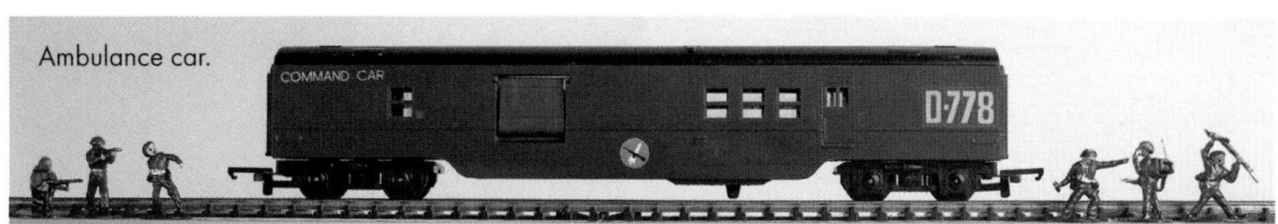

Ambulance car.

Assault tank transporter.

Bomb carrier.

Battle Space! liveried locos.

Assault tank and rocket.

Exploding car.

Helicopter launch car.

Jinty and sniper car.

Satellite launching train.

Tank rescue crane.

1970
PRE-1948 LIVERIES AND SYSTEM 6

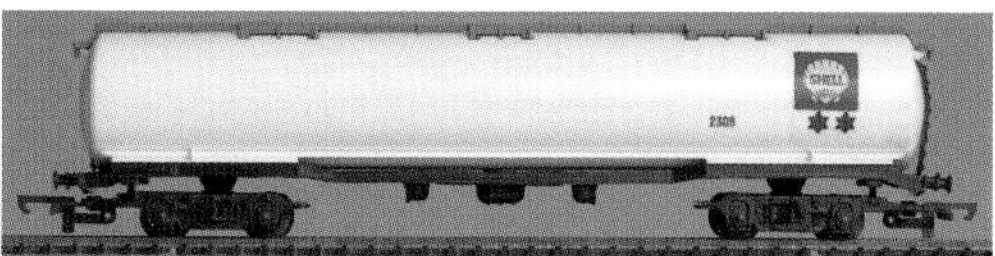

It was now two years since the end of steam on the British rail network and preservation of the remaining steam locomotives was gathering pace. Many preserved locomotives were being restored to their pre-1948 liveries.

ROVEX

A Terence Cuneo painting called 'Express Engines at Tyseley' adorned the front cover of the 1970 Tri-ang Hornby catalogue and showed GWR *Clun Castle* and LMS 'Jubilee' *Kolhapur,* both in their pre-nationalisation liveries. While models of these two locomotives were not to be found inside the catalogue, there was, for the first time, a burst of pre-1948 liveries to greet customers as they turned the pages. From just one such livery the year

The Class B12 in LNER gloss green.

The Class M7 in SR green.

The LMS blue *Coronation.*

before, there were now seven locomotives in pre-1948 colour schemes and five more in the Tri-ang Wrenn range (also included in the catalogue).

An exciting new addition to the locomotive stud was the LMS streamlined 'Princess Coronation' Class as 6220 *Coronation* in blue and silver livery. The LMS had released their first 'Princess Coronation' in 1937, built at Crewe to handle heavier loads on the London–Scotland West Coast Main Line. In all, twenty-four streamlined locomotives ('Coronations') were built, the last in 1943; the rest of the class were built without streamlined cladding ('Duchesses'). The model's arrival was late owing to difficulty in matching the complicated lining. Part was heat-printed on and the rest was hand-painted. All the class, except one, had lost their streamlined cladding by the time they passed into BR ownership. At the time of writing, Hornby have yet to produce 46243 *City of Lancaster* in BR black with 'BRITISH RAILWAYS' on the tender sides, this being the only one to keep its cladding long enough.

The LMS blue 6220 *Coronation,* LMS maroon 6201 *Princess Elizabeth,* GWR green 4983 *Albert Hall* and the SR malachite 21C151 *Winston Churchill* were all sold with a sheet of three alternative names and numbers, encouraging buyers to purchase a second model (or more) and re-name them. In the case of *Coronation,* you could re-identify it as 6221 *Queen Elizabeth,* 6222 *Queen Mary* or 6224 *Princess Alexandra.* Also available in pre-1948 liveries were the B12 4-6-0 as LNER light green 8509, M7 0-4-4T as SR green 328 and the existing LNER light green A3 4472 *Flying Scotsman.* 'Achilles' Class 4-2-2 *Lord of the Isles* was re-released in a gloss dark green GWR livery.

With new locomotive liveries, there was a need for suitably liveried rolling stock, but there were no models in the range of coaches that had been around in the 1930s and 1940s. With

The GWR 'Dean Single', *Lord of the Isles.*

The GWR 'Hall' Class, *Crumlin Hall.*

The BR Mk 1 corridor composite in Southern Railway (SR) dark green.

The LNER teak Thompson brake third.

The BR VIX ferry van.

limited money for new tooling, a compromise was required and so the existing 1950s BR Mk 1 composite and brake third coaches had to be used. Although almost one inch too long to be authentic, these were produced in fake LMS, SR and GWR livery, and the green used for the SR coaches never looked right. For LNER coaches, Thompson-style coach sides were tooled up to replace the BR sides. The 'Thompsons' did not look too bad, but they had no interior units and so always had a very empty look. The teak woodgrain effect was achieved by adding a chemical to light brown plastic which made it 'curdle'.

Sets with the LNER *Flying Scotsman* and Thompson teak coaches became one of Hornby's best-sellers. Two new wagons this year were the 100-ton Shell bogie oil tank wagon and the Anglo-Continental ferry van.

The catalogue carried a questionnaire asking customers what improvements and new products they would most like to see, and improved wheel profiles was the most frequent suggestion. Rovex had already decided to respond to customer demands for finescale track and their 'System 6' range was launched in 1970. Previous track systems had been Rovex (1950), Universal/Standard (1952), Series 3 (1958) and Super 4 (1962). All of these could be used together as they had a similar coarse rail profile. For connection to the new finer-scale System 6, an R476 converter rail was produced. Other suggestions from the customer survey were circulated and taken on-board.

System 6 was an important step on the way to turning a toy railway into a model railway for adult enthusiasts. The new track had been

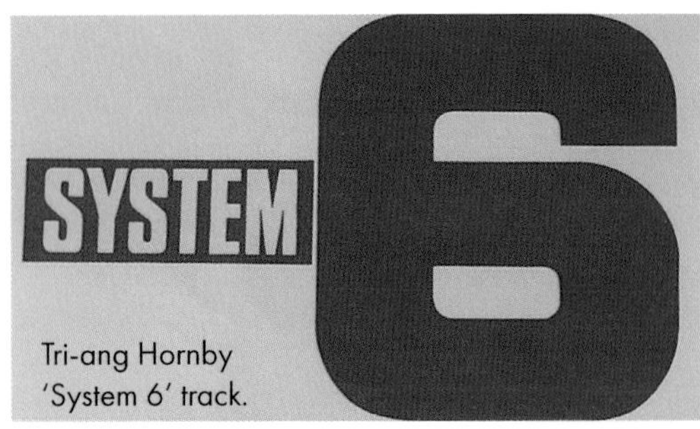

Tri-ang Hornby 'System 6' track.

A wholesale clockwork 'toy train' set.

Economy boxes.

the result of many hours of trials, because of the need for compatibility with existing locomotives and rolling stock. This had been difficult to achieve and required compromises. The points had been particularly difficult, causing a delay in their delivery. Eventually it was decided to have the track made by Roco in Austria as, by supplying several other companies, it had become economical for Roco to automate the process, thus reducing the cost.

There was always a need for cheap starter sets. The cheapest were very simple clockwork sets sold through the Wholesale Department under the Tri-ang or Rovex name to corner shops, supermarkets and by mail-order companies. Very cheap to make wagons were produced from single mouldings with clip-in wheel sets. Containers from the main range were printed with adverts for the company's products and these are sought by collectors today. A four-wheel foreign-looking coach was produced as well as both clockwork and electric versions of a Continental 0-4-0 tank engine with a one-piece body. A 'longer bodied' clockwork locomotive was planned but did not make it into production. Also, in an attempt at reducing the cost of some of the main range of wagons, five of the cheapest were sold in inexpensive brown boxes.

For the Canadian market a range of CP Rail-liveried models were delivered in May, along with the 'Polysar' bogie tank wagon. For Australia there were ACT containers and plans for Victorian Railways box cars and pulp wood cars, which did not materialise. This overseas stock was supplied in bulk and packaged on arrival by Lines Group companies in those countries.

The Australian 'ACT' container wagon.

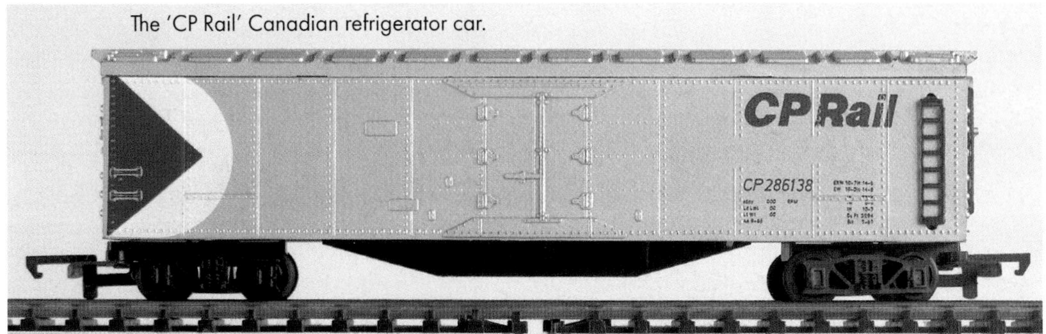

The 'CP Rail' Canadian refrigerator car.

For the Big Big 0-gauge system there was a station, log truck, caboose and a kit that could be assembled into different types of wagon and called 'Change-a-Truck'. New ideas discussed were a 0-6-0T Continental locomotive, a signal gantry, message carrier (caboose mail van), hydraulic buffer stop and a wagon-mounted animal cage with animals supplied by Scale Figures Ltd., another member of the Lines Group.

The decision had been taken in February to cease production of Minic Motorway.

HORNBY DUBLO

As indicated above, Tri-ang Wrenn locomotives and wagons were displayed in the Tri-ang Hornby catalogue, all made from former Hornby Dublo tooling. There were ten locomotives with a mixture of BR and earlier liveries, and there were sixteen wagons, almost all in private owner liveries.

1971
EVENING STAR AND LINES GROUP BREAK-UP

TRI-ANG HORNBY

The year 1971 saw the first of a new generation of models developed at Margate. BR 2-10-0 Class 9F 92220 *Evening Star* was the most complex model Rovex had ever developed. This was largely due to the need for the chassis to have ten coupled driving wheels that could manage the tight curves on a model railway layout. It was inspired by models of large American locomotives which had overcome the track radius problem. The model also needed to show a large area of daylight under the boiler and this was how *Evening Star* became the first of the company's models to be fitted with a Tri-ang Hornby version of the

The Class 9F, *Evening Star.*

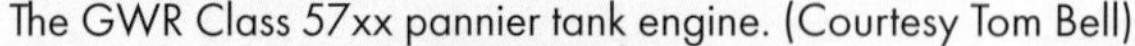

The GWR Class 57xx pannier tank engine. (Courtesy Tom Bell)

Ringfield motor in the tender, an idea that came from Fleischmann. Through reduction gears and traction tyres on some of the tender wheels, it had excellent slow running ability and could haul long trains.

During the 1970s and early 1980s, the Ringfield motor was Hornby's motor of choice over the much-dated and less efficient Tri-ang X04. That motor dated back to the 1950s and demanded more power than the Ringfield design. In the early 1980s Hornby had planned to replace the Ringfield with an imported can motor, and the first new model fitted with one was the Class 58 diesel. However, financial restrictions at the time prevented the full conversion of the fleet.

Hornby continued to use the Ringfield in its tender drive and its diesel and electric locomotives into the 1990s, but by then modellers had turned against it. They disliked a locomotive being pushed by its tender, sometimes with the valve gear locked up, and they also disliked the traction tyres. Unfortunately, the Ringfield motors sometimes developed a screeching sound and so the days of the Ringfield were numbered.

Evening Star featured in another Cuneo painting on the catalogue cover and is sometimes referred to as the last Tri-ang Hornby locomotive. However, this title belonged to the humble GWR Class 57xx pannier tank that was released late in 1971 in a gloss GWR green livery as 8751. The Tri-ang Hornby locomotive models at this time were usually finished with a coat of gloss varnish. Charles Collett's GWR 57xx pannier tank design of 1929 was a much-modelled subject, possibly because it was such a large class, 863 having been built between 1929 and 1950. As such it was an obvious choice for a model.

There was now a red version of the streamlined 'Coronation' Class (again with a choice of three alternative names) and an LMS red 'Jinty' No. 7606. The M7 tank was now in a darker Southern green and the Caledonian 'Single' returned in its splendid CR blue livery. *Britannia* was now available with a sheet of three self-adhesive alternative names and numbers. The search for realism had so far introduced synchronised smoke and

The Caledonian Railway (CR) 'Caledonian Single'.

cab fire-glow, but in 1971 went a stage further by adding exhaust sound to some models. Also referred to as 'chuff chuff', it was achieved by an economical and simple device on the underside of the tender and linked to the speed of the wheels. You could buy a replacement tender fitted with it. The LNER *Flying Scotsman*, LMS *Princess Elizabeth*, GWR *Albert Hall* and the BR black B12 were fitted with it, and on the B12 it remained a feature for many years.

The LMS 'Jinty' 0-6-0T.

A sound-fitted SR *Winston Churchill* had been intended but was not proceeded with.

Unhappy with the lack of correct model coaches for the pre-BR liveried stock, the pair of Caledonian panelled coaches (introduced with the Tri-ang 4-2-2 Caledonian Single locomotive in 1963) were now available in Southern dark green and LMS maroon. New wagon liveries were green for the single bolster wagon, BR 'Parcels' blue for the goods van and the ferry van was now in Transfesa blue livery. 'Big Four' liveries were introduced with SR for the 7-plank, LMS for the drop-door wagon, GWR for the 'Toad' brake van, and a new coke wagon was tooled up as the LNER wagon. Canada received the bogie brick wagon in CP Rail livery and the BR bogie bolster wagon with a steel rail load; not many were manufactured, and both are sought after by collectors.

The LMS maroon 'Coronation' Class, *King George VI*.

The BR 'Britannia' Class, *Robert Burns*.

The 'CP Rail' brick wagon.

The 'N.E.R' coke wagon.

The SR 7-plank wagon.

The most eye-catching introduction, however, was the Cowens-Sheldon 75-ton steam breakdown crane in red. It had a matching crew coach, which was the Thompson brake end in red.

An interesting release in 1971 was 'The Railway Children' train set, which coincided with the release of the popular film of that name. This short-lived and collectable set carried Tri-ang Hornby branding on the box lid, but a second batch in 1972 carried Hornby Railways branding. Another train set release that is sought by collectors today was the 'Wild West' train set. The locomotive was cobbled together with an obsolete clockwork 0-4-0 tank engine (known as a 'top tank'), now fitted with a cowcatcher and spark-arresting chimney and paired with a modified 'Davy Crockett' tender. Some 00-scale cowboy and indian figures, four standing and two mounted, had been bought in from The Medway Tool & Moulding Co. (another member of the Lines Group and believed to be linked to Subbuteo) at a price of twelve shillings and twenty-four shillings per hundred – ready painted.

A new series of six station sets was launched during the year, ranging from a simple island platform and shelter to a large terminus station. The former Dublo terminus station was replaced by a new and larger design which was easier to manufacture. The buildings were those introduced in 1962 but were now a bright red. Minutes of the Development Group indicate that a new girder bridge had been planned, but this was postponed until 1973. Also planned had been a Dubonnet tank wagon using the china clay slurry tank body, but this never arrived. The Battle Space! military range remained in the catalogue to clear stock and no more would be made.

In the Big Big range, the 0-6-0T battery-fitted Continental tank locomotive was released along with the animal wagon and a zoo train set.

With falling sales attributed to greater competition and changing toy fashions, coupled with problems in its overseas businesses, in 1971

The Cowans-Sheldon rail crane.

'The Railway Children' set.

The 'Wild West' clockwork train set.

Lines Bros. Ltd. were forced to call in the Receiver and the process of selling off the individual companies within the group started. Rovex was one of the most profitable and was permitted to continue trading under the name 'Pocket Money Toys'. Eventually Rovex was sold to British toymaker Dunbee-Combex-Marx (DCM) for a little under £2.26 million and the sale included the Rovex factory at Margate and the Minic factory at Canterbury. The company's name was now Rovex Ltd., and the new managing director appointed by DCM was Bob Butler.

HORNBY DUBLO

With the Lines Group being broken up and sold off, G&R Wrenn bought back their shares held by the Receiver and became an independent company again. The range of models that they were manufacturing from former Hornby Dublo tooling was renamed Wrenn Railways. George Wrenn went back to Meccano Ltd. and bought the tools for several more of the former Dublo models. It is understood that not all the remaining tooling could be found.

The R.4 Suburban Station Set.

1972

NEW OWNER, NEW NAME

HORNBY RAILWAYS

When DCM purchased Rovex for £2.26 million it gave them Hornby Railways and Scalextric, both made at Margate. It also gave them Pedigree Dolls, which included the successful Sindy range, and other products made at the Minic factory at Canterbury. Rovex also supplied them with a foot in several additional overseas markets. DCM brought new ideas to Rovex and introduced new management ideas, including ones from America.

As the Tri-ang name had been sold with one of the other Lines Group companies, it could no longer be used by Rovex Ltd., and so the system was renamed 'Hornby Railways' with effect from 1 January 1972. As the catalogue for each year is prepared during the autumn of the previous year, the 1972 edition still carried the Tri-ang Hornby branding. The cover picture was another Cuneo painting, one he had produced for British Rail to promote their Condor night freight service. The print volume for catalogues at this stage was 350,000.

The brand name on individual models did not change immediately as this required alteration to the moulding tools. An instruction was issued on 27 April 1972 that, over the following eighteen months, the name should be changed when tools had to go into the toolroom for other work to be done on them. The new inscription was to be 'Hornby Railways', unless space was restricted, in which case 'Hornby' would do. Preference was to be given to locomotives, then coaches, wagons, buildings and track, in that order.

Shown as 'new' in the catalogue was the former Tri-ang Class L1 4-4-0, which was now

The SR Class L1.

The BR Mk 1 in red and yellow.

A Caledonian brake composite coach in GWR livery.

The 'Take-a-Ticket' set.

in the dark green supposedly representing early Southern livery, as 1757. The L1 was Maunsell's successful design of 1926 for the Southern Railway and was based on the SECR L Class 4-4-0. The Mk 1 coaches were released in bright red and yellow, and the cement wagon was now bright yellow. The Caledonian coaches were available in GWR brown and cream for the first time, with the suggestion that they would be suitable for the pannier tank.

The range of starter sets now available included the 'Take-a-Ticket' electric train set. A plastic ticket, inserted into a slot in the roof

The BR 'Winkle' plate wagon.

A clockwork train set.

of the small station building, controlled a signal on the platform and altered the power supply to the track, thus determining whether the train stopped at the station or passed through. The thoughts on train control had obviously gone a lot further than the Take-a-Ticket set. Using remote control standard System 6 self-isolating points and a new pressure switch, trains passing over the switch could change the points ahead of them. This could be used to run two or more trains at the same time, switching current, stopping trains in stations, avoiding crashes on diamond crossings and even switching signals to clear the path ahead.

The year 1972 was a good one for new wagons. Besides the yellow cement wagon there were another six introductions. The first of these was the large steel mineral wagon, which was in the livery of Wm Cory, and the next was the short-lived 'Winkle' plate wagon, which would later become a breakdown crane 'runner'.

A major new van was based on an obsolete Hull & Barnsley Railway (H&B) refrigerator van and was modelled as a white

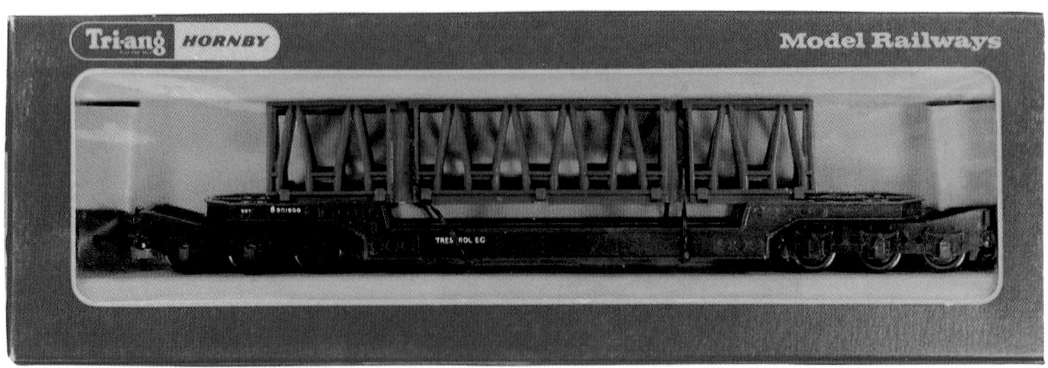

The 'Trestrol' wagon with station roof trusses.

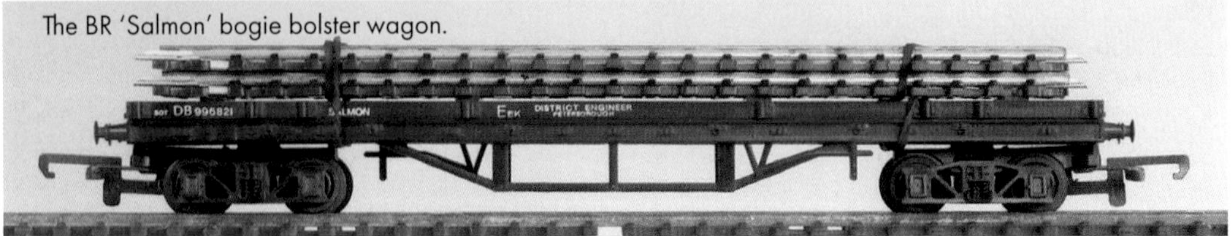

The BR 'Salmon' bogie bolster wagon.

LNER refrigerator van. Why this rare prototype was chosen is difficult to understand, especially as it would be released in a wide range of liveries in the years ahead, all non-authentic and never as H&B.

By now the Trix BRT bulk grain wagons had been replaced by a Margate-designed one, which had a slightly larger body. The rest of the new wagons made use of existing mouldings. The 'Trestrol' wagon was re-introduced with a girder load consisting of roof sections from the new terminus station. The 'Salmon' bogie bolster wagon in black carried a load of straight rails and the ferry van was now also available as a white Interfrigo freezer van.

During 1972 the co-founder of Lines Bros. and former Chairman, Walter Lines, died. Despite the disappearance of Lines Bros. Ltd., and the break-up of the Lines Group, the separation was not complete as Richard Lines, who had joined Rovex in 1951, remained with Rovex Ltd. and helped to guide the company's product range until he retired in 1995.

HORNBY DUBLO

The year 1972 was the last time that the Wrenn models were included in the catalogue as from now on Wrenn would manage their own marketing.

So, what happened to Meccano Ltd. and the Binns Road factory in Liverpool?

In 1972, Meccano Ltd. at Liverpool had been bought by Airfix Industries while General Mills of America purchased most of the shares of Meccano France S. A., renaming the French company Miro-Meccano. Meccano continued to be manufactured in France. Meanwhile, owing to competition, Meccano Ltd. at Liverpool lost much of its share of the toy market and Airfix closed the Binns Road factory in November 1979. Sixty-five years of toy-making there thus ended, leading to its demolition.

The 'Interfrigo' ferry van.

1973

SILVER SEAL AND HORNBY MINITRIX

HORNBY RAILWAYS

In 1973 Rovex had a new Director of Marketing and Sales, Karl Mueller. In the years ahead he would steer the company through choppy waters and play a major role in preventing the company from being sold overseas.

Rovex were now forging ahead and a completely new locomotive in the catalogue was an ex-LMS 'Black Five' as BR lined black 45192. As a money-saver, the model used the 'Britannia's' valve gear, but this would be corrected in 1977. It was the domeless body type and came with a sheet of self-adhesive names and numbers for both 45158 *Glasgow Yeomanry* and 45156 *Ayrshire Yeomanry,* as well as easily fitted nameplates. William Stanier's 'Black Fives' formed the largest class of LMS locomotives, 842 having been built between 1934 and 1951.

There was also a new tender-drive (9F tender) 'Britannia' Class as 70013 *Oliver Cromwell* and the Class 9F was in normal plain black with early BR decals as 92166.

All the above models were 'Silver Seal' locomotives and came in special packaging. 'Silver Seal' referred to their having tender-

The BR 'Black Five'.

Lord Westwood.

Industrial tank No.25550.

A shunter's truck.

The LNER short clerestory coach.

The LNER short brake van.

mounted Ringfield motors and finer-scale wheels that were fitted with nickel-plated tyres. An odd-ball new locomotive was the 'Hall' Class in bright red as 25555 *Lord Westwood.* The 25555 was the Rovex telephone number and Lord Westwood was Chairman of the parent company DCM. The story goes that he was delighted to be presented with one of the models fitted with an eye-patch, like the one he wore. Another Rovex number was carried in a red version of the Industrial 0-4-0T as 25550, which was the telephone number of the Hornby Service Department.

A new world record was set by a Hornby locomotive when it completed 273.84 real miles in a non-stop run at Mevagissey Model Railway between 31 July and 8 August 1973. It had run for 194 hours and 37 minutes without being touched and the feat was recorded in the *Guinness Book of Records.*

The Mk 2 coaches had been upgraded with Inter-city branding and chrome window frames. Ones used for mail-order were without the chrome and the red and cream Mk 1 mail-order coaches had lining missing. By now the clerestory coaches were also available in a teak finish with LNER branding.

New wagons in 1973 were a short grey LNER brake van (which would see much use in train sets), a grey shunter's truck (supplied with an uncoupling tool) and the H&B van, now in pale blue and marked 'Fine Fish'.

'The Minera Lime Company' lime van.

A 'Beatties' mineral wagon.

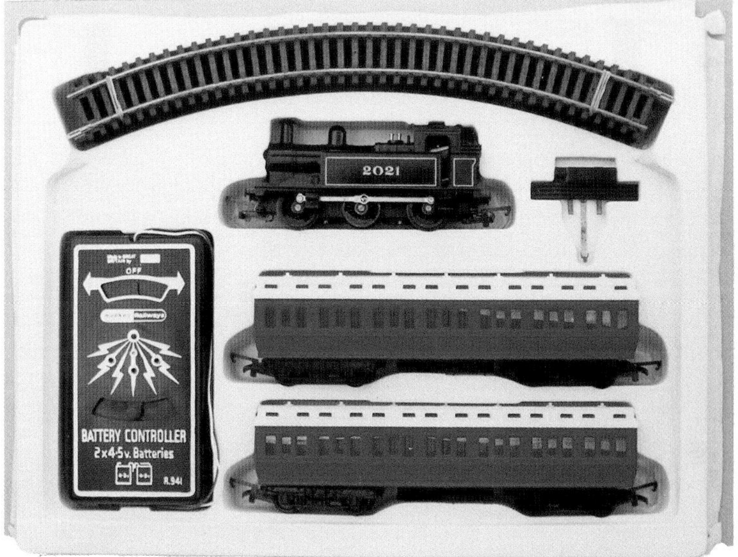

The 'Local Passenger Train' set.

These, however, were just the tip of the iceberg as there was a whole page of the catalogue devoted to a new series of nine 'Silver Seal' wagons, which had nickel-plated wheel tyres fitted. Five of the wagons were new versions of ones already in the range and these were an open 7-plank 'Lancashire Coke Co. Ltd', the cattle wagon in SR dark brown, a large hopper wagon carrying the name 'Roberts', the coke wagon 'Bannockburn' and a black NCB large mineral wagon. The remaining four wagons were all completely new and included a pale grey 'Monobloc' type tank wagon with Shell decals, a brown lime van for 'The Minera Lime Company Ltd.' and two private owner versions of a 5-plank wagon made from the lower half of the lime van. These two were a green 'A. W. Day Ltd.' and a pale grey 'General Refractories'.

The first special wagon commissioned by a shop was delivered in 1973 when 3000 yellow steel mineral wagons carrying the addresses of branches of Beatties of London Ltd. were delivered. They were to be given away with Hornby train sets sold by the company.

SR 7-plank wagons showing colour variations.

Three Hornby Minitrix locomotives.

The new versatile and inexpensive girder bridge kit was now available, and it could be made up for single or double track; further, by adding units, any length could be created. Its simple versatility was typical of a Rovex design and the supporting piers could be swivelled to fit any trackwork. The first year the bridge was made in orange plastic, after which green was used. There were also now System 6 curved points and Riko were supplying Hornby's scenic landscaping materials.

A strong emphasis on colourful train sets to attract younger enthusiasts resulted in some strange rolling stock liveries. These included bright red clerestory coaches and the ferry van with either Fyffes white and yellow livery or Ford blue and white. The seven-plank open wagon with SR branding could be found in blue, red, grey or dark brown.

The introduction of Value Added Tax (VAT) as a replacement for Purchase Tax meant that power units, as well as train sets, were now taxed at 10 per cent. Power units no longer needed to be excluded from the Hornby catalogue and the 1973 edition was the first to include these. It launched a new range of power control 'centres', which took in hand a suggestion from the public consultation.

Rovex had not wanted to get into N-gauge production but, when approached in 1972 by the German Trix company asking if Rovex would be willing to market a British Minitrix range in the UK, they saw the advantage of having their finger on the N-gauge pulse. From January 1973, Hornby Minitrix came into being and it proved a successful partnership. Rovex assisted with the choice of subject to be made and helped with design and Trix supplied the finished products in Hornby Minitix packaging. It was no great earner but ticked over nicely for several years.

Graham Farish had not been viewed as a rival until 1973 when it launched a range of 00-scale plastic wagons, mostly in private owner liveries. The company had been the first to produce a two-rail 00-gauge system after the Second World War and produced some nice locomotives with die-cast bodies – GWR 'King', SR 'WC/BB' and a GWR 'Prairie' tank. There was also a scale length Pullman car, which sold well, and some nice suburban coaches. In 1970 the company saw a future in N gauge and made a serious and successful bid for the British N-gauge market, but then decided to scale up their wagon designs for an 00 range. Two years later a range of 00 coaches followed.

1974
POSTER CAMPAIGN AND FAREWELL 'PRINCESS'

HORNBY RAILWAYS

To improve printed detail on plastic models, in 1974 Rovex changed from the use of 'hotfoil' (heat printing) and transfers to a new process called 'pad' or 'Tampo printing'. More importantly, it allowed more intricate designs to be printed onto wagons, etc., adding greatly to realism. It had been used on a few models the previous year.

Hornby posters started to appear on outdoor poster hoardings in June, July and September. This greatly increased public awareness of Hornby. One depicted the LNER *Flying Scotsman* model with the message *'Drive one this weekend'* and the other showed the GWR pannier tank with a train and the message read *'Take a different train home tonight'.*

A new locomotive in the catalogue this year was the Brush Class 47 diesel, which was in BR two-tone green as D1738. It was the first diesel model in the Silver Seal range. The locomotives were built by the Brush Electrical Engineering Co. Ltd. and introduced in 1961; they formed a large class. Also planned for release in 1974, but arriving late, was the Ivatt Class 2MT 2-6-0. This was H. G. Ivatt's mixed traffic design of 1946 and 128 of these were built between 1946 and 1952. It was the first Hornby model to have glazed cab windows including the cab-back in the tender. Compromises to keep down the tooling cost received some criticism. Another new model was the black LMS Fowler Class 2P 4-4-0 No. 690. I had been surprised to see one in a shop window the year before as it had not been in the 1973 catalogue. It must have been a late addition and turned out to be the SR Class L1 4-4-0 in LMS black livery and was a bit too large for a 2P. But when money is tight ... !

H&B vans showing hot-foil printing versus pad printing.

The BR Class 47.

The ex-LMS Class 2MT.

The SR Class L1 model as a LMS Class 2P.

Also planned was a blue version of the 'Princess' locomotive, but it appears not to have been made. However, unlined BR black, green or maroon versions of *Princess Victoria* were produced for mail order sets during the year, the maroon one being particularly rare today. These were a 'last fling' with the Princess tooling before it was laid to rest after twenty-three years. Thoughts had already turned to a suitable replacement and the only subject mentioned in Development Meeting minutes was a 'Duchess'. A temporary replacement of a large locomotive for mail order sets was needed in the meantime, and a cut-down version of the 'Britannia' model was produced and named *Iron Duke*.

After sixteen years in production the original Tri-ang Pullman cars were also about to be retired and would be replaced by more realistic 1928 steel K Class cars based on preserved *Lucille*. Both umber and cream and blue and grey liveries were to be available, but not until 1975.

While Rovex continued to manufacture its very cheap wagons from single moldings for its play sets, it required some cost effective, but better, wagons for the next range up, and three new ones appeared to serve this purpose. There was a long wheelbase van, a simplified 'Monobloc' tanker and a wagon with girder sides which carried either wheel sets or cabin cruiser. The yellow 'Shell' simplified tanker was minus its end steps and, as such, it appeared in many different liveries over the years, as did the long van. The latter started with 'Cadbury's'

The *Princess Victoria* in the rare maroon BR livery.

A stripped-down BR 'Britannia' Class locomotive as *Iron Duke*.

and 'Kellogg's' liveries. New wagons in the main range included the 14T tank wagon in 'Esso' livery and a green H&B van as 'Prime Pork'. Additions to the Silver Seal range were H&B vans 'Lyons Maid' and 'Bird's Eye' and an LMS brake van. To reduce further the cost of 0-4-0 locomotives in the cheap starter sets, mechanisms were now being bought-in from Hong Kong.

There were new building kits in the catalogue, some of which had been purchased from Pola in Germany. There were also two returns in the form of the gravity unloading bridge and the helicopter car. The former Tri-ang 'Blue Pullman' had also returned, now in its third livery of bright blue with a white window band.

There was a link with the past in 1974 when DCM bought an interest in the leading South African toy company Tri-ang Pedigree (SA) (PTY) Ltd., who, back in the 1950s, had made Tri-ang Railways at a factory in Natal. They were now Hornby agents in South Africa.

A freelance LWB van in 'Cadbury's' livery.

A girder wagon with boat.

A LMS brake van.

1975
BREATHING SPACE FOR DEVELOPMENT

Pre-production model of the international 0-4-0T as *Iron Horse*.

The catalogue celebrated the 150th anniversary of the opening of the Stockton & Darlington Railway. Several pages of the catalogue were taken up with articles about the big four railway companies and advice on landscaping a layout.

At Margate there was a declared aim to increase the range of locomotives in the catalogue to twenty-four, and a list was drawn-up of ten possible subjects that needed to be researched. The late delivery of the previous year's models meant that Rovex already had plenty to sell in 1975 and a new 0-4-0T was released to replace the 'Continental' 0-4-0T, which had been produced in vast numbers for starter sets in both clockwork and electric mode. Today, this new model is referred to as the 'International' tank locomotive. It was powered by a Hong Kong can motor and had a well detailed body. It was intended for overseas sales but sold more in the UK.

A new mainline diesel for Australia was also being investigated, to be released in 1977 in Victorian Railways and Commonwealth Railways liveries. This would replace the double-ended diesel.

Work had also started on a model of the Southern Railway 'King Arthur' Class N15 4-6-0, which would not be available until the following year. The N15 class was designed by Robert W. Urie in 1918 for the London & South Western Railway. The tender of the model was an updated

SR Class N15, *Sir Dinadan*.

A 'Consett Iron Co.' operating hopper wagon.

An 'Ocean' 7-plank wagon.

Fowler design from the LMS 3F model and initially it was fitted with an automatic uncoupling device. This consisted of a rocking coupling hook that was weighted so, if the locomotive stopped suddenly, the hook would lift and disengage. The trick was to get the locomotive to pull away before the hook descended again. It may have been the problem of getting this to work which led to a delay in the release of the model and it reached the market, without the mechanism, as SR green 795 *Sir Dinadan*. Other problems identified were the slow running of the tool and the inability to fit the Ringfield motor. This would contribute to an early withdrawal of the first 'King Arthur'.

There were some new wagon liveries. These were two 7-plank open wagons – in dark brown 'Ocean' and in red 'Princess Royal Colliery Co.'. The large mineral wagon was now blue 'Norstand', the former Tri-ang hopper wagon was a maroon 'Consett Iron Co. Limited'. The simplified yellow 'Shell' Monoblock tank wagon was joined by a red 'Texaco' version. Upgrading of models to the new fine scale 'Silver Seal' wheel standards continued. It was also reported that the tooling for the composite and brake third Mk 1 coaches was badly worn.

Work had also started on two six-wheel vans, with sliding centre wheel sets to take tight curves. These would not be available until the following year and consisted of a maroon 'Palethorpes' sausage van and a white LMS milk van. Other uses for the six-wheel chassis were considered and sample models built. One planned for 1976 had been a twin gas tank wagon, but this, and a planned operating fuel depot, did not make it into production. Gas tank wagons dated from the time when coaches were gas-lit and had clerestory-type roofs to house the gas lamps. There was also discussion about the possibility of six-wheel coaches, but sadly this idea was not followed up.

Work was also done to improve the track fishplates, modify the buffer stops, produce an improved power clip (based on one made by Jouef) and improve the X.04 electric motor used in many of the locomotives. Adaptions were being made where possible to take the Ringfield motor. What was described as a 'coal-loader' and a new turntable were also under development, as too was a new split-chassis 0-4-0 tank locomotive, which was to have a die-cast frame and be 'clip-together' for easy construction.

Following the success of the 1974 poster campaign, there was a second blitz, with new designs, which this time also included newspapers.

A 'Palethorpes' six-wheel van.

1976
NEW COMPETITION

During 1976, three new 00 model railway systems came onto the British market – Lima 00, Mainline Railways (by Palitoy) and Airfix Railways (later called GMR). All three were producing attractive, good quality, detailed models, all-over spray painted and with the numbers and names crisply printed onto the sides so finely that a magnifying glass was required to read the smallest of print. It was amazing and very exciting. This surely was what model railways were all about and by the time the models started to appear later in the year the demand was incredible.

Lima had already had some success with N gauge in the UK and, in 1973, had produced a British H0 range. The latter had not been well received and so, in 1976, Lima switched to 00 scale for the UK and were soon attracting a following. Their first locomotive was an LNER Class J50 0-6-0T, but they soon found that the demand was for new classes of diesel locomotives and modern stock for them to pull. Their first diesels were a Class 33 and a Class 55 'Deltic', which were released in 1977.

Airfix had announced their intension to enter the British 00 market in 1975 and used two manufacturers in Hong Kong to make the models; these were Sanda Kan and Cheong Tak. Their first samples were seen at the 1976 Toy Fair and the first train set was out in time for Christmas.

Palitoy launched their Mainline 00 system at the 1976 Harrogate and Brighton Trade Toy Fairs and were clearly ahead of Airfix with their development. Palitoy already used Kader in Hong Kong to manufacture toys for them and so asked Kader to produce the tools and sell them the products to market as their own Mainline brand. The fact that Kader owned the tools would lead to a very important development thirteen years later, which dramatically affected the Hornby story.

HORNBY RAILWAYS

The development of a new model railway system takes at least two years and these announcements gave Rovex two years to prepare themselves to meet the challenge. While the two factories continued to trade as Rovex Ltd., the company operated as three divisions which tended to drift apart. The Canterbury factory became Pedigree Dolls & Toys. The Margate factory with Hornby Railways, Big Big, Hornby Minitrix, Minic, Jump Jockey, Frog Kits and Scalextric was, for a time, known as Rovex Models & Hobbies. The name 'Hornby Hobbies' would not be formerly adopted until 1 January 1979, although it was used at times before that date.

To encourage exports, 'Rovex International' was formed as the third division and the largest

Hornby stamps promotion.

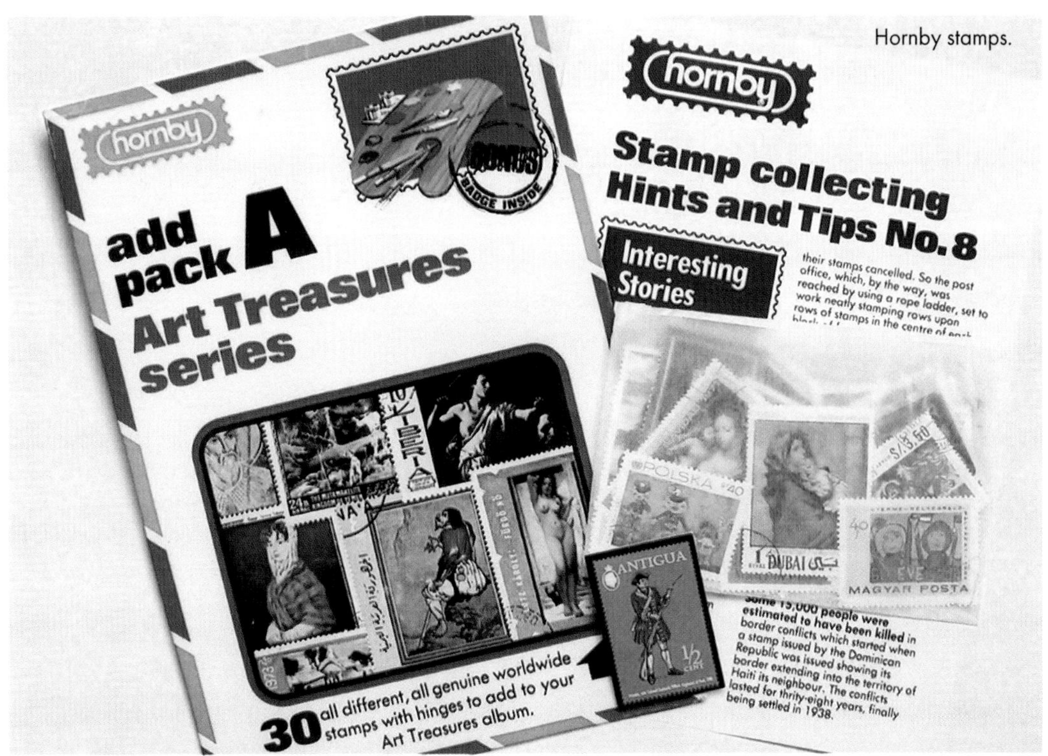

Hornby stamps.

export market was Australia with a new range of Australian sets planned each year. In 1977 these included the new GM diesel. By 1978, Hornby Railway products would be sent bulk-packed to an Australian company owned by DCM called Lidrana (Pty) Ltd., who would use them to make up Hornby train sets for local distribution. However, all was not well at Lidrana.

In April 1976, DCM acquired the American giant toy manufacturer Louis Marx which had three factories in the United States and one in Hong Kong. The company was one of America's oldest toy makers and employed 3,200 people. The purchase cost DCM over $15 million and would prove to be 'a bridge too far'. Bob Butler was sent to America to manage Louis Marx, and Karl Mueller became Managing Director at Margate. He was an ideas man and looked for ways of widening the company's product base.

New products introduced in 1976 included Hornby Stamps (thematic packets and albums supplied by Scott Publishing Co. in New York), Shipwright (kits of classic ships launched in 1976) and Minic Ships. The last of these were the re-introduction of a range of waterline die-cast 1:1200 scale ships previously made by Minic in the early 1960s. The original harbour models were re-used, but new tooling was produced for ten large battleships and liners. They were made by a DCM company in Hong Kong on a budget of £12,000. None of the three products produced enough sales and were dropped after two years.

From 1976, all Silver Seal locomotives had detachable tenders. There were three new locomotives, including the SR 'King Arthur' Class *Sir Dinadan* referred to above in 1975. The second was a new improved model of a Class 08 diesel shunter, which had the automatic uncoupling device referred to above. The third was a J83 Class 0-6-0 tank engine in LNER green as 8477, which was a replacement for the worn-out and withdrawn 'Jinty' model of 1953 vintage. In addition to these the B12 4-6-0 was now in war-time plain black with 'NE' on the tender and carried the number 1577.

Hornby Minic waterline ships. (Courtesy SAS)

The Class B12 in LNER war-time black.

The J83 model was based on an LNER rebuild of M. Holmes's Class D tank engine, of which forty were built for the North British Railway in 1900. As a replacement model it was cheap to produce as it used the existing 0-6-0 chassis and was a simple moulding lacking separate handrails.

The coaches were now all in the Silver Seal range. An important addition to the range of coaches would not interest adult enthusiasts, but was, nevertheless, to have quite an impact in the years ahead. It was a simple British-outline three-compartment, four-wheel coach in blue that appeared in the Rural Rambler train set with a blue industrial 0-4-0T numbered 7178. The body sides of the new coach were clearly based on part of the clerestory coach and the chassis was that of a brake van with its running boards. The roof and window glazing were a single clear moulding which clipped into the body from above and the roof sprayed to the required colour. In the years ahead it would be manufactured in at least ten different liveries and was used in many less expensive starter train sets.

The revised Class 08.

All wagons (including the Australian ones) were also now up to Silver Seal standard and new ones included a revised Esso 14T tank wagon, a United Dairies milk tanker and a re-tooled GWR brake van. New 900 Series power controllers arrived in 1976 as well as a new series of signals.

An Irish train set ('Sláinte Express') was sold through Kilroy Brothers of Dublin. This contained the 'Hymek' and two Mk 2 coaches in Córas lompair Éireann (CIE) orange and black livery, and the locomotive and coaches were also available solo. All parts, including Hornby branded packaging, were produced at Margate.

A new independent model magazine launched in May 1976 was *Hornby Express*. It was published by Timebridge Ltd., but from June by Embankment Press (Publications Ltd.). It was not successful and lost its 'Hornby' title a year later before disappearing altogether.

The LNER Class J83 tank engine.

The Irish CIE passenger train set.

The S&DJR four-wheel coach.

Hornby Express magazine, first issue.

1977
HST AND REGIONAL COACHES

The catalogue contained many exciting layout suggestions and introduced a new track stencil specifically designed for use with Hornby track to help you design your own layout. There was also the Hornby Railways track plans book, now in its umpteenth edition. Father and son were as busy as ever on the landscaping. Added to the plastic building kits was the huge Pola main line station with its Victorian/Continental architecture. Special attention was drawn to the play-value of Hornby with catalogue pages devoted to its operating accessories, such as the mail van TPO, gravity unloading bridge, breakdown cranes and container and car carriers, as well as a new eight-exit turntable.

There were new train sets, which were photographed to make them more appealing, and these included two large Silver Jubilee sets commemorating the Queen's Silver Jubilee. Between 1977 and 1980, train sets contained a floppy gramophone record containing a message by Bernard Cribbins about the set and how to get started with it.

During the year the gloss liveries were done away with and a matt finish adopted. This decision may have been influenced by the matt-finished Mainline and

The Hornby track stencil.

The 'Silver Jubilee' freight train set and the 'Silver Jubilee Pullman' train set. (Courtesy LSK)

Airfix models coming onto the market by then. Indeed, at the July Development Meeting, models currently marketed by the three rivals were discussed and the decision reinforced that Hornby needed to up its game: increasing authenticity was now essential. Top of the list was the need to build a comprehensive

Comic actor, Bernard Cribbins, who helped to promote Hornby Railways.

Sample model of *City of Truro*.

and balanced range of quality locomotives from small to large, steam, diesel and electric.

To meet this challenge, new models were being planned up to two years ahead, including an LNER A4 4-6-2, a 'Western' diesel hydraulic, an SR Class E2 0-6-0T, an LMS 'Patriot' 4-6-0, a GWR Class 47xx 2-8-0 and a model of the preserved GWR classic *City of Truro* 4-4-0. The last of these was to have been the first of a range of finely detailed up-market products (the '700' range) to appeal to serious modellers and a sample model was made up that still exists today. The tooling cost was estimated at £80,000, but the estimated market price was £20. Concern over cost meant that the project was abandoned in August 1978. The GWR Class 47xx was also dropped. A major updating of the wagon range in 1979 was also planned, including more modern wagons and an accurate 10-ft wheelbase with scale buffer heights. A new coupling hook was to be introduced for closer coupling.

The model of *Evening Star* also returned and, at a cost of £2,000, a tool was made to produce the correct valve-gear for the 'Black 5'. All non-Silver Seal steam locomotives were fitted with scale wheels.

Another interesting matter that was discussed at some length in September was whether any of the 1979 range of new models should be outsourced to a company in Hong Kong. This was twenty years before a move of production to China was eventually made. The suggestion may have come up as the Airfix and Mainline railway models were being made there and Rovex's parent company, DCM, had interests in Hong Kong. It seems that, back in 1977, the idea was strongly resisted.

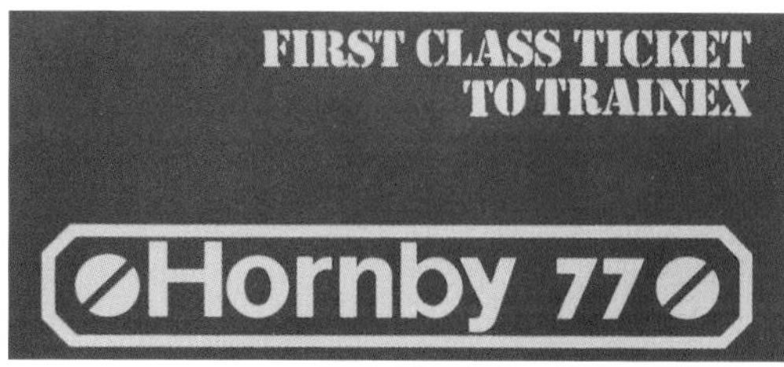

A 'Trainex' 1977 ticket.

One idea that did bear fruit during the year was a travelling Hornby exhibition on a train, appropriately named 'Trainex'. The train toured the country and was parked in stations for short periods so that invited local retailers could visit the exhibition and order stock. One of the coaches was fitted out with showcases displaying all the current range and proposed new models. Another carriage had tables and chairs where retailers sat with the Hornby sales staff and discussed the next year's orders while refreshments were provided.

The most exciting new motive power in 1977 was the BREL Class 43, which, with its trailers, formed the 'High Speed Train' (HST). HSTs went into service on the Western Region mainline in October 1976 and are still very much in evidence today on parts of the network. This highly successful BR design would also become one of Hornby's biggest revenue earners. Additional trailer cars could be bought.

Also new was the hinted at Stanier LMS non-streamlined 'Duchess' ('Princess Coronation' Class) 4-6-2, which was the replacement for the 'Princess'. It was first released as the preserved locomotive 6233 *Duchess of Sutherland* in LMS maroon.

The LMS, *Duchess of Sutherland.*

The BR Class 25.

There was also a BR-designed Bo-Bo Class 25 diesel as a replacement for the Brush A1A-A1A Class 31, the tooling for which was showing excessive wear. The real Class 25s were introduced in 1961 as mixed-traffic locomotives for the secondary routes. They were a development of the Class 24, and 323 of them were built between 1961 and 1967 at Derby, Darlington and by Beyer Peacock. From the start this model was released in both two-tone green and blue livery.

At last the 'regional' coaches were ready for release incorporating several money-saving compromises. There were shared parts to produce four sets of two coaches from a total of

LNER teak Gresley coaches.

Pre-production model of the BR Mk 3 TSO.

Pre-production sample of the BR 'Carflat'.

eight tools, with inserts to produce variations. It meant that the coaches were all the same length, had the same two seating units and shared an underframe. To begin with they were also fitted with BR bogies, but this would be corrected later. The range consisted of Stanier LMS CK and BTK (also available in BR crimson and cream livery), Collett-style GWR CK and BTK, Gresley LNER CK and BCK and Maunsell style SR CK and BTK. The GWR coaches were quite convincing, although the plastic was a bit too yellow. The LNER coaches certainly had the right shape, but the teak finish was still achieved by curdling the plastic. Sadly, the SR stock was more obviously compromised by using parts from the Collett coaches. Having said that, the new coaches were a hundred times better than the fake-liveried Mk 1 they replaced. They had been designed to allow for the fitting of internal lighting units. Also new in 1977 was the first attempt at a BR Mk 3 coach, which was rather short. A first class version would follow.

There were two new private owner liveries for the 5-plank open wagon. These were in black 'Bestwood' and in maroon 'Arnolds Sands'. Another new wagon was the BR bogie FVA 'Carflat'; the real vehicles were built on the chassis of scrapped pre-1948 coaches and Rovex were able to use the chassis of the new 'regional' coaches and a supply of Minix cars to make a cheap new addition.

A new Silver Seal motor was ready and was first fitted in the new Australian GM diesel. The Class 08 diesel shunter in NSWR maroon was supplied to Australia to join the Class 31 in the same livery, which had first been made in NSWR maroon in 1974. Several of the UK wagons were produced in Australian liveries for sets assembled in Australia and a NSWR Z class goods brake van model was also produced at Margate, but unfortunately there was a misunderstanding about the colour required and orange ones were sent. A fresh batch of correct NSWR maroon ones followed.

The government had received a request from Russia to acquire any old tooling surplus to requirements within the British toy industry. Wanting to show willing, but against advice, the management of DCM offered the tooling for the Frog aircraft kits and the Tri-ang Big Big 0-gauge railway. A deal was struck under which the tooling would be paid for with products manufactured from them, sent back to DCM to sell. It proved to be a bad deal as the tools were misused and damaged, and Rovex had to sort out the problems. The aircraft kits sent back by Russia were of a very poor quality and consequently difficult to assemble. The imported models were sold in Great Britain under the Novo brand and an organisation had to be set up to handle sales.

A 5-plank 'Arnolds Sands' wagon.

The Class 08 in New South Wales Railway (NSWR) maroon livery.

The Australian GM S Class Commonwealth Railways diesel.

1978

NEW BUILDING RANGE

There was a change of direction with the graphics in the catalogue and for box-top illustrations. The emphasis was on precision and this could be emphasised better with coloured drawings than with photographs, although they sometimes exaggerated. This was effective, making you want to own one of these beautiful models. It was also in line with Hornby's agreed target of 'greater authenticity by 1978'.

There were major changes in the range of locomotives, but unfortunately the first of these ran against the new philosophy. A model of a GWR 'King' Class, 6024 *King Edward I,* was released at the same time as a more authentic model was released by Lima – a point not missed by the press! This was a warning shot across Hornby's bows and only one batch of the model was made before the tooling went back to the toolroom. Two years later a new and better

GWR, *King Edward I*.

Pre-production sample of *King Henry VIII* to show improvements.

GWR 'King' Class locomotive appeared in the catalogue as 6013 *King Henry VIII*. The main criticism of the original Hornby model was that daylight could not be seen under the boiler, as on the real locomotive, while the Lima model had this feature.

The problem now was what to do with the sub-standard models. The answer, of course, was to sell them in a giant set with other less popular items in the storeroom and to make the set so impressive and reasonably priced that it sold. Some 1,900 giant sets were assembled with two ovals of track, sidings, three different locomotives and rolling stock for them to pull, a range of buildings and two power units. Everything was still in its original packaging and was stacked inside a purpose-made cardboard trunk to make the largest train set ever sold by the company. This was the 'Hornby King Size' train set and went on sale in 1979 with the remainder re-numbered and sold in 1980.

Another new locomotive in 1978 was the GWR Class 101 0-4-0T. Only one member of the class (No. 101) was made by the GWR and it was never to leave the Swindon yard. It was converted to oil burning as an experiment. The Hornby model of it proved to be far more successful. It provided a new inexpensive model for starter sets while also being based on a real locomotive. It would see many different liveries in its long life, but, for 1978, the model was in GWR matt green as No. 101. Most of the Hornby locomotives were now in the new matt finish, but unfortunately it had a waxy look to it that rather spoilt the effect and would lead to an important policy decision in 1980, which would greatly improve their look.

The 'King Size' train set.

There was also a new model of the LMS Class 3F 0-6-0T 'Jinty' which was more accurate than the 1953 withdrawn model and included internal cab detail. As evidence of the effort that went into getting it right, no fewer than three pre-production samples exist showing different stages of improvement. Two versions of the new model were initially made, one in LMS maroon as 16440 and the other in lined BR black as 47458.

Having produced the Class 25 diesel, the team had looked around for a different body they could fit on the chassis and had chosen the 'Sad Eyes' Class 29. The class of 20 was introduced to BR between 1958 and 1960, and was built by the North British Locomotive Co. Both green D6110 and blue 6124 model versions were produced. A 'Baby Deltic' may also have been considered as a hand-made model of one was found in the factory store.

There was now a London Transport version of the Class 57xx GWR pannier tank, although the body was red rather than maroon, and the Ivatt Class 2MT 2-6-0 was now in BR green as 46521. The GWR 'Hall' was now 5934 *Kneller Hall* and the 'Black Five' was available in LMS maroon as 4657. A Class 86 West Coast Main Line electric locomotive was originally planned, but this was postponed, possibly because the overhead catenary was no longer made.

An important addition to the coaches was a reasonably accurate model of a travelling post office (TPO) in LMS maroon along with the lineside apparatus.

Also added to the range of Collett-type coaches was a restaurant car, and the LNER Gresley coaches now had a sleeping car.

The GWR Class 101 tank engine.

The new 'Jinty' in BR lined black.

The new 'Jinty' in LMS maroon.

The Class 29.

Sample model prepared of a 'Baby Deltic'.

London Transport Class 57xx.

Internal lighting sets were introduced for coaches and powered from the track. A new wagon was the 'Prestwin' silo wagon.

An important image change came with a whole new series of clip-together plastic railway buildings to be sold in kit form. The most striking difference was that the brickwork and tiles were printed onto the surface of the plastic and looked much more realistic than earlier buildings. Items included a waiting room, booking hall, water tower, engine shed, halt station shelter, platform fencing, signal box, goods depot and buffer stop. In addition, the platform sections were re-tooled to improve surface detail but remained compatible with the earlier ones. The total tooling cost was estimated to be £58,460. There was also a new elevated track system.

It was in 1978 that the development group at Rovex set out their locomotive strategy for the next four years. It was agreed that some thirty-five model locomotives would need to be in the range by 1982. This compared with twenty-six planned for 1979. The thoughts were that for each of the Big Four, plus BR steam and BR 'modern', there needed to be a range of locomotives that 'could be said to typify the company's loco operations'. It was agreed that the range should include large and small, as well as expensive and inexpensive. It will be obvious

A BR 'Prestwin' twin silo wagon.

to the reader that this would place a heavy bias on steam outline models at the expense of more modern traction. This left the way open for Lima who designed models of seventeen of the British modern traction classes, giving them a major share of the modern image market.

The principle of a balanced locomotive stable is alive today, but it is now influenced by which real locomotives still exist in preservation and are available to be laser-scanned. Such is the demand for accuracy today when compared with forty years ago.

The Collett restaurant car.

The LMS travelling post office.

Model of a booking hall.

1979
ZERO 1 AT HORNBY HOBBIES

The start of the year saw the name of the company change from Rovex Ltd. to Hornby Hobbies Ltd.

The big story in 1979 was Zero 1, originally referred to as 'Multiple Train Control'. This sixteen-channel command control system was the idea of a Portuguese engineer, Lu D'Sa, who visited the firm to see if Rovex would be interested in it. It was based on digital technology and was a forerunner to the NMRA Digital Command Control (DCC) system, which appeared in the 1990s. A layout was built at Hornby's detached unit in Ramsgate and demonstrated to the development team. It was claimed that sixteen locomotives could be operated at the same time, independently. Although an important piece of history, Zero 1 was not widely successful. The controller units and decoder modules were expensive and the cost of replacing decoders when they failed put off people buying it. Track cleanliness was important and chip-fitted locomotives could not be used on DC systems.

There were also another four completely new locomotives in 1979. These were the LNER A4 in BR livery as 60022 *Mallard*, unrebuilt 'Patriot' 4-6-0 in LMS maroon as 5541 *Duke of Sutherland*, London Brighton & South Coast Railway (LBSC) brown Class E2 0-6-0T as No. 100 and attractively styled BR 'Western' Class 52 C-C diesel hydraulic in BR maroon as D1062 *Western Courier*. Already dropped from the range were the 'King Arthur' Class *Sir Dinadan*, the LNER J83 tank and the pannier tank in London Transport red. They were probably dropped because none of them came up to the new standards Hornby were setting.

The iconic Class A4 was bound to be a good seller. The A4 was Nigel Gresley's

The 'Zero 1' controllers.

The Class A4, *Mallard.*

The LMS 'Patriot' Class, *Duke of Sutherland.*

The Class 52, *Western Courier.*

ultimate express engine development and arrived in 1935. It was one of the most successful streamlined railway engines designed in Great Britain and one of the class (*Mallard*) still holds the world speed record for a steam locomotive.

The LMS 'Patriots' were also known as 'Baby Scots' and were Henry Fowler's mixed-traffic locomotives of 1930. Fifty-two were built at either Derby or Crewe between 1930 and 1934. The LBSC Class E2 were designed by L. B. Billinton as passenger tanks and they came into service in 1913, whereas the 'Western' mainline diesel hydraulics were designed and constructed at Swindon in 1962 to provide high-powered mixed-traffic locomotives on the Western Region.

An interesting Irish train set released this year was the 'CIE Local Goods', which included a Class 101 0-4-0T in CIE livery and the 5-plank wagon in SLNC and CIE livery, a white CIE long van and a Shell 'Monoblock' tank wagon.

There was one new coach, a BR Inter-city Mk 3 FO to go with the previously introduced SO.

New wagons consisted of a new ventilated van based on a BR VEA 'Vanwide', a 27-ton steel 'Tippler' mineral wagon and a 10-ft wheelbase

The Class E2 in London Brighton & South Coast Railway (LBSC) brown.

7-plank open wagon with a sheet rail. There was also a new modern GLW wagon chassis with two, two-wheel, bogies. This was used on the modern wagons proposed back in 1976 and the first two wagons were an OBA bogie open wagon and a 'Bogie Steel AB'.

The Hornby Book of Trains 25 Year Edition, commemorating the twenty-fifth anniversary of the Hornby Margate factory, was published by Rovex during the year and contained a history of the Rovex company along with many interesting chapters on development and manufacturing. There were pictures of models that did not get beyond the sample stage, such as the mountain railway, CN turbo train, French TEE and a coach with doors that opened when it came into the station.

A BR 'Tippler' mineral wagon.

A GWR 7-plank sheet rail wagon.

The Hornby Book of Trains – 25-Year Edition.

The SAA 'Bogie Steel AB'.

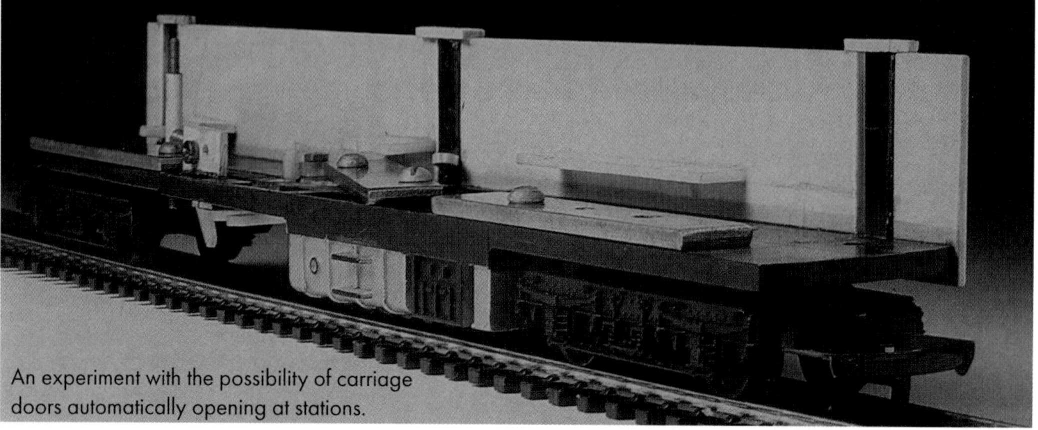

An experiment with the possibility of carriage doors automatically opening at stations.

There was a new canopy for the straight platform sections, with die-cast supports and another new set of signals. Also, Pola produced a GWR station kit exclusively for Hornby and two further GWR Pola kits were in preparation and would arrive the following year.

Hornby power units had a bad name and Hornby wanted to get the production of them away from Margate. The firm Hammant & Morgan (Systems) Ltd. (H&M) produced a very popular range of power units for model railways and Rovex wanted to get hold of their patents to improve their own range of power units. They bought H&M from Richard Kohnstamn Ltd. (the owners of Beatties stores) and sent a member of staff, Stan McCullum, to run it. Buying H&M provided a solution to everyone. It was bought by DCM and not Hornby Hobbies Ltd., and when retailers told salesmen that H&M quality would now go down, they reminded them that they were still a separate company under DCM. They even had a separate stand at the toy fair so that they would not be associated with Hornby.

Hornby encouraged the company to widen its product range and the HM Relco, a locomotive

Live steam *Rocket* with rare shop display stand.

Mrs Brenda Mahoney entertains workmates during the Meccano factory sit-in on 26 December 1979. (Courtesy *Liverpool Echo*)

testing rolling road, and an arrangement to market the American Woodlands Scenics range of scenic materials, resulted. The latter is now marketed by Bachmann. However, in 1982 H&M was absorbed into Hornby Hobbies at Margate. With the company's transfer came one of its salesmen, Simon Kohler, who went on to become Hornby's Marketing Manager. He became a very familiar figure with the public, gaining the unofficial title 'Mr Hornby', and today is Hornby's Director of Marketing & Product Development.

It was at the 1979 Toy Fair that the public got its first glimpse of the Hornby live steam *Rocket*. It was a 1/16-scale model which ran on 3½ in. gauge track. *Rocket* was the result of an idea which had come to Karl Mueller while visiting the Nuremberg Toy Fair in 1977. He wanted a prestige model to sell, which could also draw attention at exhibitions. A team of six had been assigned to it. It did cause a sensation, sold well abroad and attracted TV coverage. Although the 23,500 sets made did not cover the development costs, the publicity value it gained made up for this.

HORNBY 0 GAUGE

The Meccano factory and former home of Hornby Trains in Binns Road, Liverpool finally closed in November 1979.

The year saw the founding of the Train Collectors Society, which includes collectors of Hornby 0 gauge, Hornby Dublo, Tri-ang Hornby and Hornby Railways, as well as any make, of any age and any gauge.

1970s – A DECADE SUMMARY

Following the shrinkage of the model railway market during the 1960s, the 1970s saw a gentle revival, but not before the final round of changes in the Lines Group. Production of Minic Motorway finished in 1970 and this coincided with the move of Scalextric production to Margate and the closure of the Minimodels factory in Havant. This move was to give Rovex two strong products in the years ahead.

In 1971, the Lines Bros. Group collapsed. Overseas companies within the Group had been haemorraging money while at home the shrinking popular toy market was being undermined by cheap imports. The one reasonably healthy member of the Group was Rovex Tri-ang Ltd., with its factories at Margate and Canterbury. From January 1972 Rovex belonged to the Dunbee-Combex-Marks Group (DCM) and the model railway system was renamed 'Hornby Railways'. The years that immediately followed were dogged by a limited budget and the need for compromises in design, to save money.

The move into pre-BR liveries seemed to breathe new life into model railways and we saw a steady increase in optimism in the expanding range of new products from Margate. This was given a further boost by the arrival of competition in the form of Lima 00 scale, Palitoy's Mainline Railways and the new Airfix Railways (GMR). By the middle of the decade it was obvious that some of the early body moulds were wearing out and needed replacing. This included the original 'Princess' 4-6-2, 'Jinty' 0-6-0T, Class 08, Class 31 and the Mk 1 coaches.

The restricted budget led to economies in design in the mid-1970s, which resulted in some new models not being up to the standard needed to compete with the new manufacturers. In 1977, concern was being expressed by Hornby's management at the greater authenticity of models being produced by the three new rivals and plans were made to raise the standard of Hornby models over the next two years. The fight was on and the company went into the next decade with some new and attractive models under development, making it much more competitive.

HORNBY MINITRIX

Minitrix Electric first appeared in Germany in 1964, although the Minitrix name had previously been used on a push-along range of trains since 1959. The Wrexham-based British Trix company (by then part of the Courtaulds Group) marketed Minitrix in the UK. It was decided that there was a market for models based on British prototypes and the plastic parts for the new British range were tooled and made in Wrexham.

In 1967, British Trix was sold to Trix in Germany, but, in 1971, Trix decided to pull out of train production in the UK and the British Minitrix tooling and stocks were moved to Germany for further use. In 1972, the German company started to look for an importer in the UK. Rovex had considered going into N gauge in the late 1960s, but were not sure whether their workforce could handle such small models. Instead, in 1967, they agreed to import Lima N gauge and market it through their subsidiary company, G&R Wrenn, under the 'Wrenn Micromodels' name. With the break-up of Lines Bros. the agreement with Lima ended and so, when approached by Trix, Rovex ageed to be the marketing agents for the Minitrix in Great Britain, under the brand name 'Hornby Minitrix'. Rovex found it a good and trouble-free system and got on well with the manufacturers.

DUNBEE-COMBEX-MARX (DCM)

Dunbee had been founded in 1946, by Richard Beecham and Basil Feldman, to take advantage of the new plastics available after the war. By the late 1950s the company had a turnover approaching £1 million. Toy manufacturer Combex was bought for £250,000 and the group went public in 1962. Burbank Toys (owners of the Victoria Plum brand) was added to the group and an agreement with Mattal Inc. made them agents for Barbie Dolls and Hot Wheels in Great Britain and Ireland. In 1967 the company bought the Swansea-based UK interests in Louis Marx & Co. Ltd., and in 1971 acquired Rovex Ltd.

By now they were quite a formidable toy group, but, in 1976, DCM began a bid for the USA branch of Louis Marks, which also had interests in Hong Kong. The US giant cost them over $15 million and involved large bank loans. The German toy manufacturer Schuco was also bought that year and in 1978 kit manufacturers, Aurora Products, was added to the group.

The Chairman's Report in 1978 was the first public sign that the company was in financial difficulty. There were massive losses in America, and heavy losses at Schuco in Germany and the Australian subsidiary, Lidrana. The Receiver was appointed on 19 February 1980 and one of the few profitable companies in the group was Hornby Hobbies Ltd. (formerly Rovex Ltd.).

The year 1970.

The year 1971.

The year 1972.

The year 1973.

The year 1974.

The year 1975.

The year 1976.

The year 1977.

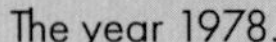
The year 1978.

The year 1979.

1970s MILESTONES

1970 – 'System 6' track, 'Coronation' Class, alternative locomotive names, 100-ton oil tanker and the end of Minic Motorway production.

1971 – *Evening Star*, breakdown crane, 'chuff-chuff' sound, 'The Railway Children' set, a new range of station sets, the end of Battle Space!, the collapse of the Lines Group, receivership and Pocket Money Toys.

1972 – Hornby Railways, DCM, 'Take-a-Ticket' set, automatic train control and the H&B van.

1973 – 'Silver Seal', 'Black 5', new 'Britannia', 25555 *Lord Westwood*, 'Monobloc' tank wagon, first BR Mk 3 coach, last fling of 'Princess', Hornby Minitrix; launch of Graham Farish 00 wagons.

1974 – First poster campaign, Tampo printing, Class 47, Ivatt 2MT, second series Pullman car and building kits.

1975 – Six-wheeled vans, automatic uncoupling device, problems with *King Arthur*; launch of Graham Farish 00 coaches.

1976 – Arrival of Airfix, Mainline and Lima 00; Hornby Hobbies Ltd., Rovex International Ltd., J83, four-wheel coach, British wagons in Australian liveries, Hornby stamps, Minic Ships and Shipwright.

1977 – Silver Jubilee train sets, HST, Class 25, 'Duchess', regional coaches, Big Big tooling and Frog kits to Russia.

1978 – GWR 'King' 4-6-0, Class 101 0-4-0T, Class 29, LMS TPO, LNER sleeping car, GWR restaurant car and a new range of printed plastic railway buildings.

1979 – Zero 1, 'Patriot', Class A4, 'Western', LBSC Class E2, GLW wagon chassis, *Hornby Book of Trains 25 Year Edition*, H&M bought, live steam *Rocket* and Railfreight livery.

BOX LID ARTWORK OF THE 1970s

'Continental' 0-4-0T.

'Jinty' 0-6-0T.

Class 37 Co-Co.

'International' 0-4-0T.

Class 57xx 0-6-0PT.

1980
PAINT FINISHES AND RECEIVERSHIP

HORNBY RAILWAYS

The year 1980 was a bad one for the British toy industry, but Hornby Hobbies still managed to make a profit. However, Dunbee-Combex-Marx, after its ambitious attempt at breaking into the American market, went into receivership with the Receiver being appointed on 19 February 1980. The management at Margate were left *in situ* and allowed to carry on trading, but nothing important could be done without the Receiver's approval. The collapse of DCM also saw the end of Hornby's Australian models; the remnant rolling stock would later be sold off cheaply in Franklin's Supermarkets in New South Wales and the locomotives through Bourkes Department Store in Melbourne. From then on Australia would receive the standard Hornby range, firstly through their new agents A. S. Scott & Co., and then through Southern Models.

On 9 March 1979 an instruction had been issued at the Margate factory that, for 1980, all locomotives, coaches and wagons were to have a paint finish. The importance of this dictat cannot be overemphasised. This was vital if Hornby were to compete with the new 00 systems, which all had paint-finished models. The paint finish did more than anything to change the products from looking like toys to serious models for the model railway enthusiast. Apart from the old pannier tank all the locomotives were now also sold with a driver and fireman.

The re-tooled 'King' Class model, 6013 *King Henry VIII*, was released, looking far better than

The CR 0-4-0 saddle tank engine.

The LNER Class B17, *Manchester United.*

The LMS Fowler 4P passenger tank engine.

Pre-production model of a LNER Class J36 (not made).

the first attempt. There were also four completely new locomotives and this time the quality was much improved. These were LNER 4-6-0 Class B17 'Footballer' as 2862 *Manchester United,* Caledonian Railway blue 0-4-0ST as 270, GWR 0-6-0PT Dean Class 2721 as 2744, and LMS maroon Fowler Class 4P 2-6-4T as 2300.

The late members of the B17 class were built for use on the LNER's Great Central Division in 1936–1937 and were named after football clubs, which gave them the nickname 'Footballers'. The Caledonian Railway 0-4-0STs were Dugald Drummond's Class 264 dockyard shunters, which first appeared in 1885, and the model was intended for cheaper train sets, breaking new ground in having a die-cast footplate, smokebox and chimney to give it extra weight. Dean's GWR Class 2721 tank engines were built at Swindon between 1897 and 1901 as saddle tanks, but most were converted to pannier tanks soon after the First World War and the LMS Fowler 4P tank 2-6-4T was so far the largest tank engine to join the Hornby Railways range.

Also planned for this year had been an ex-NBR LNER J36 0-6-0 and a BR/EE 25 kV Bo-Bo Class 87 electric (plus catenary), but they were dropped

The GWR Class 2721.

Avanced Passenger Train (APT) driving car.

to make room in the schedule for a BR Class 370 Advanced Passenger Train (APT). Both deleted models would eventually be designed by Hornby and released in 2018. Thus, 1980 was the year that the APT entered the catalogue, carrying the name *City of Derby*. Much help was received from British Rail in its development. For reasons of secrecy, amongst senior staff involved with the project it was referred to as 'Project Ramsgate' as, no doubt, it had been developed in isolation in the building the company owned in Ramsgate. The real APT was still in development and experiencing problems with its tilting mechanism, which is surprising because the Hornby one worked well!

There were two new coaches: a Mk 3 in the form of a buffet car (TRUB) and a Pullman K class brake car to go with the K class parlour car introduced in 1975. Among the wagons, there were now an LBSC brake van, a BR 'Merry-Go-Round' hopper wagon, an attractive new small tank wagon in Shell/BP livery with a 10-ft wheelbase and the BR 45-ton GLW VDA van.

The APT train set.

The BR Railfreight VDA.

The Pullman K brake car.

The HAA 'merry-go-round' hopper wagon.

Six pages of the catalogue were devoted to the digital Zero 1 and two more to the new analogue range of power units. The Pola kits now included a signal box and level crossing. Added to Hornby's own printed clip-together plastic buildings was a much-needed diesel depot. Many pages of the catalogue were devoted to showing how buildings, track and accessories should be used in a landscaped layout.

As part of the 1980 'Rocket 150' celebrations, the Hornby live steam-powered 3½ in. gauge model of Stephenson's *Rocket* was ready for release. The boiler had a thick insulating jacket to prevent burns. It was fuelled by butane gas from cigarette lighter refills. There was an attractive coach and the track consisted of asymmetric moulded plastic units, representing the fish-belly rails of the period. These could be assembled either way round, to give either curved or straight track.

HORNBY DUBLO

It was in 1980 that New Cavendish Books published the book *Hornby Dublo Trains*, by Michael Foster, which provides an extensive history of the Dublo system and a comprehensive record of the products made.

Hornby Dublo Trains, by Michael Foster.

1981
THE YEAR OF THE LOCOMOTIVE

HORNBY RAILWAYS

Following the collapse of the parent company, the staff at Hornby Hobbies waited for thirteen weeks to hear what was going to happen to them. Karl Mueller fought a long battle to prevent Hornby Hobbies being sold to a Hong Kong company and managed in the end to put together a consortium (Wiltminster Ltd.), under the chairmanship of Jack Strowger, to buy the company from the Receiver with the help of venture capital. It is thought they paid between £8 and £10 million and, on 21 May, the staff were given notice and then promptly re-employed by the new independent Hornby Hobbies Ltd. The purchase included not only Hornby Hobbies, but also H&M (Systems) Ltd. In 1982, Jack Strowger brought in Keith Ness as the new Managing Director of Hornby Hobbies Ltd., to replace Karl Mueller who had left by then.

An early requirement from Ness was the addition of more model variations to the 1983 catalogue, in order to provide some extra revenue and, as the catalogue had already been designed by then, the new items appeared on the catalogue's back cover. They included four complete passenger trains, five more wagon liveries and the Caley 'Pug' in BR lined black livery and named *Smokey Joe*. This small model would remain in the catalogue for the next thirty-five years – and counting!

Keith Ness was from Pedigree Dolls & Toys Ltd., and the Hornby board had given him the task of widening the product base of the

Smokey Joe.

company, especially by catering for girls as well as boys. Between 1983 and 1993 more than forty different ideas were tried with most not surviving for more than two years. Most were imported, but an exception was 'Flower Fairies' (based on the illustrations in the *Flower Fairies* book by Cicely Mary Barker), which was home-grown and had a slightly longer life. Another, Pound Puppies, had come from Irwin Toys in Canada, but was developed over subsequent years by Hornby. Hornby Hobbies had become importers of toys and development work on model railways and slot-cars was cut back.

Fortunately, before this change in policy, the plans for 1981 were well advanced and would not be affected by the future cutbacks. In line with the 1977 plan to develop a balanced range of first-class locomotives, 1981 was declared 'The Year of the Locomotive' and what was achieved in one year is difficult to comprehend. There were nine locomotives from new tooling! Pride of place were four 4-4-0 tender locomotives, one for each of the 'Big Four'. They had a Ringfield motor in the tender, which had a heavy die-cast chassis and traction tyres. There was a smoke unit, cabin crew and the new shorter couplings.

For the GWR there was a 'Churchward County' 3821 *County of Bedford*, for the LMS it was a 'Compound' No. 1000 in maroon livery, for the LNER the model was of a Class D49 'Shire' as 2763 *Cheshire* and, not surprisingly, for the Southern Railway it was a Class V 'Schools' as 928 *Stowe*. Was it just coincidence that all four classes had been modelled in 0 gauge by Hornby before the war? News that Airfix were producing a model of the 'Schools' Class initially led to it being dropped by Hornby, but it was reinstated and Airfix went into receivership before completing their model.

The GWR 'County' 4-4-0 was introduced by George Churchward in 1904 for express passenger duties and the LMS 'Compound' was Samuel Johnson's design for the Midland Railway of 1902 but modified by Richard Deeley in 1905.

The LNER Class D49 'Shire' locomotives were built at Darlington to one of the last of Nigel Gresley's group standard designs and introduced in 1927 for express passenger and mixed-traffic duties. Like the pre-war Hornby 0 gauge 'Shire', it would later give way to a 'Hunt' Class, although it would still end up as *Edward* in the 'Thomas & Friends' series. The SR 'Schools' Class

The GWR, *County of Bedford*.

The LMS 'Compound'.

Pre-production sample of the SR 'Schools' Class, *Stowe*.

The LNER D49/1 Class, *Cheshire*.

was the most modern of the four, having been introduced in 1930 and designed by Richard Maunsell as express passenger locomotives. It was the most powerful 4-4-0 class to be built in Great Britain.

The other five new locomotives were a re-tooled 'Britannia' as 70021 *Morning Star* (now with wire handrails and pad-printed nameplates), a new *Flying Scotsman* A1 body with wire handrails, the A4 with valences as LNER blue 4902 *Seagull*, GNR Class J13 0-6-0ST in GNR green livery as 1247 and a BR/EE Class 86 25 kv electric locomotive as 86219 *Phoenix*.

The 'Britannia' came with three alternative names and numbers as self-adhesive labels, as did the Southern BB/WC Class, which had returned after a break of eight years. It was in malachite green and carrying the identity of 21C166 *Spitfire*. The 'Black 5' was also now in LMS lined black as 5138. There were several other new liveries on existing locomotives, bringing the choice in 1981 to a staggering forty-one! Also released in a limited-edition train pack were *Lord of the Isles* 4-2-2 and three short clerestory coaches in GWR livery. Unlike earlier editions of the locomotive, this one had printed splashers instead of stickers.

An even larger list of new locomotives had been planned, including a GWR Class 45xx 2-6-2T, a GWR 'Dean Goods' 0-6-0, an LMS Class 8F 2-8-0 and LMS Ivatt Class 3MT 2-6-2T, but all had been dropped. The two GWR locomotives were postponed because

The BR 'Britannia' Class, *Morning Star*.

LNER A1, *Flying Scotsman.*

LNER A4, *Seagull.*

The Great Northern Railway (GNR) Class J13 saddle tank.

of wheel issues. With so much time spent on new locomotives, it was not surprising that there were no new coaches, wagons or lineside accessories. An unpredicted addition to the list of locomotives in 1981 was 47712 *Lady Diana Spencer,* in celebration of a certain event that year.

As previously mentioned, in 1979 and 1980, to dispose of the unwanted 'King' Class locomotive and other slow selling models, large 'King Size' train sets were sold in a specially made cardboard trunk. This must have been successful as, in 1981, Hornby introduced 'Treasure Chests'. These were cardboard boxes specially printed to look like treasure chests and filled with ready boxed obsolete or slow-moving items for bulk sales by mail order. Obviously, buyers needed to know what they were buying and so a selection of standard combinations were made up and, in 1981, buyers had a choice of fifteen of these mixes and some 16,500 sets were made up that year. It seems that some retailers were unhappy that the public were being offered discounted obsolete stock this way and asked that they might be offered bulk packages of old stock which they could re-sell. This resulted in retailers being offered a further choice of fifteen 'Treasure Chests' in 1983 and a little over 5,200 being sold.

The Class 86, *Phoenix*.

Pre-production model of a GWR 'Dean Goods' (not made).

Pre-production model of an Ivatt tank engine (not made).

As seen in the notes above, the year was also marked by the collapse of Airfix, brought on by heavy losses at its Meccano Ltd. subsidiary. Airfix was bought by General Mills of America, who already owned the British toy company Palitoy, the makers of Mainline Railways. It was arranged that Palitoy would take over the Airfix GMR tooling to extend their Mainline Railways range. Airfix and Meccano were moved to the former Lines Bros. factory at Calais, which had been taken over by Meccano (France) in 1965. Remnant Airfix GMR model railway stock was bought by a Cheshire company called Highfield Birds & Models. Two years later, in 1983, the company would be renamed Dapol Ltd.; it was owned and run by David and Pauline Boyle, who repackaged some Airfix stock under the Dapol brand and renamed some of the locomotives in order to increase the variety available for sale.

1982
RETURN OF THE GREEN

HORNBY RAILWAYS

A page in the catalogue entitled 'Your Questions Answered' dealt with five questions raised by the public. Requests included more BR liveries, more alternative names and numbers, and more locomotives that smoked. In recent years there had been little in the Hornby catalogue for BR steam-era modellers, but, in 1982, BR liveries made something of a comeback. The 'Duchess' was released in BR green as 46231 *Duchess of Atholl,* the 'Footballer' as 61656 *Leeds United* and the Fowler 2-6-4T was turned out in BR lined black as 42308.

In 1982 a fifth brand was added to the Hornby price list, called 3-D-S (three-dimensional space). It cashed in on the interest in space travel and consisted of an aerial hyperway that twisted and turned along walls and across ceilings, along which model spaceships could travel. It was not successful and was dropped two years later.

The APT had originally been available only in a train set, but now it was available in a train pack. Sadly, the controversial withdrawal of the real trains before they had been fully brought into service had a downward effect on sales of the models and the APT would be dropped after 1984. A Clayton/Beyer Peacock Class 17 Bo-Bo had been planned, and a sample made up, but it would have required a non-standard mechanism and so a BREL 2387 hp Class 58 Co-Co was developed instead, fitted with a can motor instead of the Ringfield type. Another dropped model had been a planned new Class 08 diesel shunter with correct outside frames. That would be made, but at a much later date.

The former Tri-ang Met-Cam Lightweight DMU had been finally dropped in 1979 and a new model in 1982 would be the Birmingham RC&W Class 110 DMU ('Calder Valley'), although the original plan had been for

The BR Fowler 4P passenger tank.

The Hornby '3.D.S Mission 1' set.

Pre-production BR Class 17 'Clayton' (not made).

The APT pack. (Courtesy Vectis Auctions)

the earlier version – the Class 104. DMUs were widespread in Great Britain and so Hornby needed to have them in their range. The Class 110 on this occasion was in BR refurbished white livery as a three-car unit and a further trailer car was available to buy separately. The Class 110 DMUs were built by the Birmingham Railway Carriage & Wagon Co. in the late 1950s and provided suburban and cross-country services, especially in Yorkshire and Lancashire.

The Class 58 was shown in the catalogue in large logo blue. However, the class was still under development and its planned introductory livery was still not known. Hornby did manage to change the livery of

The Class 110 DMU in 'refurbished' livery.

the model to grey in time for its release as 58007, although the livery detail was not quite right. Apparently, the running number 58007 was chosen because, when the company had to make a livery decision, as BR were still undecided, it was felt that it was right to choose a number for the locomotive which had not been built yet, therefore the livery was slightly irrelevant. During the year, the Class 47 was correctly turned out in BR large logo blue as 47170 *County of Norfolk*.

It was in 1982 that Hornby released the 'scale' GWR clerestory coaches that were a real improvement on the original Tri-ang ones of 1961, although the old ones have remained in production for cheaper train sets requiring the classical look. Completely new wagons included the end-door 8-plank wagon, an LNER refrigerator van ('Canterbury Lamb'), a short-lived 20-ft 'Conflat A' flat wagon with a 20-ft Freightliner container, a new BR standard brake van and a track cleaning coach based on the new four-wheel coach. The former shunters truck returned as a carriage wagon with a car-load. Some shops were supplied with their own limited-edition H&B vans, including Redgates, Eastbourne and Railmail.

The printed plastic railway buildings experienced a complete change in appearance simply by changing the printing. Instead of a tidy brick finish for each, they had all become stone

BR 'Conflat A' with Freightliner container.

A Class 58 locomotive.

Commissioned H&B vans by Redgates, Eastbourne and Railmail.

The 'Canterbury Lamb' refrigerator van.

A track maintenance coach.

structures, making them look older. There was also a new footbridge. The buildings were now also produced in N scale for the Hornby Minitrix range and were made in Hong Kong to Hornby designs.

Two complementing lineside accessories were the coal wagon tipper and coal conveyor. The first set contained incline piers, a Neal wagon tipping unit and an opening end-door 8-plank coal wagon in the livery of James Hargreaves & Sons. The other set contained the hopper into which the coal was tipped, together with a Crigglestone conveyor and chute for loading the coal into wagons. They were both electrically operated.

Hornby Hobbies had its own subsidiary company in the USA called Hornby Inc., and in 1982 this ceased trading and was finally wound up in April 1984.

A stone-printed station building.

In 1982, Railfreight was established by British Rail to control all network freight operations by dedicating specific rolling stock and teams to manage evolving freight traffic demands. The Railfreight division operated as a single entity for BR's rail freight until 1987 when it was split into sectors, each with its own livery. Add to these the passenger liveries and those of the later passenger and freight operating companies and this was the start of livery expansion in Great Britain which would have major significance to the model railway industry. The more livery variations there were on the real railways, the more model variations could be made without the need to produce expensive new tooling. The company which made greatest use of this fact was Lima, who produced well over a hundred variations of some of their models such as the Class 37 and Class 47. Livery expansion affected model passenger and freight rolling stock as well.

1983

PLAYTRAINS

HORNBY RAILWAYS

In 1983 the toy industry in Great Britain was in the grip of a recession and by the end of the year Hornby had cut about a third of its manufacturing, development, administration and marketing staff. This reduced the number of employees from 640 to 433.

This year there was a distinct change of policy. Until now it had been normal to have each locomotive in the catalogue in just one livery at a time. Thus, when the steam outline models were changed to pre-1948 liveries, the BR liveries disappeared. With less money to pay for tooling new models, Hornby would offer models in more than one livery and so cater for customers modelling in a wide range of eras. This widened choice and increased sales potential. It had also become obvious that most sales occurred when a model first reached the shops and that sales dropped off dramatically in the second year. By constantly changing the identity of their models they could sell far more of them. One of the new identities was the Class 47 diesel in BR blue as 47541 *The Queen Mother* and a sample was delivered to Clarence House.

The Class 47, *The Queen Mother*.

A Midland Railway 'scale' clerestory composite coach.

Hornby's 1984 unsuccessful attempt at improving the scale of the 'Coronation' model.

The same policy was beginning to apply to rolling stock with the 'scale' GWR clerestory coaches now also in MR maroon and the three LNER 'teak' Gresley coaches additionally in BR maroon. There were six new versions of existing wagons.

The 'Coronation' locomotive returned with a Ringfield motor fitted in the tender as LMS blue and silver 6220 *Coronation*. An attempt was made at this stage to produce a scale length model with a realistic front bogie, but it was abandoned, and we would have to wait until 2001 before an accurate one was marketed. A pair of Stanier coaches were produced in the blue and silver livery of the 'Coronation Express'.

A new series of building kits from the Life-Like range was planned for 1983 which, from the catalogue illustrations, looked as though they were straight out of an American catalogue. Indeed, they were marketed by Tyco in the USA as the 'Centre Street' range. The models were all urban commercial buildings with flat roofs and over-adorned with advertising. Although called 'The Hornby High Street Series' they certainly did not portray a British high street by any stretch of the imagination. However, the kits did not materialise, but four new sets of painted figures and three sets of trees did; these were supplied by Life-Like.

In line with the board's policy to develop the toy side of the company, a new range of plastic push-along 'Playtrains' (later marketed for a short while as 'Early Play') was introduced for

Life-Like 'High Street' kits (not delivered).

An 'Early Play' counter box.

sale in toy shops. Some were themed on new toy ranges that the company was developing, such as Pound Puppies, The Shoe People, Postman Pat and Thomas & Friends. Some, but not all, remained in production until around 1990. As well as sets, some of the Playtrains parts were sold loose in counter boxes.

The clockwork Continental 0-4-0T was sold in bright colours with a choice of at least ten different names on its sides – Adam, Edward, Michael, etc. There was also a whole range of differently named push-along 0-4-0 tank engines using the old 'Nellie' industrial tank body.

Another product planned but not made was 'System Plus'. The modules were designed on the Lego principle but with railway and slot-car bases on to which vehicles could be built with plug-together bricks. Two train sets were planned for release in 1983: one electric and the other in the push-along Playtrains series. The locomotives were standard models, a Class 101 0-4-0 tank called 'Terry' for the electric set and 'Pixie' for the Playtrains one. The rolling stock initially consisted of the Hornby flat wagon with a dimpled upper surface onto which the child could build a body of his or her choice.

It appears that, in 1983, the stamp company Stanley Gibbons Ltd., of The Strand, London, were considering a sideline in model railways and a series of track packs was devised that

The 'Pound Puppies' train set.

Peter.

together built a layout. Three locomotives in finishes exclusive to them were also ordered and made. However, the order was cancelled, and they were sold instead to the Beatties chain of shops. The locomotives were maroon LMS 'Coronation' *King George VI*, Class 47 diesel 47480 *Robin Hood* and black CR 'Pug' as LMS 16032.

The 'Playtrains' set and counter display box.

British Rail involved Hornby in a major business promotion in 1983, for which Hornby produced three wagons carrying slogans

The 'Postman Pat' train set.

The Hornby Caledonian Railway 0-4-0ST in LMS black as 16032.

Packaging for the British Rail marketing 'freebie' models.

encouraging business to make greater use of BR services. Each wagon was packed in an impressively designed box and they were given out at business conventions as gifts. The best-remembered of the wagons was the chrome finish Monobroc 'Think' tanker. The others were an OBA open wagon and a VDA van, representing modern wagons at the time.

General Mills, the American owners of Palitoy, decided to pull out of toy manufacturing and, in 1983, the Mainline Railways system came to an end. The former Airfix GMR tooling, held by Palitoy, was sold to Highfield Birds & Models, which became Dapol Ltd. in September 1983. Unsold Mainline stock also went to Dapol. The Mainline Railways tools were the property of Kader, the Chinese owners of the Bachmann brand, and so remained with them in Hong Kong. Of the three rivals to Hornby that had arrived in 1976 only Lima remained, but now there was also an expanding Dapol range and an independent G&R Wrenn with the former Dublo tooling. And sitting out in Hong Kong were the former Palitoy Mainline Railways tools …

1984
RETURN OF A 'PRINCESS' AND THE ROYAL TRAIN

HORNBY RAILWAYS

The reduction in staff the previous year cut the company overheads sufficiently for the operating profit to rise by a large amount even though the income was lower. The net loss over the year was halved.

A totally new 'scale' model of the LMS 'Princess Royal' Class locomotive opened the 1984 catalogue, and this was in BR green as 46201 *Princess Elizabeth* as well as LMS maroon as 6200 *The Princess Royal*. A princess was expected to visit the Hornby Hobbies stand at the British Toy Fair that year and one of the models was renamed *Princess Margaret* and mounted on a plinth with a brass plaque attached. Sadly, her royal highness did not pass the Hornby stand and the model was returned to the factory store at Margate.

On 22 March, Hornby Hobbies did, however, receive royal attention when HM the Queen was presented with a model at the gala opening of Andrew Lloyd Webber's musical 'Starlight

The uncollected *Princess Margaret* presentation model.

The Princess Royal.

The 'Starlight Express' factory copy of a model presented to HM The Queen.

Express' at the Apollo Victoria Theatre in London's West End. The model was presented by Hornby's Managing Director, Keith Ness, and it consisted of a 'Battle of Britain' Class model painted in the blue and silver theme of the show. Some time later I spied the presentation model in a showcase at the National Railway Museum.

Hornby had built a massive layout around the outside of the theatre's auditorium, incorporating 1,500 feet of track. Trains ran for an hour before the lifting of the curtain. Hornby planned to produce a complete train set based on the presentation locomotive and livery, but this was later dropped. However, the hand-painted prototype sample of the locomotive and coaches survived, and the locomotive matched the one presented to HM the Queen. An overseas set was also planned to use the Australian GM diesel and Transcontinental coaches in the same blue and sliver design.

The 'Starlight Express' presentation. (Courtesy Hornby)

The type K Pullman parlour car was now available with a sheet of self-adhesive names for all eight of the Orient Express Pullman cars. Using the BR Mk 2 and Mk 3 coaches, three Royal Train models were available in dark purple, representing the coaches and a sleeping/power brake of HM the Queen and the Duke of Edinburgh. This was the only Hornby model of the Queen's coach that correctly had a representation of the unique double doors. Hornby Pullman models were sold

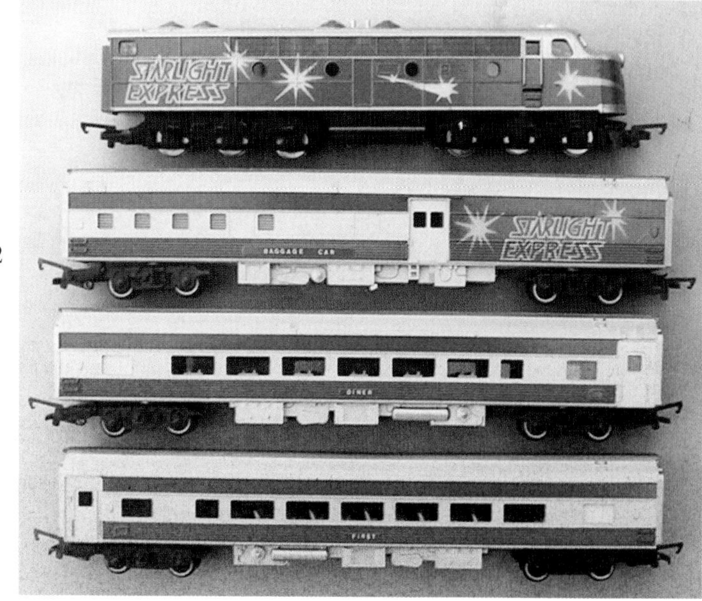

Pre-production TC 'Starlight Express' train pack. (Courtesy Killick Collection)

The 'Venice Simplon Orient-Express' train set.

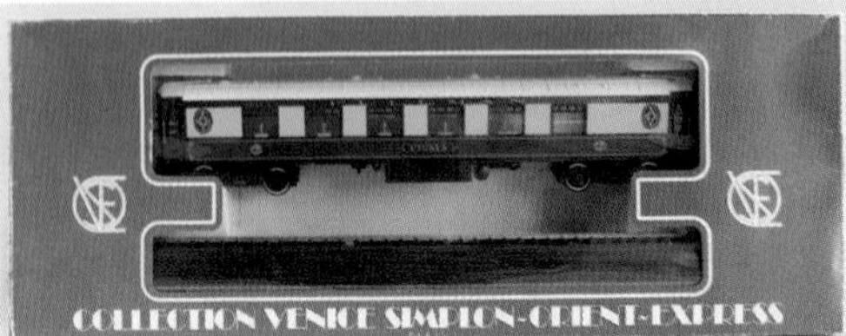

The Venice Simplon Orient-Express promotion pack sold on the train.

A 'Campbell's' PVA curtain-sided van.

on the Orient Express train, each one supplied with a plinth and taking the name of one of the real cars. The plinth carried a brass plate, which the purchaser could have engraved.

A completely new wagon was the curtain-sided PVA van in 'Campbell's Soups' livery. This was a modification of the Hornby VDA long wheelbase van of 1980. Many more variations in livery and identity were produced during the year, with the emphasis on small tank engines for the 'junior' market.

At the back of the catalogue there was an advert for a book called *The Art of Hornby* by Richard Lines. This was a year-by-year look at Hornby catalogue and advertisement artwork between 1920 and 1982, and it contained a page at the back of the book showing all the logotypes used as Hornby brands up to the date of publication.

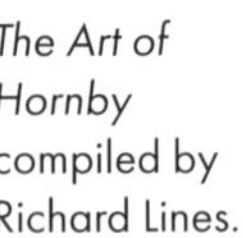
The Art of Hornby compiled by Richard Lines.

The Royal Train Mk 3, Queen's coach.

1985
'THOMAS AND FRIENDS'

The GWR 150 Class 101.

In 1985 the company's turnover increased by 60 per cent and Hornby Hobbies moved into profit.

Hornby's rather disappointing austerity 1985 catalogue celebrated the 150th anniversary of the Great Western Railway, the theme being reflected in the models. The 'King' Class model had changed to GWR 6000 *King George V*, a special edition of the Class 101 0-4-0T carried the GWR150 logo on its tanks and the GWR Class Class 2721 0-6-0PT was re-issued as 2747. What had been an LMS travelling Post Office was now released in GWR chocolate and cream and the 'scale' clerestory coaches were in a new version of the GWR livery.

As was now becoming the norm, many of the existing locomotive models were re-issued in new liveries or re-numbered and re-named. These had become too numerous to be included in this book and the same goes for the coaches and wagons too. They may all be found in *Ramsay's British Model Trains Catalogue.*

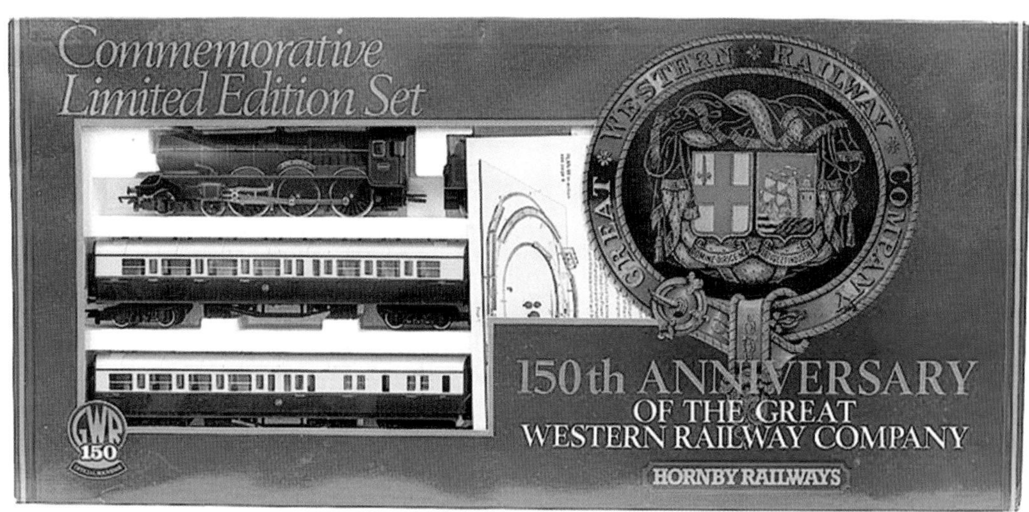

The GWR 150th anniversary commemorative set.

The GWR *King George V*.

The GWR travelling post office.

The Intercity 125 Mk 3 open first.

There were now FO and SO coaches in the BR Mk 3 range, with eight instead of seven windows each side, but still too short to be accurate. They were available in both 'Inter-City' blue and grey and in 'InterCity 125' grey and beige livery.

With the company's toy priority policy to the fore, six pages at the back of the 1985 catalogue were devoted to a new product range based on the ever-popular books by the Rev. W. Awdry and the television series of 'Thomas the Tank Engine & Friends'. The first releases were two train sets, one with Thomas and his two carriages, Annie and Clarabel, and two wagons; the second contained a green 0-4-0ST *Percy* with three wagons.

Percy had a completely new body on the electric 0-4-0 chassis, while *Thomas* was the former LBSC Class E2 0-6-0T suitably altered to look like the *Thomas* in the books and given the familiar blue livery and a smiling face.

Back in 1989, I corresponded with the Rev. W. Awdry for some time when I was researching an article on the origins of the characters in the 'Thomas' books. Awdry kindly wrote me a twenty-page account of all the models on his own layouts which had inspired the books' characters. His first 'Thomas' model (1948) had been a 0-6-0T built by Stewart-Reidpath, but, apparently, he had shown his original illustrator, Reginald Payne, a picture of an LBSC Class E2 tank engine when asked what *Thomas* should look like. When Hornby were planning their 'The World of Thomas the Tank Engine' model range, it was a coincidence that they had recently released a model of the Class E2 0-6-0T – or was it?

Many of the original samples for the faces that adorned the models have survived and

Percy, No. 6.

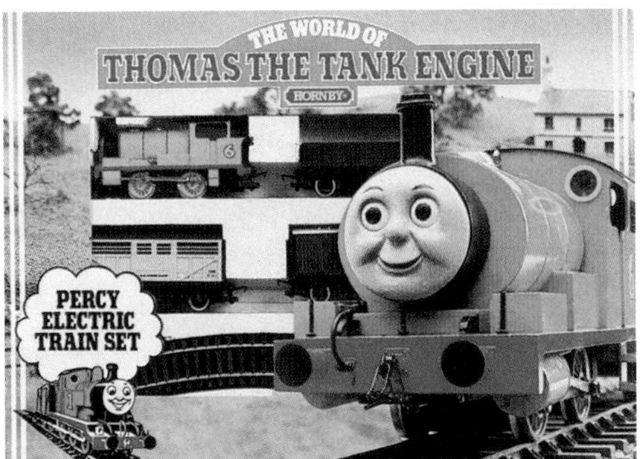

The *Percy* electric train set.

Early pre-production *Thomas* models.

The *Thomas* electric train set.

Annie and *Clarabel.*

Large scale *Percy* face.

Large scale moulds and mouldings for *Devious Diesel.*

amongst them there are larger-scale ones, which were moulded from those produced for the television and video series, using 0-gauge models built by Märklin. These face mouldings were used in the process to produce the smaller faces for the Hornby models. Prior to this Hornby had tried to hand-carve the faces, but this proved unsuccessful, which is why on some of the older *Thomas* locomotives you will

Pre-production 00-scale faces for *Thomas* and friends.

find different faces from those later produced in abundance.

The locomotives and rolling stock could be bought individually, the wagons coming from the standard range but finished to look like those in book illustrations. They consisted of an open wagon, goods van, standard brake van and a milk tanker. There was also a station, engine shed, goods depot, signal box, tunnel, signals, footbridge and water tower from the main range, but with a brick-printed finish.

From 1985 the production of Zero 1 ceased as the sales were poor.

HORNBY 0 GAUGE

It was in 1985 that New Cavendish Books published the book *The Hornby Gauge 0 System*, by Chris and Julie Graebe, which provides an extensive history of the system and a comprehensive record of the products made.

The Hornby Gauge 0 System, by Chris and Julie Graebe.

1986
FLOATATION

HORNBY RAILWAYS

On 29 October 1986 Hornby Hobbies was floated on the London Stock Exchange's Unlisted Securities Market (USM), which had been set up in 1980 for companies too small to qualify for full listing. Hornby Hobbies became Hornby Group plc and was able to raise money by share issues in order to expand. However, the first task was to pay off the secured loan notes in connection with the 1981 management buyout.

To celebrate the occasion it was decided to produce a limited-edition locomotive for the directors and others involved with the launch. An LMS maroon 'Coronation' Class was made, carrying the inscription 'Hornby USM Debut

The Hornby Group plc logo.

The 'Coronation' Class model as *The Stock Exchange*.

Hornby pre-production 'Princess' Class, *The Stock Exchange* (not used).

GWR 'Saint' Class 4-6-0, *Saint David.*

The SR 'Schools' Class, *Eton.*

December 1986' on its sides and named *The Stock Exchange.* However, it is likely that the cost of producing a limited run would have been too great and a red Caledonian 'Pug' was produced instead, with the above inscription on its tank sides in gold. A total of thirty-four were made.

There were no completely new locomotives in 1986, but the body of the 'Hall' Class had been revised to turn it into the 'Saint' Class – in this case GWR 2920 *Saint David.*

Also revised, the Class 37 diesel now had modified cab ends with split headcodes and was released in BR green as D6736. The SR 'Schools' Class also looked different as it had been released in olive green without smoke deflectors as 900 *Eton* would have looked in earlier days.

New in the coaches was a Mk 3a in the livery of HoverSpeed. This company, formed in 1981 by the merger of Hoverlloyd and BR, owned Seaspeed. Their primary service had been established by Seaspeed in 1968 between Dover and Calais with two car-carrying SRN 4 Hovercraft: *The Princess Anne* (now preserved) and *The Princess Margaret.*

This year we saw the return of two old friends from the Model-Land kit range. These were the country church (without its chimes mechanism) and the three electricity pylons, which had been modelled on one standing outside the drawing office at Margate.

The 'Thomas & Friends' range had grown and included solo models of *Gordon* (based on the Class A1) and a pair of Collett coaches in green and yellow.

Since Airfix had been bought by General Mills in 1981, it had manufactured its kits in the

The Hover Speed Mk 3a open coach.

Gordon, No 4.

Gordon's coach.

Meccano (France) factory in Calais. Following the break-up of the General Mills toy businesses, Airfix was bought by another American group in 1986. This was Borden Inc., and the purchase was made through its subsidiary, the Hull-based model paint manufacturers, Humbrol. Thus, Airfix became a subsidiary of Humbrol Ltd., in association with the French kit-manufacturer, Heller. Airfix kit manufacture was moved to the Heller factory at Trun in France.

1987 CHANGE AND CHANGE ABOUT

HORNBY RAILWAYS

Hornby Group plc had three wholly owned private companies: Hornby Hobbies Ltd., H&M (Systems) Ltd. and Hornby Industries Ltd. Hornby Industries Ltd. was incorporated on 17 October 1986 and the entire assets, liabilities and trade of Hornby Hobbies were transferred to it on 31 December the same year. On 8 January 1987, Hornby Hobbies Ltd. and Hornby Industries Ltd. exchanged names. From then on,

The SR BB-WC Class, *Fighter Pilot*.

The BR black 'Hunt' Class, *The Pytchley*.

The LNER 'Hunt' Class, *The Fitzwilliam*.

both H&M (Systems) Ltd. and Hornby Industries Ltd. were dormant companies.

By now Hornby had an established policy of producing limited runs of their locomotive models and changing their identity before the next run. In 1987 the Class BB/WC 4-6-2 switched to SR malachite green as 21C155 *Fighter Pilot* and, for the first time, carried the 'Golden Arrow' fittings. Appropriately, the Pullman cars now came with Golden Arrow/Fleche d'Or labels as well as a sheet of alternative names.

The real LNER D49 Class was too large for them all to be named after counties (shires) in the LNER region and so others took the names of local hunts. Known as 'Hunts', they had the representation of a fox on the top edge of each nameplate. In 1987 the identity of the Hornby 'Shire' changed to that of a 'Hunt' and the two initially made were LNER green 359 *The Fitzwilliam* and early BR black 62750 *The Pytchley*.

A completely new model was a BR Leyland/BREL twin railbus Class 142 – also known as 'Pacer' or 'Skipper' depending on their geographical location. These had controversial success on the BR network and Hornby went on to produce the model in many different liveries as they were relocated. By now, some diesels were being released without numbers, but with a sheet of transfers so the customer could choose their own.

On 10 June 1986, British Rail launched Network SouthEast, an organisation designed to deliver a co-ordinated train service for London and the surrounding region.

A BR Provincial Class 142 'Pacer'.

The Class 47 Network SouthEast (NSE) blue, *The London Standard.*

The first model to receive the new Network SouthEast (NSE) livery was the Class 47 as 47573 *The London Standard* and there were also Mk 2 coaches in this livery.

In the wagon section the Railfreight red and grey livery was spreading like a rash and seven models were affected, including the ferry van and standard brake van. Since the large breakdown crane turned BR yellow, it had needed a crew coach to match and this arrived in 1987 in the form of a Mk 2 brake end in yellow.

London Road station was added to the building range and this was a throwback to the large Hornby Dublo terminus/through station of 1961 and later Tri-ang Hornby 'Central Station' of 1971. It was assembled from existing parts in the stone finish and had two of the clear station over roofs.

New 'Thomas & Friends' additions were *Duck* the GWR pannier tank and *Devious Diesel*. *Duck* made use of the withdrawn GWR Class 57xx model of 1971 and *Devious* was the earlier 08 diesel shunter.

The BR yellow QPV Mk 2 BFK.

The Cowans-Sheldon rail crane.

A standard brake van.

Duck, No. 8.

Remember the tooling in China that had been used to produce Palitoy's Mainline Railways range? Back in 1984, Godfrey Hayes of Replica Railways had contacted Kader, the owners of the tooling, asking if they would use the tools to produce some models for him to sell. The first of these arrived in 1987 and a small range of good quality models followed and were sold in Replica Railways packaging.

1988
PANTOS AND CATENARY

HORNBY RAILWAYS

By the end of 1987 Hornby Group plc had been looking very strong and there was money in 1988 to upgrade the entire Scalextric range. Also, the emphasis at Margate was on streamlining the production process with computers and automation. Quality control was also improved.

With plans to expand into the leisure industry, Hornby Group plc bought the Fletcher Group, at a cost of £1.7 million. The group consisted of five companies involved in speedboat production and sales. Initially, this managed to break even, but a lot of money was spent on building the group new premises and the subsequent returns did not justify the expenditure. The business was later disposed of but left its mark in the form of two Fletcher light blue containers on a bogie flat wagon available in the Hornby Railways range during 1992–94.

In 1988 the EEC issued a directive on the safely of toys and to show compliance with the newly agreed standards, Hornby started putting the CE logo on its packaging.

The Stanier Class 8F 2-8-0, which had originally been considered for 1981, was released in 1988 in two plain black liveries – LMS 8193 and early BR 48758 – and they had firebox glow in the cab. The class had been introduced by William Stanier in 1935 to fill a serious gap in the LMS stable. It became the standard heavy freight design adopted by the War Department during

The LMS Class 8F.

the Second World War. In all, 666 locomotives were built. Unlike the Hornby Dublo model of 1958, which had a heavily rivetted tender, the new Hornby model had a tender based on the welded version with smooth sides. A new version of the BR Class 9F was released, which was very like the previous one but now had wire handrails. It was in BR green as 92220 *Evening Star*.

With Scottish modellers in mind, two Class 47 models were available in ScotRail livery as 47716 *Duke of Edinburgh's Award* and 47711 *Greyfriar's Bobby*. Two Mk 3 coaches in ScotRail livery were also available. ScotRail was the brand name for BR-operated passenger services in Scotland and extending across the border into Northern England and on to London. The corporate livery created for major express services in Scotland was the InterCity one, with the red stripe replaced by a saltire blue one.

In 1987, British Rail's Railfreight operations had been divided into sectors and a new version of the livery was used, consisting of three shades of grey and giving the sectors individual identities with logos on the sides of locomotives. They also carried depot plates, which carried the depot's logo rather than a name. The first model to receive the new livery arrived in 1988 and was 58050, which carried the triple grey livery with Railfreight Coal Sector logos and Toton depot plates. The Coal

The ScotRail Class 47, *Duke of Edinburgh's Award*.

A ScotRail Mk 3 tourist standard open (TSO).

A Railfreight Coal Class 58 with a weathered finish.

sub-sector included merry-go-round block coal train movements for power stations and provided resources for steel and cement works, fly ash and nuclear flasks.

New in the 1988 catalogue were two additional BR/BREL/GEC designed 25 kV AC electric locomotives. The first was the Class 90 arriving late that year in Intercity 'Swallow' grey and beige. A fleet of fifty was being built by BREL Crewe and all were in service by the end of 1990. In the same livery would be a model of an East Coast Main Line Class 91, which would arrive in 1990. The real locomotives were introduced with the electrification of the East Coast Main Line and the result was the IC225 trains designed to run at 225 kph. A new

The BR Class 06.

The Intercity 'Swallow' Class 90.

A 'Tilbury' PGA ballast hopper wagon.

range of catenary coaches was also planned for mid-year delivery. Another new model locomotive was a small 0-4-0 diesel shunter based on an Andrew Barclay Class 06, with a future role in low-priced train sets.

Completely new wagons included a PGA aggregate hopper wagon, available in Tarmac, Yeoman and Tilbury liveries, and a CDA covered hopper as an 'English China Clays' (ECC) wagon.

Added to the stone-finish building range was a buffet and bar with 'TEAS' painted on the roof.

James the Red Engine had joined *Thomas* and friends and brought with him his own Collett coaches in red and white.

An 'ECC' CDA covered hopper wagon.

James, No. 5.

James' coach.

1989
THE NUMBERS GAME

In 1989, alternative numbers were supplied with almost all the modern image locomotives and multiple units. The Class 47 in NSE livery came with a choice of three names supplied on a sheet with the model and the Class 110 DMU was now in BR plain blue. A second example of the new Railfreight sectional livery on a Hornby model was on 47231, which carried the triple-grey livery with Railfreight Distribution

The BR Class 110.

The ex-LMS 'Jinty' in LNER plain green livery.

The Highland Railway 0-4-0ST, *Loch Ness*.

The Silcock Express 'Cartic'.

(RfD) logos and Tinsley depot plates. RfD was responsible for non-trainload freight operations, as well as Freightliner and Intermodal services. It was also responsible for freight operations through the Channel Tunnel.

A strange livery for the LMS Class 3F 'Jinty' was to be found in the 'Suburban Passenger' train set where it sported LNER apple green with LNER lettering and the number 8400. The three coaches were short clerestories in LNER teak finish.

Another oddity was Dugald Drummond's Caley 'Pug' 0-4-0ST, branded a Highland Railways locomotive. Over the years this small model saddle tank engine would appear in the identities of the CR, L&YR, HR, MR, FR, LMS and BR as well as NCB and several private companies. The real locomotives dated from 1878 and were mostly used for shunting in dockyards.

The range of coaches remained unchanged, but there were seven new wagon liveries. Principal amongst these was the return of the articulated 'Cartic' car carrier in orange with

The High Speed Train (HST) shed.

'Silcock Express' branding. It carried twelve Ford Sierra cars in various colours.

The range of building kits was enlarged and named 'Town & Country'. It now included a pub, three houses and a pair of shops, as well as an HST shed and coach siding platforms for the gang of coach cleaners. Other than the shops the new range was produced exclusively for Hornby by the German model building manufacturer, Pola.

Additions to the 'Thomas & Friends' range were a tar tank wagon and the large breakdown crane. A 'Playtrain' 'Thomas & Bertie' set was now available in the form of a race game with plastic 'gulley' type rail and roadway. It included

The 'Town & Country' construction kits.

Bertie the Bus.

A motorised *Annie* with non-rail wheels.

a battery-powered 'Bertie the Bus' to race with a 0-4-0 *Thomas*, the latter being non-powered and pushed along by a battery-powered *Annie* the coach, which also towed *Clarabel*. In the set was a Ladybird book containing the story about the race.

It was in 1989 that the Exclusive First Editions (EFE) range of 00-scale die-cast commercial road vehicles launched. The year before, Hornby had been approached by the company for advice about the 'Heygates Grain' livery that Hornby had used in 1986 on their BRT bulk grain wagon. The information was supplied and the EFE 'Heygates Flour' road tanker was released in the first batch of EFE models.

With the thought of a possible range of EFE models in liveries compatible with other Hornby wagons, but sold under the Hornby name, several castings were supplied to Hornby by EFE and these were made up and painted in the R&D Department. Nothing came of the idea until the SkaleAuto range by Oxford Diecast arrived twenty years later. However, the EFE samples made up in the Hornby factory have survived.

In 1989 another new company was established which would make a considerable mark on the model railway market in Great Britain and prove to be Hornby's strongest rival so far. This was Bachmann Europe Ltd., a subsidiary of the Chinese firm, Kader, a major player in the American market under its Bachmann brand. As we have seen, Kader was the company that

The Hornby 'Heygates Grain' wagon and Exclusive First Editions (EFE) 'Heygates Flour' tanker.

Exclusive First Editions (EFE) castings given to Hornby.

had made the models for Palitoy's Mainline Railways in the late 1970s and early 1980s and, under the arrangement, retained ownership of the tools. These were about to be put back into use again and this time to more devastating effect. This brought to an end the manufacturing arrangement that Replica Railways had with Kader.

1980s – A DECADE SUMMARY

The decade started with Hornby's parent company, DCM, in financial difficulty resulting in Hornby Hobbies being dragged into receivership in 1980. Due to its own trading strength, the Receiver imposed few restrictions on continued production and development, and eventually Hornby Hobbies succeeded in a management buy-out in 1981. In 1986 the new independent Hornby Plc was floated on the London Stock Exchange's Unlisted Securities Market.

The emphasis for the main range was now model authenticity. The policy of model diversification saw the start of producing a suite of tools with changeable inserts so that a model could be changed to take account of physical differences between locomotives in a particular class or over a period of time. An early example was the 1981 tooling for the A4, which could be produced with or without valences. This forward thinking in tool design would grow in importance as railway modellers demanded more and more accuracy.

With a need to enlarge their share of the market, the Hornby Board appointed Keith Ness as Managing Director. Ness had come from the former sister company, Pedigee Dolls and Toys, and set about launching a range of dolls and toys under the Hornby name as a means of beating the current recession. This was a world he was familiar with, but this policy met with no great success. A whole array of cheap train sets, including push-along models, were also put on the market. Unfortunately, it took a long time before the failure of this policy was realised.

This diversification in the mid- to late-1980s had been largely at the expense of further development of the model railway and slot-car ranges. There were many redundancies as development work on those products was reduced and toys were imported, principally from across the Atlantic. Fortunately, much work had already been done to tool-up a number of new railway models before the budget restrictions were imposed, and the early 1980s had seen a host of new locomotive models released which helped to see Hornby over the lean years. However, by the mid-1980s new models were becoming a rarity, and new names, numbers and liveries were used to offer the public constantly changing choices. Indeed, the range of models in the late-1980s was larger than ever before, just by producing different versions of existing models, thus avoiding the high cost of new tooling.

The 1980s were a time for interesting new liveries reflecting a fast-changing scene on the real railways – InterCity, HoverSpeed, Railfreight, Network SouthEast, ScotRail, Speedlink and the Royal Train – and Hornby did well to keep up with the changes. Also, new locomotives and rolling stock sometimes appeared in model form before the real item arrived on the railways, examples being the APT and Class 58 diesel.

The introduction of pad (Tampo) printing in the 1970s made it possible to greatly improve the detail on models, and a major breakthrough in 1980 had been the policy of giving every locomotive and item of rolling stock a paint finish with pad-printed lining and other detail. At one stroke, toys became models. The 1980s showed the versatility of pad printing, allowing wagons to be available in an ever-changing array of liveries and when this versatility was applied to pad printing the finish on buildings, it became possible to alter the era of an entire range of railway buildings almost overnight by changing the print design.

Outside the Hornby bubble, the world of model railways was seeing changes. In 1981,

Airfix went into receivership and its GMR system was abandoned. In 1983 it was the manufacturers of the rival Mainline Railways range, Palitoy, that closed down. From these losses came a new firm, Dapol Ltd., and, by the end of the decade, the biggest rival yet, Bachmann Europe plc. Hornby's slowdown in product development left it vulnerable with room for a new player. That opportunity would not be missed.

The year 1980.

The year 1981.

The year 1982.

The year 1983.

The year 1984.

The year 1985.

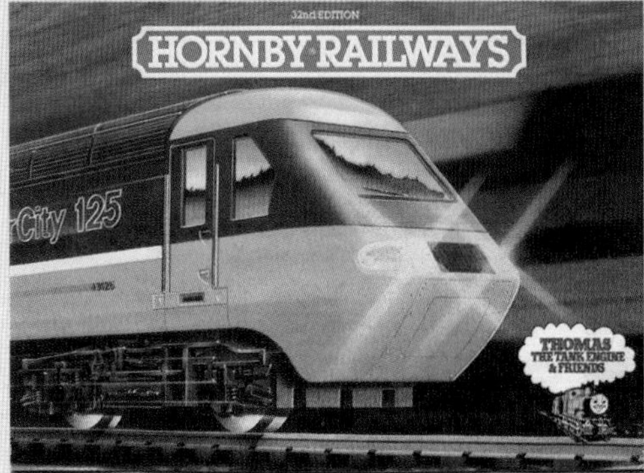

The year 1986.

The year 1987.

The year 1988.

The year 1989.

1980s MILESTONES

1980 – In receivership again, paint finishes, new 'King', 'Footballer', Caley 'Pug', GWR Class 2721 pannier tank, LMS 'Fowler' 2-6-4T and APT.

1981 – Management buy-out, 'Year of the Locomotive', 'Schools', 'Compound', 'Shire', 'County', J52, new 'Britannia', Class 86, re-tooled A1/A3, A4 with valences and Treasure Chests; the end of Airfix GMR and birth of what would become Dapol Ltd.

1982 – BR liveries return, Class 110 DMU, Class 58, 'scale' clerestory coaches, coal conveyor, etc., LNER refrigerator van and stone-finished buildings; 3-D-S.

1983 – Multiple liveries, Hornby High Street Series, 'Coronation Express', 'Playtrains' and expanding toy range; end of Mainline Railways and deal with Stanley Gibbons.

1984 – New 'Princess' model, Royal Train livery, Orient Express, PVA van and *The Art of Hornby.*

1985 – GWR 150, Thomas & Friends, BR Maunsell coaches and eight-window Mk 3s.

1986 – Hornby Hobbies floatation, 'Saint', InterCity grey, HoverSpeed and *Gordon.*

1987 – Class 142, NSE livery, Golden Arrow, 'Hunt', domed 'Black 5', *Duck* and *Devious.*

1988 – Classes 90 and 06, LMS 8F, revised 9F, ScotRail livery, PGA, CDA and *James the Red Engine.*

1989 – Alternative numbers, strange liveries, first BR Express Blue locomotive, RfD livery and 'Thomas & Bertie' set; birth of Bachmann Branchline.

THE WORLD OF THOMAS THE TANK ENGINE IN THE 1980s

Bill and Ben.

Devious Diesel.

Duck.

Edward.

Gordon.

Henry.

James.

Oliver.

Percy.

Stepney.

Toby.

Thomas.

1990
ENTER THE DRAGON

It was in 1990 that Hornby's new rival, Bachmann, released its first European catalogue and, as predicted, the first models were produced from the former Palitoy's Mainline Railways tooling. As time passed, these were improved and quickly Bachmann Europe developed new models designed in their UK drawing office at Barwell, Leicestershire. This came at a time of a depressed economic climate. Over the following years the two rivals would push each other on to produce better and more accurate models and the friendly rivalry would prove to be of great benefit to the British railway modelling community.

HORNBY RAILWAYS

The Class 91 was finally available in 1990, having been developed in co-operation with British Rail. It was in Intercity 'Swallow' white, grey and beige, a livery the model carried through many name changes, including as a promotional model for BBC Radio One FM. For its initial release it was un-named, but with a choice of numbers – 91001, 91008 and 91010.

To go with the new locomotive there were three BR Mk 4 coaches and a driving van trailer (DVT) – all in Intercity 'Swallow' livery. They were fitted with BT41 type bogies. These enabled modellers to form miniature replicas of the East Coast mainline expresses.

The Intercity Class 91.

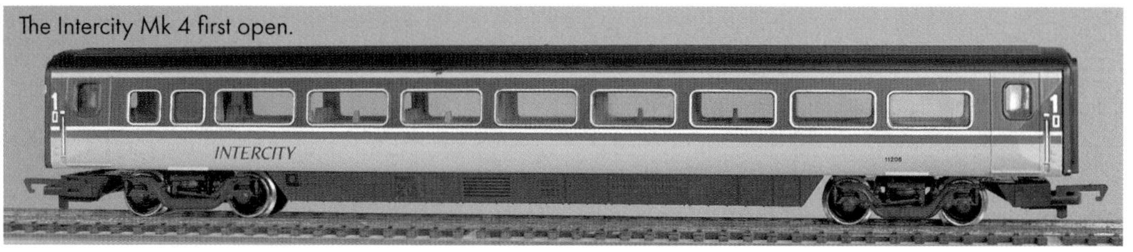

The Intercity Mk 4 first open.

The Railfreight Class 86, *Halley's Comet.*

A third version of the Railfreight revised livery appeared in 1990 and this was on 86504 in triple grey with Railfreight General Sector logos and Willesden depot plates. The sector covered any operations not assigned to either Trainload Freight sub-sectors or Railfreight Distribution. However, with only four locomotives carrying this livery, after two years it was absorbed by Railfreight Distribution in 1989.

There were no fewer than five different versions of the Class 47 model in the catalogue that year, four having been carried over from the year before and a new one in the 'Freightmaster' train set. This was the first model to carry Railfreight Construction Sector triple grey and was 47079 with Canton depot plates. The Class 58 was now available in Freightliner Coal Sector grey with a choice of three different numbers applied in the factory.

In addition to producing existing models in new identities for general release, from time to time Hornby have produced special runs for organisations. One example occurred in 1990 when a limited edition of 1,267 models was created for the Buckley and District Round Table. It was a standard R333 Class 86 electric locomotive in Intercity grey and beige livery as 86220 *The Round Tabler* and no doubt was sold to members to raise money for charities.

The Intercity Class 86, *The Round Tabler.*

The Railfreight Construction triple-grey Class 47.

1991
RECESSION BLUES

In 1991, Hornby Railways and Scalextric continued to be strong and represented 60 per cent of the group's entire sales. Despite this, group profits were halved and much of the problem had been with the failing speedboat business.

Despite the recent cut-back of the development budget, a new mainline steam locomotive was released during the year, although it had relied heavily on borrowed tooling. This was the GWR Class 28xx 2-8-0 heavy freight model, which made use of LMS Class 8F parts, including the firebox glow.

The 28xx was George Churchward's heavy long-distance freight locomotive of 1903 and Swindon built eighty-four of them to the original design. A further eighty-three were later built there, to a revised design by Charles Collett and these are referred to as the 38xx Class.

The new model was released in GWR green as 2859, and the year also saw the return of the 'Churchward County' 4-4-0 as 3825 *County of Denbigh*.

There was a brand new 0-4-0 tank engine released during the year, based on a steelworks locomotive that worked in South Wales, known as a Class D. These were used to feed blast furnaces and haul cradles of molten iron. The model, in red and numbered 40, authentically carried the name *King George V*. Its real steelworks partner, 43 *Queen Mary*, would take the model's identity the following year.

The GWR Class 28xx.

The GWR Churchward 'County' Class, *County of Denbigh*.

The new Class D tank engine, *King George V*.

The Crewe & District Quarries Class 101 tank engine.

In addition, the GWR Class 101 0-4-0T was released in three private owner liveries, these being Crewe & District Quarries No. 2 (blue), H. A. R. Wood & Co. No. 4 (green), named after one of Hornby's Sales Managers, and Lion Works No. 6 (black).

To go with the last of these, the 27-ton 'Tippler' mineral wagon was also released in black with Lion Works branding as a limited edition. Both the names on the 'Tippler' and the Lion Works locomotive were inspired by the old Spear & Jackson works in Sheffield.

The H. A. R. Wood & Co. Class 101 tank engine and trucks.

The Lion Works Class 101 with Lion-branded mineral wagons.

1992
DEVOTION TO EXCELLENCE

HORNBY DUBLO

In 1992 George Wrenn retired and sold the G&R Wrenn business to Dapol, and although the former Hornby Dublo locomotives were not returned to production again, the former Dublo wagon tooling was put to good use, which led to many more variations of the wagons under the Dapol name. For example, in the next twenty-two years the company would produce 184 versions of the former Hornby Dublo six-wheel milk tank wagon and 464 versions of the Dublo 5-plank open wagon!

HORNBY RAILWAYS

The 1992 Hornby Railways catalogue opened by reminding the public of the brand's heritage. A two-page spread showed the pre-war Hornby 0-gauge LMS crimson lake model of *Princess Elizabeth,* posed beside the present-day Hornby 00 model of *Princess Beatrice.* The text nicely summed up the link between the two models by saying: *'Hornby's tradition of craftsmanship lives on through the generations. The size and construction methods are certainly different, but the devotion to excellence remains undiminished.'*

It was this devotion to excellence that had ensured that the brand survived through successive recessions in the toy market and it was needed to be strongly felt now. Although Hornby would lose another of its rivals with the retirement of George Wrenn, its new rival based at Barwell was already nibbling at Hornby's customer base by its concentration on raising the level of authenticity with its models. The main market was with adult modellers and they were also rail enthusiasts and quickly picked up mistakes made by model designers. This was also becoming harder to avoid as Hornby were familiarising themselves with the new liveries that were springing up on the railways.

Two iconic Hornby train sets arrived in the shops during 1992, both based on

The 'Coronation Scot' train set.

The 'Silver Jubilee' train set.

The LMS Stanier BTK in Coronation blue and silver.

Freightliner revised livery containers.

Royal duties: *Britannia*.

famous trains of the inter-war period. The 'Coronation Scot' train set contained the streamlined 'Princess Coronation' Class in blue and silver, as 6220 *Coronation*, with two blue and silver Stanier coaches, while the 'Silver Jubilee' train set contained LNER A4 Class *Silver Link* in silver/grey with two silver coaches. The Gresley coaches would not have looked like the real coaches of this famous train and so Hornby used Stanier ones instead. Additional coaches in both liveries were available to extend both trains to acceptable lengths.

Whilst there were no new locomotives in 1992, as usual there were plenty of livery changes. One example was 70000 *Britannia,*

A 5-plank 'Hornby Railways 1992' wagon.

which returned with early BR decals, but was also released during the year as a limited edition, with a white cab roof as required when pulling the Royal Train to help airborne security personnel keep it in sight.

This was the year that the 30-ft Fletcher containers arrived and the 20-ft containers in striking Freightliner red and yellow; in both cases they were sold on the bogie container flat wagon. There were several other new wagon liveries and, worth mentioning, was the 5-plank open wagon in red and inscribed 'Hornby Railways 1992'. This was the first of what became a tradition of producing a different wagon each year in Hornby livery with the year printed on it – and this is still practised today.

A series of card building kits was released during the year, the first subjects being a station, island platform and a goods depot.

The 1992 catalogue launched 'Team Hornby', a club you could join to keep up to date with Hornby Railways and Scalextric news. In reality little news was supplied and the club, run by a marketing company, seemed to be more interested in selling members stationery, T-shirts and other mementos. It was replaced in 1998 by 'The Hornby Collectors Club'.

Team Hornby 'freebies'.

1993
COLOURFUL BATTERY POWER

A new battery-powered Hornby Railways toy range was launched in 1993 called 'Station Master', which consisted of models from the main range in bright colours.

A train set contained an oval of standard track, a Class D tank engine, two large mineral wagons, a four-wheel coach, a station and tunnel (with a roof car park). By clever design, the station and tunnel clipped together to form a carrying case. The 0-4-0T, wagons and coach were available solo, along with a Class 06 diesel, 'Monobloc' tank wagon, LMS type brake van, signal box and signal, island platform, engine shed and goods depot. The colours were red, yellow and blue in mixed combinations.

The 'Station Master' electric train set.

The LNER A1, *Flying Scotsman* (1924–1928).

The LNER A1, *Flying Scotsman* (1928–1936).

The BR A3, *Flying Scotsman* (1961–1963).

The LNER A3, *Flying Scotsman* (1966–1973).

Special attention was given to *Flying Scotsman* in 1993, with four versions of the locomotive covering different periods in its life. For 1924–28 the model was an A1 with the number on the tender and the coat-of-arms on the cab-side. For the period 1928–36 it was still an A1, but with the number on the cab sides. For 1961–63 the model was an A3 in late BR green with German smoke deflectors. The fourth version, for 1966–73, caused the most excitement as it was a model of the locomotive in Alan Pegler's ownership, with two tenders and an LNER green livery.

The Class 90 was in a new livery – Rail Express Systems (RES) as 90018. The new RES livery came into being in 1992 for trains transporting mail and parcels. This was red and dark grey, with pale blue and grey flashes. The livery was carried on the rolling stock, together with several locomotives that were dedicated to mail and parcels traffic, made up mainly of Classes 47 and 90.

For the second 'year' wagon, the OAA open wagon was used, again in red. There were six other new liveries, including the PVA curtain-sided van in Railiner yellow, the 5-plank open wagon in engineer's brown with a green flash and the ventilated van as the Eastleigh red tool van.

The Class 90 in 'Parcels' livery.

The 5-plank wagon in departmental livery.

The Hornby pre-production VEA British Railways (BR) tool van.

A Hornby OBA 'Hornby Railways 1993'.

A Hornby PVA van 'Railiner' yellow TRL6950.

1994
DECISION TIME

Like all toy companies, by 1994 Hornby had been squeezed by three trends in the market. The first of these was the rise of the American multinationals, such as Hasbro and Mattel-Fisher Price, which had made it difficult for smaller companies to compete on marketing budgets. Second, imports from low-cost producers in the Far East had taken their toll. As late as 1978 Great Britain was still a net exporter of toys, but, in 1993, imports accounted for nearly half of the country's billion-pound toy industry. Third, the final blow was the rise of electronic toys, initially in the early 1980s and then the second wave ten years later with the phenomenal success of the Sega and Nintendo video game machines.

Serious consideration was now being given to moving production to the Far East, and two projects were set up. The designs for a new locomotive model had been sent to Sanda Kan in China asking them to produce the tooling, manufacture the model and supply it ready for sale. The second project was to send existing tooling to the same company and ask for the model to be produced with a high-quality finish ready for the 1996 catalogue. The new model to be tooled in China was the Class 92 electric locomotive, built for channel tunnel traffic, and the tooling sent out to China was that for the former Tri-ang Class B12 of 1963 and the LMS Class 2MT first produced in 1975. Sanda Kan had been chosen for the proven quality of their work as seen on some of the models which they had tooled and manufactured for Airfix.

Following the *Flying Scotsman* spotlight the previous year, 1994 was to be the year of the LNER Class A4 with seven different examples. Besides the two already in the range, the five added were early BR green 60019 *Bittern* in the 'Tees Tyne Pullman' train set, late BR green 60010 *Dominion of Canada* and three different versions of *Sir Ralph Wedgewood.* These were 1939–42 LNER blue with valences, 1945–47 wartime black with the abbreviation NE on the tender, and 1962–65 in late BR green. Three thousand of each were made. This was the first

The 'Sir Ralph Wedgwood' presentation set. (Courtesy Vectis Auctions)

The Class 35 in BR blue.

Class J83 in LNER green.

A Railfreight VDA van in 'Dutch' livery.

time that Hornby had offered three locomotives as a set and with a wooden case to house them.

Once again there were no completely new models in the catalogue, but plenty of new liveries, plus some old models returning with improved finishes. These included the Class J83 0-6-0T as LNER green 8473 and the 'Hymek' in BR blue as D7093.

At the time of sectorisation of Britain's railways in the mid-1980s, most secondary passenger routes, which did not fall under the InterCity or NSE banner, were re-designated as Regional Railways (originally Provincial Railways) and the Hornby model of the Class 142 'Pacer' was now in Regional Railways grey livery.

After 1987, the 'Dutch' yellow and grey livery was introduced to Britain's railways for engineering stock and this started to appear on some Hornby wagons in 1994. The ex-Tri-ang SR utility van made a reappearance after twenty-five years and for the first time it was in Southern Railway livery. Both olive green and malachite versions were produced. However, the die-cast buffers with stocks were no longer available, the buffer stocks on more recent models were now an integral part of the buffer beam moulding and so the re-introduced utility vans were issued without buffer stocks!

A SR malachite ex-Tri-ang utility van.

1995

A BIT OF CHINA, A BIT OF FRANCE

A new model for the year was the BR/Brush Co-Co Class 92 25 kV AC electric locomotive that had been tooled and manufactured in China by Sanda Kan. This highly detailed model was in Railfreight Distribution Tunnel Services livery as 92009 *Elgar* and carried Crewe Electric depot plates. In all, forty-six real locomotives were built by Brush Traction for Railfreight Distribution, Eurostar and SNCF, and can operate from four different power systems. At £3 million each, the Class 92 at that time was the most expensive locomotive design ever built in Great Britain.

Passengers travelling through the Channel Tunnel were carried on Eurostar trains and a model of one also arrived in 1995. It was not a 00-scale model built by Hornby, but the French Jouef/Mehano H0 model, repackaged. The real GEC-Alstom Class 373 trains were a co-operation between the British, French and Belgian railways and connected the countries' three capitals. Hornby offered a four-unit train both in a train set and as a train pack. The model had dummy pantographs and non-working lights.

For the first time in twelve years 'British Railways' appeared on Hornby locomotives and these were BR experimental 'purple' Class A4 60028 *Walter K Whigham* and BR green Class J83 0-6-0T 68472. Another wooden locomotive case was on offer, this time with a limited edition of the Southern malachite green 'West Country' model 21C101 *Exeter,* of which 4000 were made. This was to celebrate the real locomotive's fiftieth anniversary and the model was also released in BR green as 34054 *Lord Beaverbrook*. The first Hornby model locomotive to carry Railfreight Metals Sector livery was 37885, which had Canton depot plates.

The 'Railfreight Distribution' Class 92, *Elgar*.

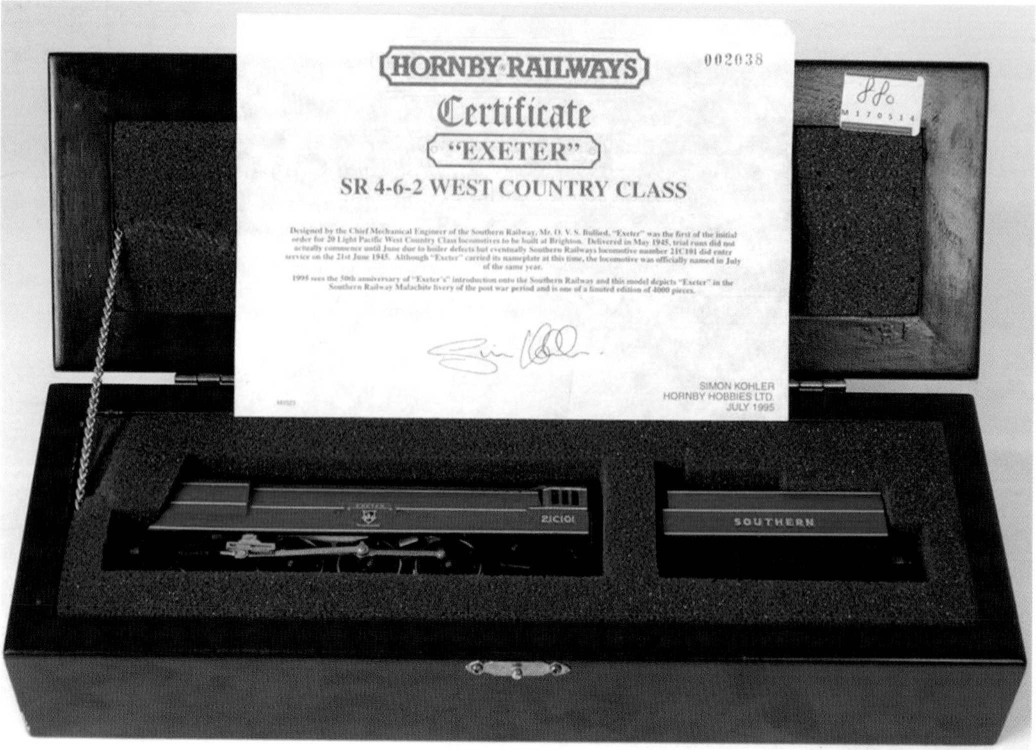

The BB-WC, *Exeter*, in a presentation box. (Courtesy LSK)

The Hornby Class A4 in an early BR experimental 'purple' livery as *Walter K. Whigham*.

A new attempt at improving the quality of Hornby wagons was launched. This was a series of three 'Authentic Rolling Stock First' open wagons, the first to be designed with Computer Aided Design (CAD) technology. More importantly, they were replicas of early 9-ft wheelbase wagons and were more suitable for the early private owner liveries, which were in growing demand from the public. The wagons were 3-, 4- and 6-plank models.

The Cowans Shildon breakdown crane had returned to red livery and the 'year' wagon was the small tanker. The ventilated van now sported a yellow spot indicating its use for banana traffic. Also, there was now a 'Thomas & Friends' version of the battery-powered 'Station Master' train set.

Richard Lines retired during the year having been with the Rovex company since it was bought by Lines Bros. in 1951. He had brought to the company an understanding of the toy industry that had been instilled in him from an early age through his father, uncles and cousins, who were all involved in the family toy business.

An 'Edwin W. Badland' 6-plank wagon.

An 'H. Hotson' 4-plank wagon.

A 'Turner & Sons' 3-plank wagon.

The VEA 'Yellow Spot' banana van.

Richard's was a steady hand, which had much to do with the success of Rovex and later Hornby Hobbies. I once asked him what his job title was, and he assured me that he had none. In the early days he had been referred to as 'Mr Richard', but after 1971 he was 'Mr Lines' or just 'Richard' to his colleagues, and he was held in high regard. In retirement he occasionally runs his Hornby 0-gauge railway for the amusement of his grandchildren – and himself! In recent years he has been a willing source of information for those researching the toy industry and Rovex in particular.

HORNBY DUBLO

In 1995 the former Hornby Dublo machinery had been installed in the new Dapol factory in Llangollen and production of wagons had started. Whilst Dapol were moving to their new premises a fire broke out at their Winsford base in Cheshire, destroying much stock and tooling.

1996
MANNA FROM HEAVEN

Following the fire, Dapol needed to raise money quickly, and the valuable asset that they could sell quickly was their tooling. This included the Airfix tools they had bought in 1983 and tooling for their own locomotives and wagons. In 1996, David Boyle approached Bachmann, but was unsuccessful in agreeing a sale.

HORNBY RAILWAYS

Hornby were feeling the effects of having Bachmann in the market and realised that major changes were needed. Keith Ness retired and was replaced by Peter Newey, who became Chief Executive and Chairman. His thoughts were that Hornby should focus on what the company was known for – model railways and slot car racing – and he set about restructuring the whole company with this notion in mind. The toys were axed and, because of this, many of the staff left, including several in senior positions.

The standard of finish and intricate lining on the B12 made by Sanda Kan was better than any we had seen before and the model went on sale in 1996 to rave reviews. Sadly, the LMS Class 2MT did not achieve the same fate as it was felt that the model was not accurate enough in design to justify the modification costs. Satisfied with the Class 92 and B12 models produced by Sanda Kan in China, discussions began about the possibility of outsourcing production to that company and closing the factory at Margate.

With new determination and money once again directed to model development, a public consultation process followed to find

The LNER B12 model that was made and finished by Sandra Kan.

The LMS black, *City of St Albans* and Royal Doulton plate.

out what railway modellers wanted from Hornby ... and the public responded. It was clear that they wanted authenticity and that must now be the priority. New subjects were wanted, and existing models needed to be upgraded. It would take time to develop a new range of high-quality models and something needed to be done in the meantime. It was then that Hornby was approached by David Boyle from Dapol, wanting to sell his tooling. It must have seemed like manna from heaven.

After an inspection of the tools and a sorting out of what Hornby felt would be of use to them a deal was struck under which most of the tools were purchased and almost immediately prepared for use. They included all but one of the former Airfix locomotives and most of the coach and wagon tools. They also included four locomotives developed by Dapol and the tools of several wagons that Boyle had arranged to be copied in China in 1982. This way Hornby gained the tooling to thirteen new locomotives they could add to their catalogue. The purchase included the Dapol Class 150 DMU, but it was such a poor model that it was not put into production. Also, the former Trix Class 124 Trans-Pennine DMU, which was out of scale, and the Class 31, which was incomplete. The Airfix rebuilt LMS 'Royal Scot' Class would have been useful, but the tools for it had been lost in China and had not been acquired by Dapol. Hornby were interested in buying the former Airfix railway kits, which Dapol owned, but they were not for sale. With the purchase came the decision that because many of the tools were already in China the tooling improvements and model manufacturing should be carried out there. This was the beginning of the end of model railway manufacturing in Margate.

The big surprise for 1996 was the 'Royal Doulton 50th Anniversary Collection'. Four locomotives in immediate post-war livery had been chosen and were the subjects of four pictures, which were reproduced on Royal Doulton plates. Limited editions of the four models were produced by Hornby and sold specially packaged with a sample of the relative plate. The locomotives were LNER blue A4 No. 1 *Sir Ronald Matthews*, LMS post-war black 'Duchess' 6253 *City of St Albans*, GWR green 'King' 6018 *King Henry VI* and SR malachite 'Schools' 905 *Tonbridge*. Three thousand of each were made and were almost all sold during the first year.

The takeover of Jouef by Lima saw the end of H0 Eurostar supplies and so Hornby tooled up their own model which was correctly to

The two Eurostar train packs, H0- and 00-scale.

The 00-scale Eurostar train pack.

00 scale. The model was designed and tooled in record time. Drawing commenced on the 2 January 1996 and the Eurostar set and pack were launched in September of that year!

In the early 1990s the government had divided the train-load business into three regionally based companies: Loadhaul, Mainline Freight and Transrail, and established the parcels and mails under a fourth organisation, Rail Express Services (RES). Freightliner was subject to a management buy-out and separated from its former Speedlink owning partner, Railfreight Distribution.

The first of the new regional train-load liveries appeared on Hornby models during 1996 and were 58050 in Mainline blue and 37424 in Transrail triple grey, while 86417 was in RES livery.

The larger locomotives were now being sold in dark brown boxes with the 'Top Link' logo and an illustrated lid design. The two-tender 'Scotsman' was in a later livery, with a blue and grey second tender, as run by 'Flying Scotsman Enterprises', again as a limited edition, and to go with it there were three Mk 2 coaches in a limited-edition coach pack.

The last time there had been BR Mk 1 coaches in the catalogue had been way back in 1982. This was because the most used tools were worn out. Now, fourteen years later, they were back and much improved in appearance. They had flush glazing and benefited from the higher standard of finish now given to Hornby models.

The Class 37 in Transrail triple grey.

The Class 58 in Mainline blue as *Toton Traction Depot*.

The Class 86 in Rail Express Services (RES) red and grey.

As before, they consisted of a CK, BSK, BG, RMB and SLE.

Late in 1996, with a new budget for marketing, Hornby attended their first Warley exhibition and this was to be the first of a whole new programme of exhibition appearances for the Hornby marketing team.

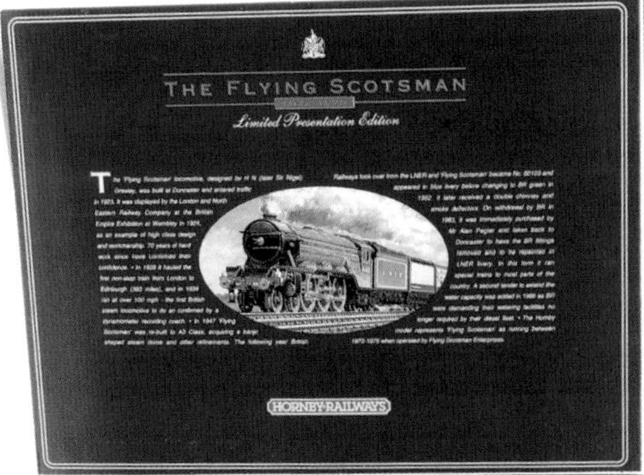

The LNER A1 'Flying Scotsman Enterprises' presentation edition.

'Top Link' packaging.

BR Mk 1 sleeping car (SLE), revised.

1997
GAME CHANGE

HORNBY

The year 1997 saw the start of the renaissance of Hornby's model railway system. It seemed that having disposed of the toys to be able to concentrate on model railways and slot-cars, and having restructured the staff base of the company, a new image was required. To start with, the name of the railway products changed from 'Hornby Railways' to just 'Hornby' and the catalogue took on a new look, with everything photographed against a white background.

In addition to eleven train sets there were now an additional eight train packs, each being a passenger train. Two of these packs contained the first of the re-issued former Airfix/Dapol models, one having early BR 'Castle' 5042 *Winchester Castle* with three carmine and cream Centenary coaches, the other with GWR 'Hawksworth County' 1004 *County of Somerset* and the same three coaches, but in GWR chocolate and cream livery.

Three of the train packs were in a new 'Great British Trains' series and each was

The BR 'Hawksworth County' train pack, ex-Airfix and Dapol.

based on a famous British named train service. They came in a standard flat green box and the first three were: 'The Royal Scot', comprising LMS maroon 6208 *Princess Helena Victoria* with three Stanier coaches; 'The Bristolian', comprised of 'Britannia' Class 70023 *Venus* and three crimson and cream Mk 1 coaches; and 'Heart of Midlothian', with BR green A4 60020 *Guillemot* and three maroon Mk 1 coaches. Several more of these packs were added over the years.

There were also former Airfix and Dapol models available solo, including former Airfix GWR Class 14xx 0-4-2T, B-set non-corridor coach and the autocoach, along with the two Centenary coaches. Also added to the catalogue were the former Airfix GWR Macaw bogie bolster wagon, GWR 'Conflat A' and container,

The GWR autocoach, ex-Airfix.

The GWR Class 14xx, ex-Airfix.

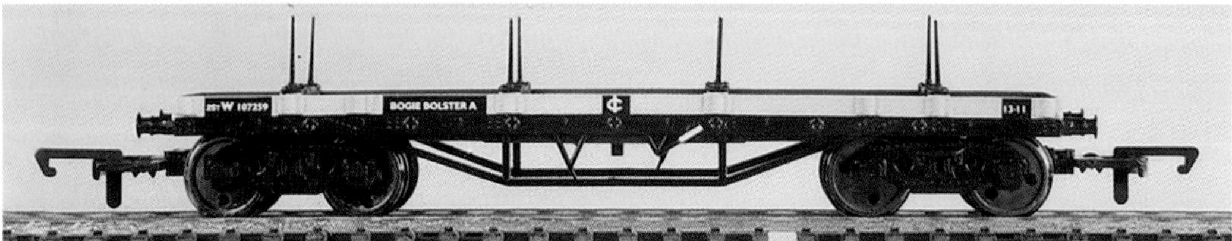

The BR 'Macaw' bogie bolster wagon, ex-Airfix.

A BR 20-ton hopper wagon, ex-Airfix.

The 'Ketton Cement' PCA 'Presflo', ex-Dapol.

The LMS Conflat plus container, ex-Airfix.

a 20-ton hopper and 20-ton tank wagon. From the Dapol wagon range came the PCA 'Presflo' (V-tank) wagon and the GWR double vent van.

Released late in the year was a completely new EMU in Network SouthEast livery. This was a model of the two-car Class 466 'Networker' which had been on the Kent Link service since its introduction in 1993. It is thought to have been suggested by the Chairman, who travelled along that route. Owing to the class's limited distribution it was a strange choice and not a big seller.

Also new in 1997 were the first signs of privatisation of the railways in the form of EW&S maroon and yellow on the Class 58 as 58033 and the Class 37 as 37057. There was also GNER navy blue livery on train packs containing the Class 43 (HST) and Class 91 as 91030 and the Mk 3A and Mk 4 coaches.

The Network SouthEast Class 466.

The English, Welsh & Scottish Railway (EW&S) Class 58.

Another new feature this year were triple wagon sets. Each set had a different private owner name and a different number on each wagon. The sets were 7-plank (Charles Stott), 5-plank (Cumberland Granite Co.) and coke wagon (Dinnington).

The lineside accessories were not forgotten. There were many track packs, which built up into a large multi-circuit layout. The grand Victorian suspension bridge was back and a new series of the railway buildings with self-adhesive surface finishes was now available. These had a 'aged' brick or stone finish and replaced the former stone finish range, looking more realistic. Also new was the TrakMat, which was a printed plastic sheet that would be included in train sets. It was a clever marketing idea as it showed track beds and places for buildings and served to encourage beginners to fill up the spaces by buying the parts needed.

During the year the 'Team Hornby Club' was wound up and replaced by 'The Hornby Collector Club', directly controlled by the company's Marketing Department. Membership entitled you to a bi-monthly magazine containing news, articles, fun features and special offers; also, the first 5,000 enrolling received a free exclusive locomotive during the year. The first year it was the Caley 'Pug' with 'British Railways' on the tank sides and numbered 56038.

The Hornby Collector club magazine, first issue.

1998
CATERING FOR COLLECTORS

By now it was clear that Hornby's main market was with serious railway modellers and collectors. During the year Hornby Collectors Centres were established. These were retailers through which limited edition models would be channelled.

The remaining three ex-Dapol locomotive models were put into production in 1998. The first of these was the little Lancashire & Yorkshire Railway 0-4-0ST in LMS black as 11232. The Aspinall Class B7 'Pugs' were designed and built at Horwich. The first of the fifty-seven built started work in 1891 and were usually found in dock areas where their short wheelbase was essential for the tight curves.

The second ex-Dapol locomotive was the London Brighton & South Coast Railway 'Terrier' 0-6-0T in SR olive green as W2 *Freshwater*. This popular subject was designed by William Stroudley as his Class A1, but the model is of the ones modified by Earle Marsh as the Class A1X. Some fifty 'Terriers' were built between 1872 and 1880 for suburban and branch line duties.

The final Dapol-designed tank engine model was the Riddles 'Austerity' 0-6-0ST of the Second World War, the model being in LNER black as 8006. The real locomotives were based on the Class 50550 design by Hunslet and 391 of them were built for the government during the Second World War, using various locomotive builders. After the war seventy-five were bought by the LNER as their Class J94 and many others were acquired by the National Coal Board and other industries.

Three more of the former Dapol-copied wagons were also put back into production in 1998 – 14T tank wagon and the 'Mogo' van, as well as the Dapol-designed HEA hopper wagon.

More former Airfix models were brought into use by Hornby during the year. These were the 1883 GWR Class 2301 'Dean Goods' 0-6-0 as 2468 in GWR green (featured on the front of the 1998 catalogue), Henry Fowler's 1911 MR/LMS Class 4F 0-6-0 as late BR black 44331, the GWR 'Siphons G & H', the 5-, 7- and 9-plank wagons and the GWR large steel mineral wagon.

The Airfix Mk 2D coaches were now available, but only in Virgin Trains livery.

The LMS ex-L&Y dockyard tank, ex-Dapol.

The SR 'Terrier' tank, *Freshwater*, ex-Dapol.

The LNER J94, ex-Dapol.

GWR 'Siphon G' van, ex-Airfix.

The final new addition was a BREL 2400 hp Class 56 Co-Co diesel, which had been tooled late by Palitoy and was sold to Dapol in 1984. Hornby released it during the year as both 56100 in black and orange Load Haul livery and 56058 in EW&S maroon and yellow.

A Great Western Railway (GWR) 'Mogo' van, ex-Dapol.

An English, Welsh & Scottish Railway (EWS) hopper wagon, ex-Dapol.

The Class 4F, ex-Airfix.

The GWR 'Dean Goods', ex-Airfix.

A LNER 9-plank wagon, ex-Airfix.

The Virgin Mk 2D tourist standard open (TSO), ex-Airfix.

The Story of Rovex, Volume 2, 1965–1971, by Pat Hammond.

The real Class 56 owed its existence in major part to the oil crisis in the early 1970s and the expected increase in the demand for coal. The first thirty Class 56 locomotives were built by Electroputere at Craiova in Romania, but the remaining 105 machines came from BREL at Doncaster and Crewe. They were introduced between 1976 and 1984.

The year also saw the publication by New Cavendish Books of *The Rovex Story Volume 2 – Tri-ang Hornby 1965–1971,* which provided an in-depth history and comprehensive record of Tri-ang Hornby products produced over the seven years the brand had been used.

1999
FAREWELL MARGATE

The last model was made in the Hornby factory during 1999; all other production was carried out by Sanda Kan in China. The final model is thought to have been an Eddie Stobart promotional model for the Trafford Model Centre.

Completely new were two super-detailed models tooled in China for the Gresley LNER A1/A3 and the Class A4. They had finely detailed chassis and bodies and came with extra details for the customer to fit if required, including cab doors, front coupling and dust shields. They also had ready-fitted brake rods and brake pipes and finer profile wheels and coupling rods.

The practice had developed of producing only enough train sets to last two years and so half the train sets in the catalogue were new each year. So popular were certain subjects, such as *Flying Scotsman* and the HST, that replacement sets of these had to always be on the list, but these needed to be different to the ones they replaced. With the HST this could be done by changing the livery, as several different railway operating companies used HSTs. With the *Flying Scotsman* it was not possible because buyers usually wanted it in LNER green.

A Palitoy-designed model that used the Airfix 4F tender was Henry Fowler's 1928 LMS Class 2P 4-4-0. Tooling had not belonged to Kader and so

The last model made in the Margate factory: container flat 'Eddie Stobart Ltd'.

The LMS Class 2P, ex-Airfix.

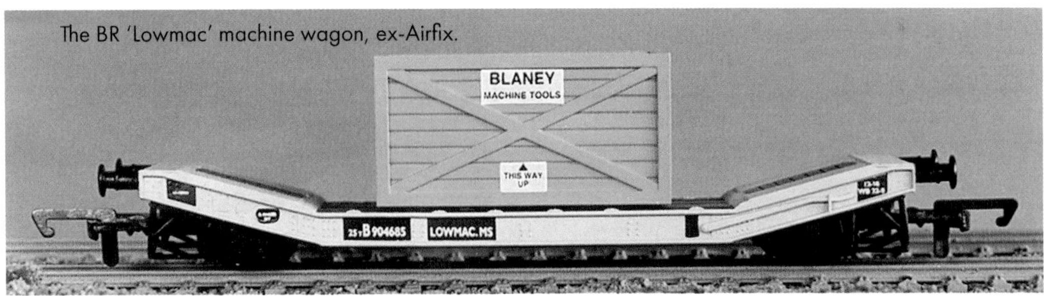

The BR 'Lowmac' machine wagon, ex-Airfix.

The LMS twelve-wheel dining car, ex-Airfix.

The LMS Class 61xx, ex-Airfix.

The Metro Class 155, ex-Dapol.

was amongst the Airfix tooling bought by Dapol and sold on to Hornby. It was now being released in the Hornby range as LMS lined black 579.

Other Airfix-originated models added to the Hornby catalogue this year were the LMS twelve-wheel dining car in LMS crimson lake, the 'Lowmac' machine wagon in BR grey, and both GWR and LMS brake vans in both pre- and post-nationalisation livery.

Also available during the year was the former Dapol Leyland Class 155 'Super-Sprinter' two-car DMU in Metro maroon and a late arrival was Charles Collett's 1931 GWR Class 61xx 'Large Prairie' 2-6-2T as GWR green 6113.

New scale-length Great Western Trains (GWT) Mk 3 standard open car.

The Colliery Set train pack box lid.

An unusual train pack commissioned by wholesaler A. B. Gee was called 'The Colliery Set'. It contained a BR Class 4F, five BR seven-plank open wagons and an ex-LMS brake van. All were from former Airfix tooling and one thousand packs were released.

A surprise arrival was the return of the earlier Class 29 'Sad Eyes' model in two-tone green as D6130.

A much-welcomed arrival in 1999 was a new range of Mk 3 coaches which, for the first time, were to scale length. They consisted of a standard open (SO or TSO), first open (FO) and buffet car. Later, the Lima TGS and SLEP as well as a DVT would be added. These proved to be good revenue earners for Hornby and were produced in many different liveries. In 1999 they were in GNER, Virgin and Great Western Trains livery.

After several years without new models in the 'Thomas & Friends' series, 1999 was marked by the introduction of an additional new clockwork range with a simplified indestructible track and accessories, all of which fitted on a specially designed Playmat. The clockwork locomotives were *Thomas, Percy* and, new to the series, *Toby* the tram engine and two more new characters – twins *Bill* and *Ben.* These last two were based on a china clay industry 0-4-0 saddle tank. This generated a new demand for the 'Thomas' range resulting in substantially increased sales.

'Thomas & Friends' revised.

Also, following the successful launch in September of battery-operated 'Noddy' sets that included both road and rail features, Hornby were looking at ways of further boosting sales in the younger market the following year. New junior versions of the Hornby railway system and Scalextric were planned for the second half of 2000.

The Tri-ang Society was formed in 1999 and caters for collectors of Tri-ang Hornby, as well as other Tri-ang products.

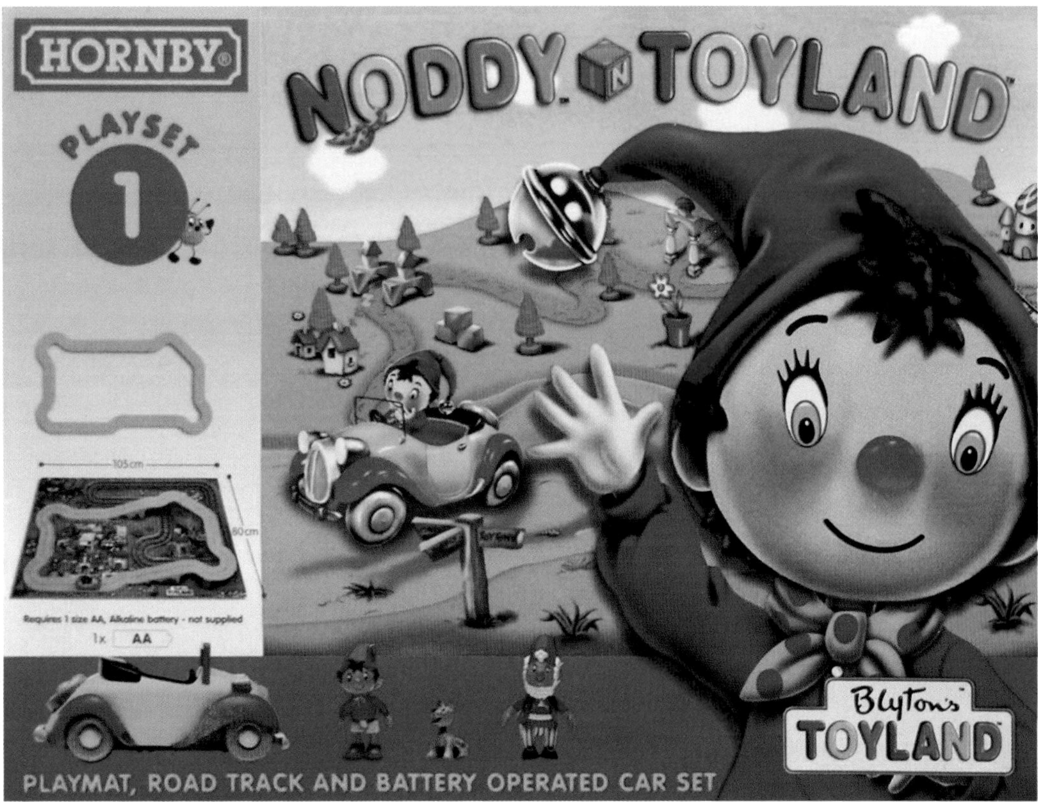

The *Noddy* play set.

1990s – A DECADE SUMMARY

The decade started during a recession in the toy industry. The company was committed to selling a wide range of toys at the expense of its historically successful model brands. Investment in new tooling for the company's model railways was at an all-time low. The gap in new models was being filled with the existing range of models being reproduced with different liveries and identities. Effort was also going into producing simple toy trains for toy shops.

In the meantime, a new rival had started to release good-quality models for the British market. They were manufactured in the Far East and model railway enthusiasts were eagerly buying them. This was the Bachmann Branchline range, designed in Great Britain by Bachmann Europe plc and manufactured in China by the company's owners – Kader Industrial Co. Ltd.

Only just in time, Hornby Hobbles realised the error of its policy and took steps to rectify the situation. The toys were dropped, and the staffing severely reduced at all levels. Money was once again directed to the company's two most successful products – Hornby Railways and Scalextric. Hornby needed new tools rapidly and Dapol were urgently in need of money after a serious fire at their works. Hornby bought most of Dapol's own tools plus the former Airfix tools, which Dapol had bought in the early 1980s. This gave Hornby thirteen new locomotives, six more coaches and about a dozen new wagons. After testing, and in some cases extensive modifications, all the newly acquired tooling was put into production.

In planning the next step, major decisions had been taken. The main and most stable model railway market was with British enthusiasts and they needed to be Hornby's main focus. 'It's what has been called the Harley-Davidson effect,' as Frank Martin, Hornby's Chief Executive during the successful years ahead, would say at a press conference. 'Middle-aged men with lots of disposable cash dream of reliving part of their childhood.' While simple trains were needed to encourage beginners and cater for those on a lower budget, Hornby's main customers wanted accurate models and the accent needed to be on super-detailed ones.

In order to compete with its rivals, the company needed to reduce its costs whilst increasing its model's fidelity. It needed to move production to the Far East. Sanda Kan Industrial Ltd. in China was chosen, and some test models made. The company catered for over sixty other manufacturers and were arguably the premier model railway manufacturer in the world. They had seventeen dedicated factories and 12,000 staff, and American customers included Lionel, K-Line, Life-Like, Atlas, USA Trains, Weaver and Williams.

Sanda Kan was later owned by New York venture capitalists, Morgan Stanley, and one of its factories in Guandong Province became entirely dedicated to manufacturing Hornby. By the end of the decade, all production had been moved to China and already four super-detailed model locomotives had been tooled up and delivered by Sanda Kan. Regrettably, the closure of the Hornby Margate factory resulted in approximately 170 redundancies over a period

The year 1990.

The year 1991.

The year 1992.

The year 1993.

The year 1994.

The year 1995.

The year 1996.

The year 1997.

The year 1998.

The year 1999.

of four years. This figure would have been a lot higher but during that time many of the older staff had retired and others had sought alternative employment. Numbers had temporarily been made up with agency staff.

Since the early 1950s, railway livery changes had been very infrequent. By the 1990s the situation had changed completely. Through sectorisation, regionalisation and finally privatisation, the trains of the day were constantly changing in appearance, giving model makers an unlimited supply of options; this would continue to expand for the foreseeable future. Reproduction of post-privatisation liveries required the permission of the owning company and in some cases a licence fee was requested.

The decade finished on a high note, a success story being the new Hornby locomotives for the enthusiast and collector, which were selling well. The Chairman also reported that the outsourcing to China had achieved significant savings in overheads.

1990s MILESTONES

1990 – Class 91, Mk 4 coaches and DVT, Rft General, Rft Construction and LNER green A4.

1991 – Class 28xx, BR maroon 'Duchess', D Class 0-4-0T and Parcels Sector livery.

1992 – 'Royal Scot' and 'Silver Jubilee' train sets, Royal Train *Britannia*, Hornby 'Year' wagons start, card building kits and launch of Team Hornby Club.

1993 – 'Station Master' series, *Flying Scotsman* year, two-tender Scotsman and RES livery.

1994 – Planned Far East move, B12 tools to China, A4 year, 'Dutch' livery and SR utility van.

1995 – SD Class 92, H0 'Eurostar', CAD and 'First' nine-foot wheelbase wagons.

1996 – Royal Doulton, Airfix/Dapol tooling, pre-privatisation liveries, 00 'Eurostar', Top Link packaging, HVR and retooled Mk 1 coaches.

1997 – 'Hornby', new look catalogue, train packs, 'Networker', ex-Airfix and Dapol: 'Castle', 'County', 14xx, GWR coaches and wagons; 'Great British Trains' packs, post-privatisation liveries, triple wagon sets, new building finishes, Trak-Mat and Hornby Railway Collectors Club.

1998 – Hornby Collector Centres, SD A1/A3 and A4, ex-Dapol L&Y 'Pug', 'Terrier' and J94, ex-Palitoy Class 56, ex-Airfix 'Dean Goods' and 4F, 'Syphons', etc., Mk 2 coaches and building packs.

1999 – Last model made at Margate, GWR 61xx 2-6-2T, LMS 2P, LMS Diner, scale Mk 3 coaches, ex-Dapol Class 155 DMU, re-birth of 'Thomas & Friends' and arrival of *Bill* and *Ben*.

YEAR-DATE WAGONS FROM THE 1990s ONWARDS

1992.

1993.

1994.

1995.

1996.

1997.

1998.

1999.

2000.

2001.

2002.

2003.

2004.

2005.

2006.

2007.

2008.

2009.

2010.

2011.

2012.

2013.

2014.

2015.

2016.

2017.

2018.

2019.

2000
THE WOW FACTOR

HORNBY

In 2000, Hornby released their first brand-new high-quality model – the BR 'Rebuilt Merchant Navy' 35028 *Clan Line*. The Hornby marketing team had invited the public to suggest what it would like Hornby to make and this subject had come way out on top. The model boasted sprung buffers, a detailed cab interior, an excellent five-pole motor and many separately fitted components. There were also other parts supplied with it for the purchaser to fit.

This was to a standard of realism never seen before on a steam outline model carrying the Hornby name. It was also the most highly priced locomotive produced by the company and yet it was an instant success. It showed that Hornby were once again going to be a force to be reckoned with and, from that point onwards, Hornby became the trendsetters. I recall a statement made by Simon Kohler when we gathered at the press launch at Stewarts Lane Shed (with the real *Clan Line* in the background): that from now on every new model from Hornby was going to be better than the one before. That was quite a target for anyone to set themselves, but it made for some very interesting years ahead – and some wonderful models.

The re-built 'Merchant Navy' Class, *Clan Line*.

The re-tooled super-detailed Class 9F.

The LNER A3 103 *Flying Scotsman* millenium limited edition. (Courtesy Vectis Auctions)

Also arriving from China to celebrate the fortieth anniversary of the completion of the last British mainline steam locomotive, 92220 *Evening Star*, was the re-tooled super-detailed model of the Class 9F 2-10-0. In addition to *Evening Star* the model was immediately available in black as 92158. The new model had a much-improved chassis, blackened metalwork and a choice of tenders. Because of the need to preserve daylight under a long stretch of the boiler, the locomotive still had tender-drive.

The official Millennium commemorative model was also available and was an LNER green model of Class A3 103 *Flying Scotsman* with 18-ct gold metalwork. The running number and livery were the final ones it carried immediately before nationalisation

The BR Class N2 tank engine, ex-Airfix.

The 'Battle Zone' electric train set. (Courtesy Vectis Auctions)

of the railways in 1948. It had also been intended to release the re-tooled 'Coronation' Class this year, but its arrival was delayed and so this was released in 2001.

Arriving from China during the year were the improved ex-Airfix Class N2 0-6-2T and a fourth version of the 'Britannia' Class model. The latter was similar to the 1981 model but had a finely detailed chassis and, on some, the later-style smoke deflectors with handhold cut-outs instead of handrails. It still had the Ringfield tender-drive, but a high-quality model was planned and would arrive in 2006. Some models were supplied with the BR1 tender with its pinched top and some with the high-sided BR1D tender, as paired with the last ten members of the class. From 2005 the models would have DCC decoder sockets fitted.

Two themed sets to appeal to youngsters were released. The 'Dinosafari' set was themed on dinosaur hunting with a buff-coloured diesel locomotive and road vehicles and the 'Battle Zone' set was military with khaki green models. Both used non-standard Hornby track, which is probably why these sets were not very successful. The sets were classified as toys and did not appear in the main catalogue.

Ironically, in contrast to the successful delivery of the new products programme, there was a stir amongst the pigeons at a shareholders meeting when it was voted that the company should put itself up for sale! Fortunately, this decision was later withdrawn.

The Hornby 'Virtual Railway' DVD.

It was in 2000 that Hornby released the revised edition of the simulation game of the Hornby Virtual Railway (HVR2) series. This was an attempt at keeping pace with the digital age.

During 2000, Bachmann Europe plc bought the Graham Farish N-gauge system and set about raising the standard of N gauge to that of their existing 00 range.

2001

'HOGWART'S EXPRESS'

HORNBY

Hornby had successfully obtained the licence to produce models related to the Harry Potter films and the first *Harry Potter* 'Hogwarts Express' train set and solo models were released in 2001. These were an instant success, bringing in much-needed revenue. The locomotive in the books is called *Hogwarts Castle,* but, for the film, a 'Castle' Class locomotive was unavailable and so *Olton Hall* was used, having been repainted red. Hornby by now did not have a model of a 'Hall' as theirs had been converted to a 'Saint' and so they used their ex-Airfix 'Castle' Class model instead, naming it *Hogwarts Castle.*
The set contained two Mk 1 coaches, track, station, power unit and a *Harry Potter* TrakMat. The following year the locomotive and coaches were also available separately, but in themed packaging.

Between 2001 and 2010 the models and the set were re-issued with each new film in the series and each time the packaging design was renewed accordingly. Thus, in 2001 it was 'The Philosopher's Stone' followed by 'Chamber of Secrets' (2003), 'Prisoner of Azkaban' (2004), 'Goblet of Fire' (2005), 'Order of the Pheonix' (2007) and 'Half Blood Prince' (2010).

Three more super-detailed models arrived from China, all of them replacements for Pacific locomotive models already in the range. These were the LMS 'Coronation' (delayed from the year before), LMS 'Princess' and Oliver Bulleid's non-rebuilt light Pacific SR 'Battle of Britain'/'West Country' Class.

The models which arrived in the first batches were as follows: 'Coronation', LMS blue 6220 *Coronation,* LMS maroon 6225 *Duchess of Gloucester* and 6235 *City of Birmingham*; 'Princess', LMS maroon 6207 *Princess Arthur of Connaught* and BR green 46203 *Princess Margaret Rose*; BB/WC: SR malachite 21C123 *Blackmore Vale* and BR malachite

The *Harry Potter and the Philosopher's Stone* train set.

The re-tooled super-detailed LMS *Coronation.*

The re-tooled super-detailed LMS *Princess Arthur of Connaught.*

The re-tooled super-detailed SR BBWC Class as 92 *Squadron.*

The SR BBWC in photographic grey as 21C164 'Fighter Command'.

34081 *92 Squadron.* A limited run of 1,000 of the Class BB/WC in 'works grey' was produced for a retailer and released the following year.

Unannounced new characters joined the 'Thomas & Friends' range during the year. They were electric versions of the three new clockwork models that had arrived the year before. There were *Bill* and *Ben* which, compared with the real china clay industry locomotives, were over-scale, but they represent twins that appear in later books and play tricks by swapping identity. There was also an over-scale *Toby.*

Bill and *Ben.*

Toby the tram engine.

HORNBY DUBLO

In 2001, the G&R Wrenn business was bought from Dapol by Mordvale Ltd., a company set up for the purpose by Maurice Gunter and his partners. The purchase included some of the wagon tooling that Dapol did not want and the Wrenn archive. Some former Dublo wagons were subsequently released under the Wrenn Railways name in different colours. By now the demand was solely from collectors.

2002
DIGITAL COMMAND CONTROL

HORNBY

Hornby announced their first DCC-compatible locomotive model. This was a re-tooled model of the famous LMS 'Black 5' Class due for release during the year. It was offered as 'DCC Ready', which meant that it was designed to take a decoder chip, but that one was not factory-fitted. Space for the decoder was in the smokebox.

The re-tooled super-detailed Class Black 5.

The re-tooled super-detailed LMS *Duchess of Buccleuch*.

A BR HBA hopper wagon.

The new 'Black 5' was a super-detailed model with a five-pole locomotive-mounted motor and the suite of tools produced would allow Hornby to produce many of the variations that occurred in this large class of mixed-traffic locomotives. The initial releases were LMS lined black 5055, BR black 45908, BR lined black 45253 and BR weathered black 44762 and 44781.

Another super-detailed model from China which arrived during the year was the new 'Duchess' Class as maroon LMS 6230 *Duchess of Buccleuch*, BR blue 46224 *Princess Alexandra* and BR green 46228 *Duchess of Rutland*. It was also available through Collectors Centres as BR maroon 46245 *City of London*. The Queen's Diamond Jubilee was celebrated with a model of 6201 *Princess Elizabeth* in LMS maroon with gold metalwork and 5,000 were sold.

Also new this year were an HBA 'Merry-Go-Round' coal hopper wagon with a hood and the former Dapol quad vent meat van. The latter model is hard to find as there were problems with the tooling and only two versions were made, 1,200 of each being produced.

In 2002, Hornby released the only train set they ever produced exclusively for Hamleys of Regent Street. It contained the 1998 A3 locomotive in bright red with 'Hamleys' on the tender and numbered 1760; presumably the date the store opened.

To the 'Thomas & Friends' range *Henry* was added using the old 'Black Five' tooling and two new grey 7-plank long wheelbase open wagons as the 'Troublesome Trucks'. These had moulded faces added, but without the faces they went on to become more widely used in mainstream train sets as freelance private owner wagons.

The *Hamley's Express.*

Henry.

A quad vent meat van, ex-Dapol.

Although the Zero 1 patents were still relevant, Hornby had not let any licences out for the use of Zero 1 knowhow and were unlikely to pursue infringements. Hornby were aware of the importance of DCC both then and in the future, but recognised that many of their customers would find it complicated and expensive. At that time, they had no immediate plans to provide DCC equipment, but said they would continue to make new models DCC-ready.

During the year there were signs that the Italian Lima Group was in financial difficulty. Lima management approached the Hornby Board with an offer to sell Hornby the considerable collection of tooling they had produced for their British 00 range of models. However, the price they wanted was too high.

Trading results for the financial year saw Hornby earn a profit of £5.4 million on a turnover of £34.5 million. This was up about £14 million on 2001. Dividends were appropriately high, and the City loved Hornby. By this time, Hornby shares were largely owned by Hornby collectors, including Martin Hughes, a former Credit Lyonnais banking analyst (with 29 per cent and the largest holder) and Peter Wood, founder of Direct Line insurance with 13 per cent. They agreed with Hornby's Board of Directors in wanting to raise the design standards and production engineering of Hornby models year by year.

During the year, Lima ended its association with its British importer, The Hobby Company.

2003
LETTING OFF STEAM

HORNBY

Largely through good *Harry Potter* sales, Hornby reported record profits and the value of Hornby's shares doubled.

In association with Hornby, the German Märklin company launched their *Harry Potter* train set in October for their three-rail AC range. The set used the Hornby models with modifications that included fitting a central slider pick-up for Märklin stud-contact track. The set included a TrakMat, a large oval of track with a couple of points, transformer, locomotive with a decoder and two BR Mk 1 coaches. Märklin adapted the bogies to take European-type couplings instead of the tension lock ones Hornby fitted.

Back in the year 2000, Chief Executive Officer (CEO), Peter Newey, asked what their next ground-breaking project should be. Then, out of the blue, they heard about someone who had designed a 00-scale live-steam locomotive that used a current from the track to boil water to make steam. That was Richard Hallam and contact was made through his agent. His 'Black 5' model was sent out to China and a search was started to find a heat-resistant plastic for the moulded body.

Nearly three years of research and development followed before a commercially marketable product was ready and I went down to the

The *Mallard* 'Live Steam' train set. (Courtesy Vectis Auctions)

launch. This was performed by Pete Waterman with Hornby's new CEO, Frank Martin, on 5 September 2003 at the Goodwood Motor Event. It was certainly impressive to watch the A4 locomotives pulling their trains of Gresley coaches. The first subject they had chosen was the record-breaking *Mallard* and this was followed by several other live-steam locomotives based on the LNER Gresley A3 and A4 classes. The reliability and quality of the engineering were outstanding, and the sets found an international market. In January 2004 the company was awarded the British Association of Toy Retailers Award for 'Innovative Toy of 2003' for its 'Live Steam'.

I later met Richard Hallam when he turned up at our local model show with his 00 steam-powered layout and we had a long chat. He told me of

Launch of 'Live Steam' at Goodwood.

A 'Live Steam' scene. (Courtesy Hornby)

the difficulty he initially had in selling the idea, including writing to Bachmann, and it had been his agent who finally sold the idea to Hornby, although I am told that the marketing and development teams at Hornby needed very little persuasion.

By the summer of 2003 plans were in place to sell the Margate site to B&Q for an enlarged store and for Hornby to develop a headquarters office building on part of the old B&Q site. However, the planning application was turned down by the local planning authority as the B&Q site was zoned for retail use and the Hornby site for industry. This was confirmed by the Secretary of State when it went to appeal.

The year 2003 also saw the launch of the Skaledale building series. These were cold-cast resin models manufactured by another company in China and came ready painted. The moulds could only produce short runs and so many new subjects were added to the range each year. At one stage we were being offered a new set of station buildings each year and each set was in a different regional style. Likewise, the buildings for individual industries such as a gas works, coal mine, waterworks, fuel storage depot and several farms were added.

Especially attractive was the set of parts to create a stretch of canal with locks, bridges, lock keeper's cottage and canal boats. This was released in 2007 and added to in 2008. Numerous high street shops have been modelled over the years, covering every conceivable trade. Skaledale buildings have become a collectable series and now include many hundreds of models. Amongst the largest models have been a railway coaling tower and a windmill. The latter was a model of the real one in Margate and the clocktower in the range was also a miniature of the one on the seafront. I understand that most of the models are based on existing buildings. A range of wagon loads was also made in the Skaledale range.

The first super-detailed tank engine arrived from China and this was the Fowler 2-6-4T. It had a new chassis and a five-pole skew-wound motor and was DCC-ready. Other improvements included much more detail, a sliding cab roof vent

The Skaledale buildings series.

and sprung buffers. Initial releases were 2311 in LMS maroon and 42355 in BR lined black.

Another addition to the growing list of new super-detailed locomotives was the GWR

A Skaledale windmill.

'King' Class, with the same motor and was also DCC-ready. The tools allowed for both single- and double-chimneyed versions and, from 2005, it would have blackened metalwork. The first to arrive were GWR 6029 *King Stephen* and late BR 6002 *King William IV*, plus an exclusive Collectors Centre model of 6028 *King George VI* in BR blue livery. A third replacement locomotive was the Sanda Kan tooled super-detailed LMS Class 8F and the motor details were the same as the others. This was initially released as LNER black 7675, LMS black 8510 and early BR black 48154.

The LMS Fowler Class 4P passenger tank engine.

The SR Class Q1.

The Hornby Class 50, *Achilles*.

The Hornby Class 50, *Resolution*.

A completely new locomotive was the SR Class Q1 0-6-0. This was Oliver Bulleid's wartime austerity design of 1942. The model was well detailed and BR versions included the moving lubricating gear where appropriate. Again, it had a five-pole motor and was DCC-ready. The first models to arrive were SR C8, BR 33037 and weathered BR 33009.

The Class 50 arrived from China during the year and this was another completely new subject and a high-quality model. The Class 50s were built by English Electric during 1967 and 1968 and, although normally associated with the Western Region, they started life on the LMR on the West Coast Main Line. The class has had a cult following, which might explain why eighteen of the locomotives have been preserved. Initial releases of the model were BR blue 50018 *Resolution*, BR large logo blue 50035 *Ark Royal*, NSE 50045 *Achilles* and Railfreight General 50149 *Defiance* (for *Rail Express* magazine).

The first of the new super-detailed coaches arrived from China in 2003. These were the newly tooled K Type Pullman cars and included five different types – first parlour car, third parlour car, first kitchen car, third kitchen car and third brake car. A bar car would eventually be added later. They were beautifully modelled with full interior detail.

The new high-quality models were now coming thick and fast and included new wagons. Completely new was the 'Coalfish' open box

The new super-detailed Pullman brake car No. 106.

Bert and Arry.

The EW&S 'Coalfish' MHA.

wagon, but unfortunately there was a height error and it was re-tooled the following year. Also new in 2003 were improved versions of the CDA china clay hopper wagon, HAA 'Merry-Go-Round' coal hopper wagon and HBA/HFA covered version.

To the 'Thomas' range was added a pair of identical diesel shunters in Sodor Ironworks green and yellow livery. These were *Bert* and *'Arry* and were based on the 1976 Class 08. Another character added was *Diesel*, a green Class 37.

In June, Hornby announced the second version of their Virtual Railway (HVR2), but it probably did not arrive in the shops until 2004. The sequel was somewhat more realistic looking than its predecessor and contained more elements to use, such as scenery, new rolling stock and new engines (including the Virgin 125). Also, you could download stations and additional locomotives and rolling stock.

During 2003, the Lima Group went into receivership.

Diesel.

2004
LATIN HARVEST

HORNBY

Hornby were going through a trading high spot, and the share price of the existing Hornby ordinary shares in 2004 had risen by over 600 per cent since the beginning of 2001. With trading being the best it had been for a long time the Hornby Board believed that there existed substantial opportunities for further broadening of both product ranges and to continue to grow profitability within their core hobby business. Having consolidated Hornby's position in the UK over the previous three years, the Board believed it appropriate to explore suitable acquisition opportunities. In the collectables and models sector, European markets tended to be fragmented, with highly specialised operators. The opportunity to consolidate certain parts of the market and to apply the lessons learned by Hornby in the UK led to the announcements that Hornby intended to expand into both the Spanish and Italian markets.

The Electrotren logo.

Electrotren S.A., of Madrid, was acquired on 31 March for €7.5 million. This was Spain's leading model railway manufacturer and the Spanish distributors of Hornby's Scalextric under the name 'Superslot'. The acquisition was mutually agreeable. The Hornby Board was impressed by the incumbent management and by the opportunities for future growth in the business. Hornby Espana S.A. would later be formed to handle distribution within Spain.

Having turned down the overpriced Lima 00 tooling two years earlier, Hornby bought the required assets of Lima S.p.A (in liquidation) in

The Lima logo.

The Jouef logo.

The Arnold logo.

The Pocher logo.

2004. This included approximately 10,000 items of N-, H0-, 00- and 0-gauge tooling, which were moved to Margate, and the intellectual assets of the Lima, Rivarossi, Jouef and Arnold brands and top-end kit manufacturer Pocher, all for €8 million.

Hornby International was formed to look after the marketing of the continental European brands, and its first subsidiary, Hornby Italia, was formed to handle distribution in Italy. About 1,000 tools went out to China immediately in order to get the first lot of models into the shops for the following Christmas. Most of the British-outline former Lima 00 models underwent modification to improve their running quality so that they could be absorbed into the Hornby range.

The Hornby catalogue, fiftieth edition.

The fiftieth edition of the catalogue was issued in 2004 and a limited-edition hard cover version in a slip case was also available. When it was being prepared, I was asked to write an introduction for it and an illustrated review of the previous forty-nine catalogues for the front section of the book. For the article, I photographed the covers of all forty-nine issues on a sunny day in my garden while standing on a garden bench, much to the amusement of my wife!

The year 2004 saw the first 'Premier' train set, which was in a red box with pull-out drawers containing a high-quality locomotive, three super-detail coaches, two ovals of track, points, a twin power unit and the Hornby Virtual Railway CD-Rom. The first of these contained the rebuilt 'Merchant Navy' BR green 35012 *United States Lines* with three of the new Type K

Premier boxed set 'Orient Express'.

Revised Class A4 flangeless rear pony wheels. (Courtesy Hornby)

Revised A4, *Golden Plover*. (Courtesy Hornby)

Pullman cars – *Iris, Minerva* and *Cygnes*. This was sold as the 'Orient Express'. Other 'Premier' train sets would follow.

During the year the third version of the A4 was delivered. It was much like the super-detail model tooled in China and released in 1998, but this one was fitted with a DCC socket and had a fixed pony truck with broad flangeless wheels on a Cartazzi axle, thus removing the view of daylight beneath the cab, which never looked right.

The model was supplied with an alternative flanged wheel set for the pony truck, to be substituted if the model was to be a static exhibit. The new model was first released in LNER silver-grey as 2512 *Silver Fox*, LNER blue as 4468 *Mallard,* NE black as 4901 *Sir Charles Newton* and BR green as 60031 *Golden Plover.* It had been intended to release similar versions of the A1/A3 during the year, but these were not delivered until 2005.

Also arriving in 2004 were the re-tooled super-detailed Gresley coaches. Gone was the chemical-induced curdled plastic for a kind of woodgrain effect. Now each coach had undergone multiple printing to produce a very realistic teak finish. The work involved in achieving this had to be reflected in the premium for the coaches, but this did not appear to deter buyers as they really were superb. The types were first corridor, third corridor, brake composite, buffet car and first class sleeper.

The re-tooled LNER super-detailed Gresley sleeping car.

2005

MORE MOVES TO CHINA

Lima Group and Electrotren production were moved to China, and Hornby bought the French model kit manufacturer MKD to form Hornby France, with the purpose of handling Hornby International business in France.

The year 2005 was a great one for new locomotives – six in all! The LNER A1/A3 super-detailed model, modified with a Cartazzi pony truck, arrived fitted with a DCC socket. In A1 mode, the first version released was LNER green 1470N *Great Northern* and in A3 mode there were LNER *Flying Scotsman,* as it was in June 2004, and BR green 60077 *The White Knight.* Also, a 'Live Steam' version of the A3 was now available as LNER 4472 *Flying Scotsman* and BR green 60096 *Papyrus.* A two-tender 'Live Steam' *Flying Scotsman* would be available in 2008.

The MKD logo.

There were also several new super-detailed locomotive models. The first of these was a GWR 'Grange' 4-6-0 with four versions arriving. The 'Grange' was Charles Collett's 68xx intermediate passenger locomotive design of 1936, and eighty were built at Swindon between 1936 and 1939. More had been planned, but the Second World War intervened. The first batch of models included GWR 6818 *Hardwick Grange,* BR black 6862 *Derwent Grange,* BR green 6879 *Overton Grange* and weathered BR green 6869 *Resolven Grange.* Unaware that Hornby were about to release this model, Bachmann were already designing one, but were able to modify their plans to produce a GWR 'Hall' instead.

Next, we had three newly tooled high-quality diesels. A Class 31 A1A-A1A was released in both normal and 'Skin-head' form. Some 263 members of the class were built by Brush Electrical Engineering Company plant at Loughborough between 1957 and 1962, and

The modified BR A3 weathered *Flying Scotsman.*

The ex-GWR 'Grange' Class, *Derwent Grange*.

The retooled Class 31 in Fragonset livery.

The EW&S Class 60.

were intended for mixed-traffic duties, originally on the Eastern Region. This high-quality model was another originally intended for release in 2004. These were weathered blue 31174 and 'Skin-head' BR green D5512. The model was also released through *Model Rail* magazine that year as Railfreight 31130 *Calder Hall Power Station.*

Then came the heavyweight Class 60, only one version of which arrived during the year – EW&S 60026. The rest of the batch, which arrived the following year, included Loadhaul black and orange 60007, Mainline grey 60077 and Mainline blue 60078. One hundred Class 60s were built by Brush Traction in Loughborough between 1989 and 1993 as heavy-duty freight locomotives.

The third newly tooled diesel was controversial as one already existed in the Bachmann range. It was the Class 08 diesel shunter. Hornby argued that the duplication was warranted because it was by far the most common shunter in use in Great Britain and their range would be unbalanced without one. Admittedly, there had been a model in the range since the early 1950s, but this was embarrassingly inaccurate with totally the wrong chassis.

Following the super-detailed K Type Pullman cars and the Gresley stock, it was the turn of

The super-detailed BR Class 08 diesel shunter.

A BR Stanier first class corridor coach. (Courtesy Tony Wright)

A LMS Stanier parcels van.

the Stanier coaches to be introduced as high standard models. These were a corridor first, corridor third and a brake third in both LMS maroon and BR red and cream livery. An LMS bogie parcels van was also released in LMS and BR maroon.

Added to the wagon range were the former Airfix double vent van and, brand-new, a YGB 'Seacow' bogie hopper wagon. The latter was highly detailed and would be followed in 2006 with the equally good 'Sealion' version. To add play-value for junior modellers, a deal was struck with Life-Like to market two of their action wagons – a bogie tipping timber wagon and a gravel tipper. They came with the operating lineside apparatus for each.

A 'Forest Lumber Co.' bogie lumber wagon by Life-Like.

EWS and Mainline 'Seacows'. (Courtesy Tony Wright)

In the 'Thomas' range *Flying Scotsman* arrived with a face. As with *Gordon* in the same series, the 1981 version of the Class A1 model was used. Also new this year in the 'Thomas' range were ex-Dapol 'Terrier' 0-6-0T as *Stepney*, the GWR 14xx 0-4-0T as *Oliver* and the Class 35 diesel as *Hymek* – each of them with the appropriate face. There was also a return for the battery-fitted *Bertie the Bus*, and 2005 was also the year that the circus train wagons were added to the 'Thomas' range.

One of several different circus vans released during the year.

The year 2005 also saw the publication by New Cavendish Books of the third volume in the Rovex trilogy titled *The Story of Rovex Volume 3 – 1972–1996*, which covered the DCM years and those of Hornby Hobbies prior to the restructuring of the company, the name change and the transfer of production to China in the late 1990s.

'Thomas & Friends' series *Flying Scotsman.*

Hymek.

Oliver, No. 11.

Stepney, No. 55.

The Story of Rovex Volume 3 – 1972–1996, by Pat Hammond.

Former Lima employees in Italy formed ViTrains and included 00-scale models of the British diesel classes 37 and 47 among their products for sale in the UK. These were made from new tooling as the original Lima tools for these two models were held by Hornby.

2006
AIRFIX COMES HOME

HORNBY

Heller S.A. were still producing most of the Airfix kits in France when it went into receivership in 2006. Without a supply of kits to sell, on 31 August

The Airfix logo.

The Humbrol logo.

2006, Humbrol went into administration and thirty-one of the forty-one employees were made redundant. On 10 November 2006, Hornby Hobbies Ltd. announced it was to acquire the Airfix and Humbrol brands for £2.6 million and re-launch them the following year. In 2008, the former Humbrol factory in Hull would be demolished. Hornby's Chief Executive, Frank Martin, had been the Managing Director of Humbrol before moving to Hornby and knew the Airfix business well.

The deal included all Humbrol's model kits and accessories, the 'Young Scientist' brand and their associated assets. Humbrol have an international market and had worldwide sales of £6.5 million in 2005. A condition of the sale was that Hornby received the Airfix tooling, which was held by Heller. Hornby restructured and re-invigorated their new acquisitions and transferred the companies' distribution, sales and marketing operations to Margate. Manufacturing, on the other hand, was transferred to India. Their aim was to focus both on traditional products for modellers and invest in new products for the younger market, as was the policy with Hornby's existing brands.

The Virgin Class 43 in Hornby livery.

The re-tooled super-detailed 'Britannia' Class, *William Wordsworth*. (Courtesy Tony Wright)

The re-built BBWC Class, *Plymouth*. (Courtesy Hornby)

Thus, the tools of two well-known Airfix ranges came back together under one ownership – the GMR model railway tools, acquired from Dapol in 1996, and those of the famous Airfix plastic kits.

The railway spot-hire company, Cotswold Rail, had Class 43 HST power car 43087 on short-term hire and in 2005 had painted it in a bright red Hornby livery, with the giant Hornby trademark in each side. This was superb publicity for Hornby as, besides being blatant advertising, it had press appeal. In 2006 Hornby released their 'Hornby Virgin Trains 125' train set, which included 43087 as a miniature version of the real locomotive.

The 'Britannia' class was BR's 4-6-2 principal standard passenger express locomotive and fifty-five were built at Crewe. The first arrived in 1951, and all but one had names. The first super-detailed BR 'Britannia' Class models arrived from Sanda Kan with four versions immediately available, which showed off the versatility of the suite of tooling. These were 70000 *Britannia*, 70030 *William Wordsworth*, 70013 *Oliver Cromwell* (as preserved) and 70052 *Firth of Tay*.

Another super-detailed model arriving from China during the year was the SR Class M7 0-4-4T, in both long- and short-frame forms. The long-frame ones were SR olive green 111 and BR black 30051, 30031 and 30108 (weathered). With the short frame was SR olive green 357. In addition, a rebuilt BB/WC

The re-tooled Class M7 tank engine.

Class was released as 34003 *Plymouth*, and a comparison between this and the 1961 Dublo model of 34005 *Barnstaple* shows how far model development has come in forty-five years, based on customer expectations.

After undergoing improvements at Margate, the first eleven former Lima models re-appeared, upgraded as Hornby models, including the classes 59, 67, 73, 101, 121, 156 and the GWR AEC railcar. Also added were BR Mk 3 coaches TGS and SLE, as well as the bogie 'Presflo' and BR CCT. Lima Group continental models were also re-introduced through Hornby International.

The Class 59 as *Village of Chantry*, ex-Lima.

The Class 67 as *Queen's Messenger*, ex-Lima.

The Class 73, ex-Lima.

The Class 121, ex-Lima. (Courtesy Tony Wright)

The GWR AEC railcar, ex-Lima.

The BR Mk 1 CCT, ex-Lima.

The Class 101, ex-Lima.

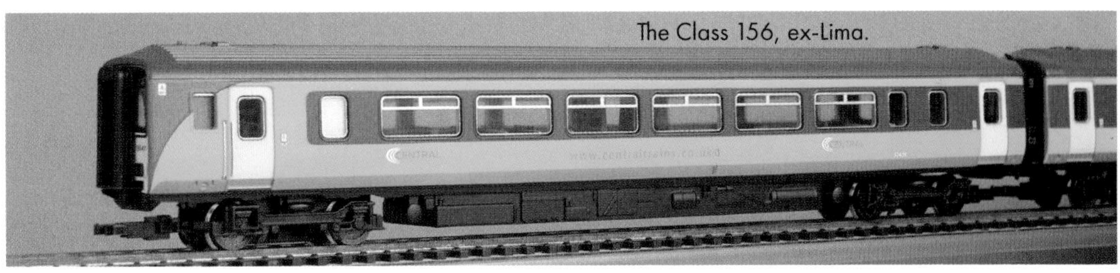
The Class 156, ex-Lima.

A PDA twin Presflo 'Croxton & Garry', ex-Lima.

The ScotRail Mk 3 sleeper (SLE), ex-Lima.

During the year Hornby bought the German model railway accessories firm Heico-Modell and formed Hornby Deutschland to market Hornby Group products in German-speaking counties. Heico had been founded in 1996 and had over 1,200 active customers accounts with independent retailers throughout Germany. It was well-known for its trackside buildings and wagon loads. As Germany is Europe's largest model railway, slot-car and kit market, and claimed at the time to be six times larger than that of the UK, it was important for Hornby to have a foot in the door.

As an off-shoot of the 2003 Skaledale painted resin building range, in 2006 a similar N-scale range called 'Lyddle End' was added. This consisted of N-scale versions of existing models in the 00 range, but also some unique ones.

The 'Thomas' series received another locomotive, which was the missing *Edward* from the early books. This model made use of the 'Shire' model tooling of 1981. Using Hornby tooled parts, Märklin launched the first of their 'Thomas & Friends' range for the Austrian, German and Swiss markets.

The Heico logo.

Corgi Classics, who owned the Bassett-Lowke brand and had re-introduced a range of 0-gauge metal locomotives and wagons, turned to ETS in the Czech Republic to produce future designs for them.

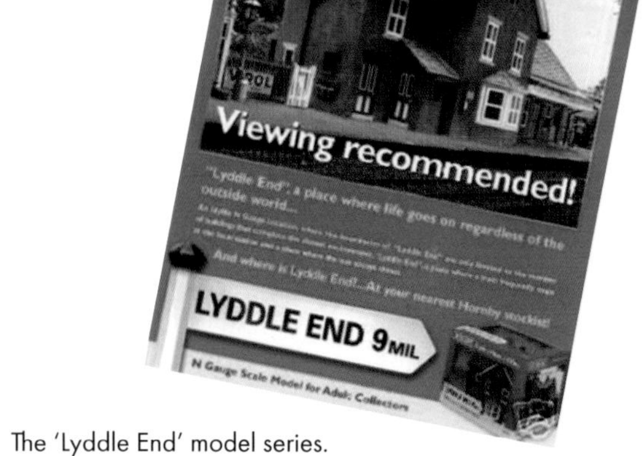

The 'Lyddle End' model series.

Edward.

2007
FOR THOSE ON A LIMITED BUDGET

HORNBY

A problem faced by Hornby, with its wide range of products designed to meet the need of both enthusiasts and those of simpler requirements, was that Hornby's cheaper models were being unfairly criticised by experts for their simpler design, even though they were sold at a considerably lower price. It was felt that only by separating the models into two distinct ranges could this criticism be neutralised.

So, in 2007, we saw the launch of RailRoad by Hornby, which is a budget range within the main Hornby catalogue. It has allowed Hornby to keep their new super-detailed models as the main

The 'RailRoad' catalogue.

The Class 55, *The Duke of Wellington's Regiment*, ex-Lima.

RAILROAD

The RailRoad logo.

Hornby range and to push any models that did not come up to that new standard on to the RailRoad pages. It has also provided a home for some of the older British-outline former Lima models that Hornby had brought back into production after 2004, such as the 'Deltic' and 'Warship' diesels. The RailRoad range has become popular with people on a lower budget and those insufficiently knowledgeable about the real locomotives to want to pay for greater accuracy.

During the Hornby renaissance, which had started in the late 1990s, there was a major effort to improve all the mechanisms in existing Hornby locomotives. The Ringfield motor was updated with five-pole armatures, improved gearing and extra pick ups. However, eventually, as models were replaced or moved into the RailRoad range, the Ringfield motor was replaced with a superior can motor in the body of the locomotive.

During the year, more highly detailed locomotives arrived from Sanda Kan, including an LMS rebuilt 'Patriot' 4-6-0, LMS rebuilt 'Royal Scot' 4-6-0 and LMS Stanier 2-6-4T, none of which had previously been modelled by Hornby. The initial batch of rebuilt 'Patriots', all in BR green, included 45531 *Sir Fredrick Harrison*, 45545 *Planet* and 45512 *Bunsen* (weathered). There were initially four rebuilt 'Royal Scots' – LMS maroon 6100 *Royal Scot* (as preserved), LMS black 6133 *The Green Howards*, BR green 46102 *Black Watch* and 46146 *The Rifle Brigade*. The Stanier tank arrived as LMS black 2546, BR black 42468 and 42437 (weathered). The locomotives had five-pole skew-wound motors and DCC sockets fitted.

A new super-detailed SR 'King Arthur' Class 4-6-0 was also delivered. The real 'King Arthur' Class locomotives varied in design between the twenty originally built for the L&SWR and fifty-four later built by Richard Maunsell for the SR. These differences were built into the suite of tooling that Sanda Kan made. The differences involved chimneys, cabs and, most obvious, the tenders; early ones had eight

The BR re-built 'Patriot' class, *Sir Frederick Harrison*.

The LMS re-built 'Scot' class, *Royal Scot.*

The LMS Stanier 2-6-4T.

The SR Class N15, *Pendragon.*

wheels and later ones six. The models delivered in 2007 were SR olive green 736 *Excalibur*, SR malachite green 746 *Pendragon*, BR green 30764 *Sir Gawain* (weathered), 30803 *Sir Harry le Fise Lake*, 30737 *King Uther*, 30799 *Sir Ironside*, 30778 *Sir Pelleas*, 30453 *King Arthur* and, for the National Railway Museum, 30777 *Sir Lamiel*. For Hornby this was a record number of models from one suite of tools to be issued in one year, and was attributed to delays with the first batch, which the batch following caught up with.

Another brand-new locomotive from China was the retooled Class 56 diesel. The model that Hornby released in 1998 had been tooled by Palitoy for their Mainline Railways range in 1983, the year in which Palitoy closed down. The virtually unused tooling had been sold to Dapol and then sold to Hornby in 1996. The new suite of tooling by Sanda Kan was designed so that examples of the locomotives built at Doncaster, Crewe and in Romania could all be modelled accurately.

The re-tooled Class 56 in Railfreight Coal livery.

The Class 390 'Pendolino'.

The GB Railfreight (GBRf) Class 66, ex-Lima.

You will remember the APT tilting train, development of which BR had abandoned owing to difficulties with its tilting mechanism, but which Hornby had modelled back in 1980. A successful tilting train had been developed in Italy and was called the 'Pendolino'. Virgin Trains ordered the Italian version for the West Coast mainline. Hornby, always keen to be first with models of the new trains, decided to launch a model of a 'Pendolino'. They visited Alstom to study drawings of the units. It was expected to appeal particularly to children, as the HST and Eurostar had done previously. Because of this, the model was produced with slightly less detail than had become normal for Hornby, but this did not stop the serious modellers from buying it.

Another new addition was a simplified Class A1. This was the old 1998 model, which had a Ringfield motor in the tender, but had now been modified to loco-drive. This was intended as a low-cost model of *Flying Scotsman* suitable for train sets and as a solo model in the RailRoad budget range.

The new locomotives did not end there as there were three more former Lima diesels added to the Hornby range in 2007. These were the classes 47, 55 'Deltic' and 66. The Class 47 tools being used by Hornby at the time were the original ones of 1975. These were now

The re-tooled SR Maunsell corridor first.

The SR Maunsell Van C.

Emily, No. 3046.

replaced by the better Lima tools and any Class 47 models from 2007 onwards would mainly be made with these. The 'Deltic', on the other hand, was a very early Lima model and was not good enough for the main range. Other former Lima models added to the Hornby range that year included the Mk 1 GUV, Super GUV, six-wheel milk tank wagon, large rail crane and 'Palvan'. Of these, only the large crane went to the RailRoad range.

The latest super-detailed coaches to arrive from China were the SR Maunsell stock, which consisted of a corridor third, corridor first, composite first// third, six-compartment brake third and the four-wheel 'Brake Van C'. To these would be added the six-compartment composite brake in 2008 and the four-compartment third brake in 2009.

The latest addition to Hornby's 'Thomas & Friends' range was *Emily,* for which the Tri-ang *Lord of the Isles* tooling was used.

2008
CORGI JOINS TOO

Hornby bought the Corgi brand, tooling and intellectual property rights from NASDAQ in May 2008 for £7.5 million. It included Vanguards, The Original Omnibus Company, Trackside and several other series. Hornby now owned four great British toy brands.

Coincidentally, this was the year that the delightful SkaleAutos, made by Oxford Diecast, first appeared in the Hornby catalogue. These used existing models from that company's 00 range but were finished appropriately for the Skaledale street scenes. Thus, you had lorries and vans, which carried the names of Skaledale high street businesses, railway vehicles for the station yard, taxis for the stations, farm vehicles for the Skaledale farms, etc. Sadly, this attractive range would become overshadowed by Hornby's purchase of Corgi and would shortly disappear. So far, it has not been replaced by an equivalent Corgi 00 range.

The Corgi purchase brought with it the Bassett-Lowke 0-gauge trains, which, between the wars, were rivals to Hornby 0 gauge in the upper end of the market. This part of the Corgi business was transferred to Hornby Hobbies for

The four great British brands now owned by Hornby.

SkaleAutos. (Courtesy Hornby)

future development. It seemed strange that after so many years the two rival brands should finally come together under a single ownership.

The fifty-fourth edition of the Hornby catalogue was a highpoint in good design. The problem of poor product deliveries was still to arise, as were the dramatic price rises. The pages clearly illustrated how the product selection had become extensive, with new and planned additions being both exciting and innovative. The RailRoad range was included for the first time, having been launched the previous September.

Hornby locomotives factory-fitted with sound chips were announced this year; the sounds recorded were correct for each model. The first three 'sound' locomotives to be sold were 'Duchess' Class BR green 46249 *City of Sheffield* and the two diesels: Class 56 Railfreight Coal Load triple-grey 56125 and Class 60 EWS 60048.

Two years earlier, voters in the 'Wish List Poll', run by internet magazine *MREmag*, made a super-detailed HST Class 43 their most wanted new model, and this arrived from China in 2008. The two locomotives (one motorised and the other non-motorised) were released as a pair in five liveries: Inter-City 125, Intercity Executive, GNER, Virgin Trains and Grand Central. Also released were the former Lima HST Class 43

Bassett-Lowke by Corgi, *Flying Scotsman* with two tenders.

The sound-fitted *City of Sheffield.*

The sound-fitted Class 56.

models, which went straight into the RailRoad range. This allowed for the scrapping of the original Hornby tooling, which dated back to 1978. Mk 3 coaches in suitable liveries to go with the train packs were also available.

The pool of super-detailed locomotives grew further with the release of an LSWR Class T9 4-4-0 and a replacement model of the SR 'Schools' Class express passenger 4-4-0. The T9 was a Dugald Drummond design of 1899, and different

The re-tooled Class 43, *John Wesley.*

The SR Class 79.

cab widths and tender types were allowed for by the suite of tools. Initial releases by Hornby were SR olive green 120 and 729 and BR lined black 30724 and 30310. In each pair, one had the eight-wheel 'Watercart' tender and the other had the later six-wheel tender. The 'Schools' model was far more detailed than the 1981 model, which now slipped into the RailRoad range. The first of the newly tooled models to arrive was the BR lined black 30932 *Blundell's* in 2008, but eight more versions arrived from China in 2009.

RailRoad also gained a new Class A4 with economies made on detail, although the motor was still the five-pole skew-wound version found in the main range model. A new version of the Class 9F 2-10-0 was also produced for RailRoad and was now fitted with a powerful loco-drive five-pole skew-wound motor.

The Lima Class 37 was now ready to join the Hornby range and in doing so it dislodged the former Tri-ang Hornby tooling, which dated right back to 1966. Other former Lima models joining the main Hornby range were the Class 20, GWR Express Parcels railcar and Class 153 'Super Sprinter' railcar.

A re-tooled 'Schools' Class showing cab interior detail.

There were five special commemorative limited-edition locomotives released in 2008 in special packaging. To mark the seventieth anniversary of *Mallard* setting the current world speed record for a steam locomotive, the valanced A4 in LNER Garter blue as 4468 *Mallard* was released with 18-ct gold-plated metalwork.

The BR Class 20, ex-Lima.

The GWR AEC 'Express Parcels', ex-Lima.

Marking the seventieth anniversary of Hornby Dublo, the A4, *Sir Nigel Gresley*.

LNER A3 4472 *Flying Scotsman* arrived as it looked when, in 1988, it ran in Australia, for the Australian Bicentenial. The Hornby 'Coronation' model as LMS maroon 6229 *Duchess of Hamilton* was produced to commemorate the conversion of the real locomotive back into its streamlined form and the un-rebuilt 'West Country' in SR malachite green as 34006 *Bude,* with a black ex-LMS tender, was released to commemorate the 1948 locomotive exchange trials. Finally, a special commemorative model of LNER Class A4 4498 *Sir Nigel Gresley* in LNER 'Garter Blue' was produced, in imitation Hornby Dublo period packaging, to mark the seventieth anniversary of the introduction of the original Hornby Dublo model in 1938. This anniversary was also commemorated on the 'date' wagon for 2008.

Completely new wagons from China included a beautifully detailed 'Shark' brake van and three open wagons – a ZBA 'Rudd' ballast wagon, ZCV 'Clam' ballast wagon and 'Tope' coal hopper wagon. Re-introduced from the Lima range were the car transporter and bogie tippler, which both went to RailRoad.

Marking the seventieth anniversary of the world speed record, the LNER A4, *Mallard*.

Marking the Australian Bicentennial, the LNER A3, *Flying Scotsman* as it ran in Australia.

The 'Hornby 2008' ferry van in Dublo blue.

The sixtieth anniversary of locomotive exchanges.

The commemoration model of the LMS 'Coronation' being re-streamlined.

An A4 appeared in the 'Thomas & Friends' range painted grey as the character *Spencer* who was not in the original books by the Rev. W. Audrey, but who did appear in the later video stories.

The SkaleAuto selection consisted of fifty-three die-cast vehicles in 00 scale, including twelve Bartellos' circus vehicles. A memorable train set was 'Bartellos' Big Top Circus', which had a card kit to assemble as a circus tent, and a train that incorporated one of the SkaleAutos circus vehicles as a load. Also new in the catalogue were SkaleScenics and SkaleLighting. SkaleScenics was a large range of trees, bushes and surface scatters for landscaping layouts and SkaleLighting included lighting units, wiring and plugs for putting working lights into trackside buildings.

The 'Shark' brake van.

The 'Tope' hopper wagon.

Spencer.

The 'Bartellos' Circus' set box.

The 'Bartellos' Circus' set.

The impact of an important event in 2008 was not appreciated at the time but would lead to a threat to the survival of the company in the next decade. When, in 1997, Hornby chose Sanda Kan to manufacture its new super-detail models, it rightly believed it was choosing the best in the world. The models Hornby received over the next ten years supported this view and comforted Hornby in their choice. No doubt there were those at the time who questioned the wisdom of the company placing all its eggs in one basket, but the full danger of this was probably not appreciated. However, after a while it became apparent that Sanda Kan was experiencing severe production and debt problems after it had been taken over by J. P. Morgan private equity.

In November 2008, Kader, the owners of the Bachmann brand, bought Sanda Kan for US $8.50 million (equivalent to £5.7 million). Sanda Kan was its nearest competitor for precision model railways in the Hong Kong-based ODM business. Hornby was Sanda Kan's biggest client and Bachmann was Hornby's biggest rival in Great Britain. Concerns were expressed and assurances given that the two businesses would be kept separate and confidentiality would be maintained. Sanda Kan also manufactured for Lionel,

The SkaleScenics catalogue.

Atlas, Life-Like, Brawa, Märklin and some fifty other model railway companies. Hornby's Managing Director pronounced the acquisition a welcome outcome which removed the uncertainty over the future of Sanda Kan.

2009
PLUS 0 GAUGE

After a double-page spread showing 00-scale models built from Airfix kits and painted with Humbrol paints, the 2009 Hornby catalogue introduced the Bassett-Lowke 0-gauge model railways. These had been revived by Corgi on a limited scale with just a few locomotives and the start of a series of wagons. Unfortunately, the model engineer who had developed the range for Corgi had already left the company and joined Ace Trains, taking his knowledge and skills with him.

Hornby contacted the Bassett-Lowke Society for advice on future development, and one problem that was identified was the small size of the market for coarse-scale trains in 0 gauge. It was also a market with two or more other players meeting demand and with Ace Trains already in a dominant position. The locomotives, like their pre-war predecessors, were made in metal and this, along with the limited market, created doubts in the minds of Hornby's management, as the company was used to mass production. However, it was a long-held tradition of the company to give new products a fair trial and so it would be with the Bassett-Lowke 0 gauge.

Six pages of the 2009 catalogue were devoted to the range and showed six classes of locomotive to be available. The first of these was the LNER Class A1/A3, which was represented by two models – an LNER green A1 as 4475 *Flying Fox* and a BR green A3 as 60103 *Flying Scotsman.* Next there was a Southern Railway N Class 2-6-0 in SECR grey livery as 810, an LMS maroon rebuilt 'Scot' 4-6-0 as 6100 *Royal Scot* and a BR rebuilt 'Patriot' 4-6-0 as 45534 *E. Tootal Broadhurst.* The final two locomotives were an ex-LNER J39 0-6-0 as BR black 64744

The Bassett-Lowke 'Patriot' Class *E. Tootle Broadhurst.* (Courtesy Vectis Auctions)

The Bassett-Lowke LMS preserved *Royal Scot*. (Courtesy Vectis Auctions)

The Bassett-Lowke Peckett tank, *Wenman*. (Courtesy Vectis Auctions)

and a Peckett 0-4-0ST as *Joseph/Wenman*. How many of these were inherited Corgi stock we do not know, but the J39 appeared to be a new model and we know that the Peckett saddle tank was new.

There were also metal wagons, which included inherited 3- and 7-plank open wagons and a goods van. There was also a new small tank wagon to be released in several different liveries and a brake van. The open wagons were in BR grey as well as LMS, LNER, SR liveries and private owner versions as well. The goods van was in BR brown as well as LMS, LNER and SR colours.

Bassett-Lowke tank wagons. (Courtesy Tony Wright)

The BR 6MT, *Clan Buchanan.*

The SouthEastern high speed Class 395 'Javelin' EMU.

Added to the Hornby 00 super-detail locomotives was the BR standard 'Clan' Class 4-6-2. This was a smaller boilered version of the 'Britannia' Class and only ten had been built. These were intended for the Scottish Region and all carried names of Scottish clans. Released in 2009 were 72000 *Clan Cameron* and 72008 *Clan Macleod.*

Also new was the high-speed Hitachi 'Javelin' Class 395 EMU, some of which were given the names of famous modern British Olympians as they would be used by overseas visitors attending the London Olympics in 2012. Two versions of the train were produced in 2009 – a super-detailed version and a simplified one for less expensive train sets called the 'Blue Rapier'.

The third new model from China was the Robert Riddles' standard Class 4MT 4-6-0, which had been planned for the previous year,

The BR Class 4MT 75005.

but was late arriving. Fifty of the real locomotives were built between 1951 and 1957. Unfortunately, Bachmann had been working on a re-tooled model of the class to replace their former Mainline Railways one. The feeling was expressed at the time that the Hornby model was the better of the two. The first examples received were 75005 in BR black with a BR2 tender, 75062 lined black with a BR2A tender and 75070 in weathered black with a BR1B tender.

The latest former Lima locomotive to join the Hornby fleet was the West Coast Main Line 25KV AC Class 87. This model was initially available in BR blue as 87004 *Britannia* and in Intercity Executive livery as 87010 *King Arthur*. Also new this year was a former 0-4-0 freelance tank engine, which started life as *Thomas the Tank Engine*, but was now in BR lined black as 43209.

There were some new Pullman cars, including the *Diamond/Daffodil Bar*, the very finely detailed 'Devon Belle' observation car and a set of H class twelve-wheel Pullman cars. These were a first class parlour car, third class parlour car, first class kitchen car, third class kitchen car and a third class brake car.

The Class 87, *King Arthur*, ex-Lima.

The twelve-wheel Pullman first kitchen, *Neptune*. (Courtesy Tony Wright)

The 'Devon Belle' Pullman observation car.

The K Class Pullman Daffodil Bar car, *Diamond*.

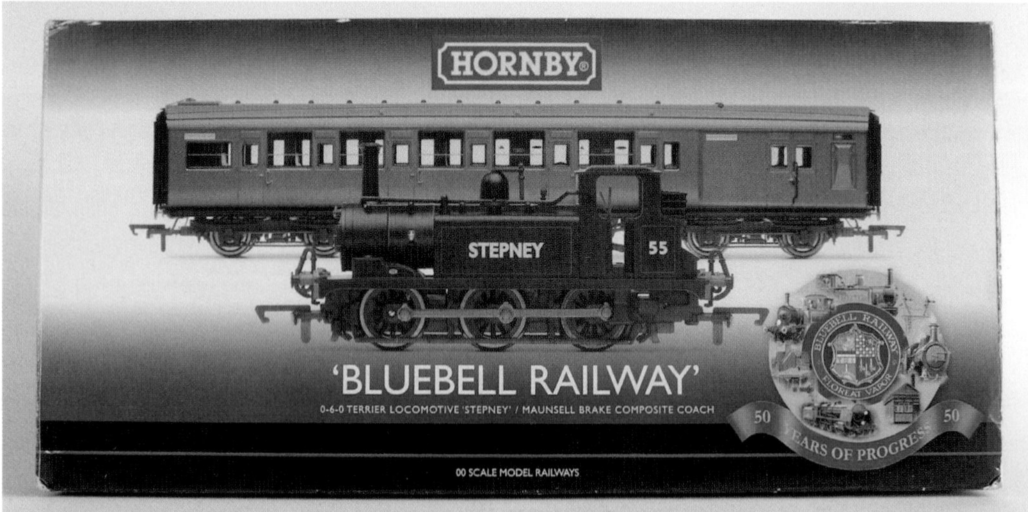

The 'Bluebell Railway' fiftieth anniversary train pack.

An attractive train pack produced for the Bluebell Railway, to commemorate the fiftieth anniversary of its formation, contains a black 'Terrier' tank as 55 *Stepney* and a blue painted Maunsell brake end coach. This was how they must have looked as the first train over the line after it had been acquired for preservation.

The year 2009 saw the launch of the A4 Commonwealth Collection. To quote from the 2009 Hornby catalogue: 'In 1937, and to celebrate the Coronation of George VI, the LNER inaugurated "The Coronation" service, which operated between London King's Cross and Edinburgh Waverley.' Each model was produced as a limited edition of 1,000 pieces,

The 'Pete Waterman Collection', *Royal Scot*. (Courtesy Tony Wright)

complete with an authenticating certificate. The models for 2009 were 60013 *Dominion of New Zealand* in BR green with early decals and 60012 *Commonwealth of Australia* in BR green with late decals. *Dominion of Canada* and *Union of South Africa* followed in 2010, with *Empire of India* bringing up the rear in 2011.

There were proposals to release three brand-new wagons this year, but all were found to be so diverse in design that it was hard to decide what a typical one looked like. The OTA timber carrier was eventually modelled, but did not arrive until two years later, while the ZCA 'Sea Urchin' and ZCA 'Sea Horse' were both abandoned as non-starters.

The mistaken image the public have of adult men 'playing with trains' was addressed by Hornby during the year by launching the Pete Waterman Collection. This was a series aimed at raising public awareness of railway modelling as an adult hobby. The idea was to link the Hornby range of exquisite models with a well-known personality who is himself a keen modeller. Record producer and television personality, Pete Waterman, agreed to provide that link. He was asked to select five of his favourite locomotives, which Hornby could produce from their tooling range. The five he chose were 'Black 5' Class 45190, 'Castle' Class 5053 *Earl Cairns*, rebuilt 'Royal Scot' Class 46100 *Royal Scot*, 'King Arthur' Class 30452 *Sir Meliagrance* and 'Princess Royal' Class 46201 *Princess Elizabeth*. The models came with a themed box design.

The disruption at Sanda Kan was already beginning to affect deliveries, with planned models slipping into the following year. While Hornby's management were hoping the Kader take-over of Sanda Kan would correct the situation, it recognised its vulnerability in having only one supplier. It therefore started the search for alternative suppliers in case the need arose. Hornby also warned that due to the economic recession prices were going to have to rise again owing to the fall in the value of Sterling against the US dollar. The company bought 90 per cent of its products in currencies linked to the dollar and sold only a quarter in dollars or euros. To add to the company's problems, Hornby shares fell 20 per cent to 76.5 pence, their lowest in more than six years.

The year finished with something to cheer up everyone – the James May's televised *Toy Story* ten-mile long model railway. May attempted to build the world's longest model railway between Bideford and Barnstaple in Devon and Hornby provided ten miles of their 00 track. Helped or watched by some four hundred enthusiasts, May hoped that a train would run successfully along the length of the track, but it was disrupted by vandals and thieves who interfered with the track, shorting it out with coins, while parts of the track were stolen. Five trains set off, but none made it, the last one (a 'Javelin') gave up the ghost at Instow. It was good entertainment and showed Hornby's community spirit.

Track for James May's record-breaking attempt in Devon. (Courtesy Hornby)

Setting up James Day's record attempt sponsored by Hornby. (Courtesy Hornby)

2000s – A DECADE SUMMARY

The first decade of the new millenium was one of expansion for Hornby, involving the purchase of the leading model railway brands for Italy, France and Spain and their tooling, the leading N-gauge brand in Germany and the Airfix, Humbrol, Corgi and Bassett-Lowke brands in the UK. Hornby International was established to deal with the overseas brands, with their marketing and distribution handled through subsidiary companies in Italy, France, Germany, Spain and the USA.

In Great Britain there was a quick development of a range of high-quality and well-detailed models tooled and built by Sanda Kan in China, plus the absorption into the Hornby range of many models previously developed by Airfix, Lima, Dapol and Palitoy. By the end of the decade the Hornby locomotive stud had grown to over fifty steam engines and more than forty diesel and electric locomotives and multiple units. That does not include those in the RailRoad and 'Thomas & Friends' ranges, which take the total to well over a hundred. These were supported by super-detail GWR, LNER, LMS and SR mainline coaches as well as a large range of Pullman cars and BR standard designs. In addition, there were over eighty wagons (not counting early ones not were recently available).

Other new concepts included the division of the Hornby models into a main range and a new budget series called RailRoad. There was also now 'Live Steam', digital train control, engine sound and the inclusion of Bassett-Lowke 0-gauge trains in the Hornby catalogue. Other new ideas included the Skaledale and Lyddle End resin buildings, SkaleAutos, SkaleScenics and SkaleLighting; all large ranges of accessories and materials catering for the serious railway modeller.

The decade started with Hornby in a good place with good profits, a rising share value and with the *Harry Potter* range dominating the children's market. By its end things were looking a bit different, largely due to the earlier decision to use only one main supplier in China. When things started to go wrong at Sanda Kan, deliveries were not getting through on time and planned models were being postponed. The decade ended with Hornby's main supplier owned by Hornby's main rival, a raging recession, rising prices and falling sales. But there was always hope that the good times would return.

The year 2000.

The year 2001.

The year 2002.

The year 2003.

The year 2004.

The year 2005.

The year 2006.

The year 2007.

The year 2008.

The year 2009.

2000s MILESTONES

2000 – SD Rebuilt 'Merchant Navy', SD 9F, Millennium gold A1, N2, new 'Britannia', Hornby for sale ... then it's not; Dinosafari and Battle Zone sets and HVR2.

2001 – 'Hogwart's Express', SD streamlined 'Coronation', SD 'Princess', SD Streamlined BB/WC, *Bill*, *Ben* and *Toby*.

2002 – First DCC-ready locomotive, SD 'Black Five', SD 'Duchess', HBA MGR, meat van, Hamley's set, *Henry* and profits up.

2003 – 'Live Steam', Märklin Harry Potter, launch of Skaledale, SD Fowler 2-6-4T, SD GWR 'King', SD 8F, Q1, Class 50, SD K Type Pullman cars, 'Coalfish', CDA, HAA, HBA/HFA, *Bert* and *'Arry* and record profits; Lima in receivership.

2004 – Hornby buys Lima Group assets and Elecrotren, fiftieth edition catalogue, Cartazzi A4, SD Gresley stock and first premier train set.

2005 – Cartazzi A1/A3, 'Live Steam' A3, 'Grange', SD Classes 08, 31 and 60, SD Stanier stock, double vent van, 'Seacow', 'Thomas & Friends', *Flying Scotsman, Stepney, Oliver* and *Hymek*, circus train wagons, etc., and Skaledale wagon loads.

2006 – Hornby buys Airfix, Humbrol and Heico, Lyddle End, real 'Hornby' Class 43, SD 'Britannia' SD M7, rebuilt BB/WC, Märklin/Hornby 'Thomas' set, classes 59, 66, 67, 73, 101, 121, 156 and GWR AEC autocar, Mk 3 TGS and SLE, bogie 'Presflo', 'Sealion', *Edward*, Hornby 'Select' and 'Elite' digital control and return of Caley 'Single'.

2007 – RailRoad, SD 'King Arthur', rebuilt 'Patriot', rebuilt 'Scot', Stanier 2-6-4T, SD Class 56, 'Pendolino', simplified A1, Class 47, 'Deltic', GUV, Super GUV, six-wheel milk tank, large Lima crane, 'Palvan', SD Maunsell stock and *Emily*.

2008 – Hornby buys Corgi and Bassett-Lowke, 'SkaleAutos', 'ScaleScenics', 'SkaleLighting', sound fitted locomotives, five commemorative models, SD Class 43, T9, SD 'Schools', RailRoad A4 and 9F, Classes 20 and 37, parcels railcar, Class 153, car transporter, bogie coal hopper, Bartello's circus and *Spencer*; Kader buys Sanda Kan.

2009 – Bassett-Lowke re-launched, BR 4MT 4-6-0, 'Clan', 'Javelin', Class 87, Pullman bar car, observation car and H class six-wheel stock; A4 Commonwealth Collection, deliveries worsen, prices rise and sales fall; James May's *Toy Story*.

HARRY POTTER IN THE 2000s

2002, *The Philosopher's Stone* coaches.

2002, *The Philosopher's Stone* loco.

2003, *The Chamber of Secrets* loco.

2003, *The Chamber of Secrets* coaches.

2003, *The Chamber of Secrets* set.

2004, *The Prisoner of Azkaban* set.

2004, *The Prisoner of Azkaban* playmat.

2007, *The Order of the Phoenix* loco.

2007, *The Order of the Phoenix* coaches.

2007, *The Order of the Phoenix* set.

2010, *The Half-Blood Prince* set.

2010
'DESIGN CLEVER'

HORNBY

As the quality and accuracy of models increased there were more parts which had to be added by hand, and these models cost more to produce. The move of production to China in the late 1990s was made because these labour-intensive models could not have been made in the Margate factory owing to the lack of expertise as well as labour costs. As the years passed the cost of manufacturing in the Far East gradually increased due to the strength of the Chinese economy, rising material costs and the falling UK pound. The new hi-tech industries in China were able to pay workers far more than the more traditional manufacturers. Whilst the cost gap between manufacturing in China and the UK was still large, Hornby, like other manufacturers, was constantly being criticised for the rising cost of their models, which were out of step with the British Cost of Living Index.

During 2010, in order to try to reduce these costs, consideration was given to how the assembly time could be reduced. Was it necessary to have so many parts separately moulded and added by hand? Providing detail parts in a polythene bag in the box for the purchaser to fit had only been partially successful and was unpopular with modellers and particularly collectors. This led to an attempt to simplify models without losing the overall realistic appearance. The Hornby marketing team were unhappy with the decision to 'dumb down' the models, believing it was a retrograde step, but the Hornby Board were insistent and left it, perversely, to the Marketing Department to 'sell' the idea to the modellers, hence they came up with the term 'Design Clever'.

The first model to be designed this way was the A1 Trust 'Peppercorn' Class A1 *Tornado,* the finished models of which would arrive in 2011. The new design philosophy was applied, and the model was sold in the RailRoad budget range. It did not have pick-ups on the tender to save assembly time and there was a reduction in livery. There was a lack of separately fitted parts, no sprung buffers and RailRoad standard packaging. The retail price was to be £77, and a second version with enhanced livery would be available for £93. As it happened, both versions sold well and showed what could be done with a little bit of design thinking.

In light of this success, thoughts would move to designing models for the main Hornby range, but the whole issue would come to a head with the large eight-coupled GWR tank engines for release in 2013. The already prepared highly detailed designs were modified in accordance with the 'Design Clever' principle, but when these much-wanted models were released, the public and reviewers gave them the 'thumbs down'. The hard-won reputation which Hornby had striven for since the beginning of the Millennium was tarnished. Add to this the growing difficulty which they were having in obtaining products from China, and the rising prices; it seemed that things could not get much worse.

The LNER Class L1 mixed-traffic tank.

The re-tooled GWR 'Castle' Class, *Great Western*. (Courtesy Tony Wright)

A previously designed, completely new locomotive this year was Thompson's large mixed-traffic tank engine, the Class L1 2-6-4T. As the real locomotives were a late design in the run up to nationalisation they were built by British Railways and only four carried LNER numbers. Four ordered models arrived from Sanda Kan in 2010 and were LNER green 9001, early BR in light green as 67717 and BR lined black 67772 and 67722. Because the models had been designed many months previously, they were spared the ravages of the 'Design Clever' dictate.

There were two re-tooled models replacing existing ones in the range. The new GWR 'Castle' Class replaced the 1997 model and was super-detailed with a choice of tenders, single or double chimneys, five-pole motor, sprung buffers and DCC ready or fitted, with the possibility of sound. The first versions to arrive were BR green 4098 *Kidwelly Castle*, 5068 *Beverston Castle*, 7007

The re-tooled ex-GWR Class 28xx.

The BR Class 33, ex-Lima.

The Virgin Mk 3 DVT.

Great Western, 7037 *Ince Castle* and for the 'Steam' Museum in Swindon – 7037 *Swindon*.

The other replaced model was the GWR Class 28xx 2-8-0 of 1991. The new model was again super-detailed with a suite of tools, which allowed for modelling variations, including the 38xx Class plus all the new benefits enjoyed by other models arriving from China. The first releases were GWR plain green 2818 and 3803 as well as BR plain black 2810 and 2891. Also announced was a super-detailed LNER B17 to replace the 1980 model, but this would be held up for two years with the production problems at Sanda Kan.

Yet another former Lima model arrived during the year. This was the Class 33, which went into the RailRoad collection. Another arrival was a DVT (driving trailer) for the Mk 3 coaches.

The Caledonian 'Single' was re-released in LMS maroon livery in a limited-edition train pack with three of the original Caledonian coaches, which were also beautifully finished in LMS maroon. Celebrating GWR 175, the Dean 'Single', in GWR green as 3012 *Great Western* with two scale clerestory coaches, was re-released. It was also available as a limited-edition solo model as 3064 *Duke of Edinburgh*.

The Class 101 0-4-0T was available again in GWR colours sporting the 'GWR175' logo on its tanks and, as we have seen, the 'Castle' was available in BR green with early decals as 7007 *Great Western*.

The last single wheeler train pack. (Courtesy Tony Wright)

This late in the day, the only GWR coaches available in the Hornby catalogue were early clerestory stock, the under-scale Collett coaches released by them in 1977 and some made from former Airfix tooling of similar date. Bachmann had a set of better Collett coaches already on the market, so when the public demand for GWR coaches designed by Hawksworth came top of the annual *MREmag* wish list, Hornby responded. These arrived in 2010 and consisted of a corridor third, corridor first, corridor first/third, brake first/third, brake third and a full brake. The real coaches were late arrivals and went straight into BR crimson and cream livery, although a selection of them had been temporarily painted in GWR chocolate and cream livery for photographing. Realising that there would be a demand for a set in true GWR livery, Hornby released them in this livery as a single batch in 2011.

When Simon Kohler met Barry J. Freeman at an exhibition held at the National Railway Museum, he was fascinated by the breathtaking reality of Freeman's railway paintings and the seed of an idea led eventually to a series of five limited-edition (1,000 of each) train packs based on five of these paintings. In each case the train in the picture was replicated by the models in the pack, which also contained a print of the picture. The first three due in 2010 were 'Rare Bird' (BR blue A4 60024 *Kingfisher* plus Gresley coaches), 'Days of Red and Gold' (maroon LMS 'Coronation' 6239 *City of Chester* plus

The GWR 'Achilles' Class, *Duke of Edinburgh*.

The 'GWR 175' version of the Class 101 0-4-0T.

The Hawksworth corridor third class coach.

Stanier coaches) and 'Fireworks at Chilcompton' (BR 'West Country' 34042 *Dorchester* plus maroon Mk 1 coaches). They were followed a year later by 'A Date with the Duchy' (BR green 7036 *Taunton Castle* plus chocolate and cream Mk 1 coaches) and 'Duchess at Carlisle' (LMS maroon 6233 *Duchess of Sutherland* plus Stanier coaches).

Hornby Live Steam was winding down, with only LNER A4 2509 *Silver Link* and LNER A3 4472 *Flying Scotsman* still available. There was now a choice of six diesel and six steam locomotives fitted with sound and the RailRoad series now boasted twenty-one different locomotives and a good selection of rolling stock. The first few Corgi 'Trackside' series models appeared in the Hornby SkaleAutos range during the year.

With the London Olympics of 2012 only two years away, Hornby had been awarded the contract to be the official supplier of themed toy/model-related merchandise. Unknown at the time was that there would be inadequate control on imported souvenirs, which would swamp the

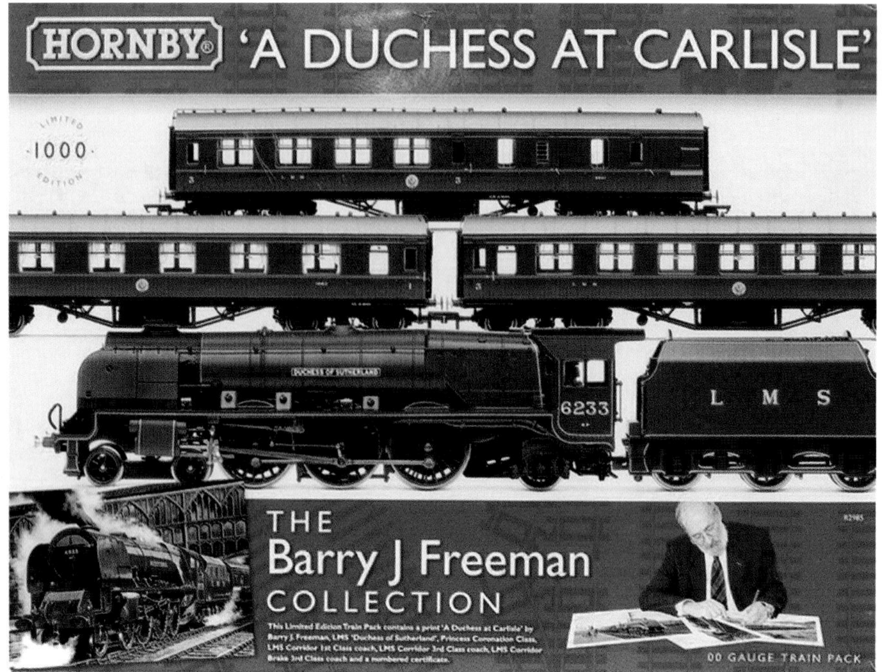

The Barry Freeman collection, 'A Duchess at Carlisle'. (Courtesy Vectis Auctions)

The 'London 2012 train pack'. (Courtesy Vectis Auctions)

Corgi Trackside for SkaleAutos Scammell. (Courtesy Tony Wright)

The Hornby Visitor Centre.

The Hornby Visitor Centre logo.

The Skaledale ferro-concrete coaling tower. (Courtesy Tony Wright)

market, leaving Hornby with large unsold stocks at the end of the Games and heavy trading losses. In the lead up to the great event, Hornby released their Hitachi Class 395 'Javelin' in a train pack. It was white, carrying the 2012 London Olympic and Paralympic logos, featuring pictogram designs representing many of the sports and disciplines of the games. The official souvenir train set would arrive the next year with a purple Class 395, which had a different pattern of symbols.

The Skaledale range continued to grow and now included a spectacular ferro-concrete coaling tower for the locomotive yard.

July 2010 saw the opening of the Hornby Visitor Centre, which provided – and still does – a wet weather attraction where children can be inspired by the Hornby working model railways and Scalextric racing circuit, together with the many models on display. Adults can enjoy the nostalgia of Hornby, Scalextric, Airfix and Corgi models that they remember from their youth and learn more about the companies which developed them. There is also a shop where many of the current models and kits may be bought and the 'Just the Ticket' café adjacent to the centre.

The supply problem in China worsened and prices continued to rise.

2011

TRAINS BY MAIL

'The Royal Mail Great British Railway Collection', marking the Royal Mail's historic link with the British rail network, was one of the themes for 2011 and was the result of co-operation between Hornby and the Royal Mail. The latter issued stamps featuring different steam locomotives and Hornby released models of three of them. They were each sold in a quality box with a lift-off lid. An envelope carrying the stamp relating to the locomotive was included in the box. The subjects were GWR 6002 *King William IV*, 'King Arthur' Class SR olive green 785 *Sir Mador de la Port* and Class A1 LNER green 4476 *Royal Lancer*.

Similarly, Hornby released their models of *Thomas*, *Percy* and *James* in the 'Thomas & Friends' series to correspond with the Royal Mail releasing commemorative stamps depicting scenes from the Rev. W. Awdry's books. As with their main range, Hornby produced special packaging for each of the three locomotives and included in the pack an envelope with the stamp depicting the relevant character.

Live Steam was finally dropped from the catalogue as, too, was the Bassett-Lowke 0 gauge. The end of Live Steam was not unexpected as the demand had been met and stocks run down. The tooling remains available should a new demand arise in the future.

There are many who condemn Edward Thompson's locomotive designs, but the one that has received universal praise is his Class B1 4-6-0. In 2011 the Hornby super-detailed models of the B1 started to arrive from China. The first three releases were LNER lined black 1040 *Roedeer*, BR lined black 61138 and 61243 *Sir Harold Mitchell*. One of the reasons for the

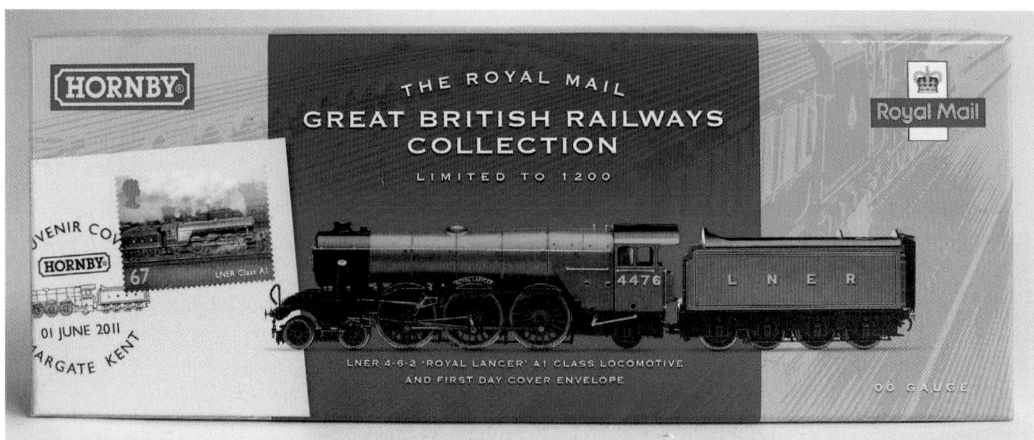

The LNER A1, *Royal Lancer*, Royal Mail series.

Royal Mail 'Thomas & Friends' stamps.

'Thomas & Friends' Royal Mail packs.

The ex-LNER Class B1, *Sir Harold Mitchell*.

The A1 British Railways blue *Tornado.*

B1's choice was that it had compatible tooling with the recently released Thompson Class L1 large tank engine.

The previously announced model of the A1 Trust's new-build 60163 *Tornado* also arrived. It was the first 'Design Clever' model on the market but did not attract the scorn which later ones would encounter, possibly because from the start it was advertised as a RailRoad model. It was in LNER green, but with 'British Railways' on the tender. It arrived with three more versions with greater detail. One of these was in the same livery, but with full lining and etched metal nameplates; another was the same,

The Network SouthEast (NSE) Class 423/1 4-VAP train pack.

The British Railways (BR) Class 423/1 4-VEP.

but in BR Express Blue livery, and the third was in BR green and in the 'Tornado Express' train pack with three maroon Mk 1 coaches.

Hornby had not paid much attention to older 'slam-door' electric multiple units (EMUs) and had some catching up to do. The first of these was a BR 4-VEP (Class 423), which had been built at BR York from 1967 onwards. They were intended for outer suburban services and stopping trains to Bournemouth. Initially, two versions arrived, both DCC-ready. They were unit 7733 in BR blue and unit 3185 in Network Southeast livery. BR blue and grey set 7830 would arrive the following year. A model of the 'Brighton Belle' EMU was also announced but would not arrive until 2012.

A fourth completely new locomotive was a Brush Bagnall 0-4-0DS and it was initially only available in the 'Thomas & Friends' series as the character *Dart* from one of the later films. It was one of the first of the new models not to have been produced by Sanda Kan. Another new 'Thomas' character to arrive from later stories was *Murdoch,* which was based on a Class 9F 2-10-0, but coloured orange. The former Lima breakdown crane replaced the Hornby one in the 'Thomas' series. This was also the year that the *Toy Story 3* train set was released, based on the popular Disney Pixar film of that name. All the models were tooled exclusively for the set.

A 'Legends' range of locomotive models was announced in 2011, being originally put together for Argos catalogue shops. Although the thinking was sound, there were problems in the take-up by retailers. The models were GWR 5029 *Nunney Castle,* BR green 9F 92220 *Evening Star,* LNER blue A4 4468 *Mallard* and LNER green Class A1 4472 *Flying Scotsman.* The first two were released in 2011, with the others following in 2012. The excess models were eventually sold through the normal retail outlets as specials.

After quite a long wait, the Lima Class 40 was ready to join the catalogue and went onto the RailRoad pages. It seems likely that 40152 left the factory late in 2010. The Lima PGA aggregate hopper wagon was added to the wagon

The Brush Bagnall 0-4-0DS, *Dart.*

Murdoch.

Toy Story 3.

The *Toy Story 3* train set.

The Legends series, *Evening Star*. (Courtesy Hattons)

pages and was similar to the Hornby-designed one that it replaced. The reason for the similarity was that back in the mid-1980s when the subject was suggested for the Hornby Railways range, someone went out and bought four Lima models and repainted them in four suggested liveries for the Hornby new products group to see. Those repainted Lima samples survived in the Margate stores and are among several sample models preserved.

The Class 40, ex-Lima.

An ex-Lima PGA in 'Yeoman' livery.

A LNER Gresley suburban composite coach.

Having provided a set of super-detailed mainline coaches for each of the 'Big Four', Hornby turned their attention to suburban stock and released four types of Gresley coaches for suburban services. The four were a first class, third class, composite and brake third. These were initially made in both LNER teak livery and BR maroon.

Concerning teak coaches, there were two new train packs celebrating the Olympic Games, or more precisely the London Olympic Games of 1908 and 1948. The former had the 'Churchward County' as GWR 3818 *County of Radnor* and two scale clerestory coaches, but the 1948 pack consisted of a Class N2 0-6-2T with two of the Gresley teak mainline coaches with BR numbers, and were cleverly printed to appear time-worn and with occasional panels replaced; a great example of realistic model decorating.

'London Olympics 1908' and 'London Olympics 1948' train packs.

A GWR horsebox.

A LNER 'Trout' hopper wagon.

The year 2011 was marked by the introduction of six new wagons tooled in China. The first of these was a 25T ZFO/ZFP 'Trout' ballast hopper dating from 1926 when they were built for the LNER and LMS. The next was a GWR horsebox to replace the Tri-ang model of 1956. Like its predecessor, it was based on a 1937 design. The OTA timber transporters were made from the chassis of surplus air-braked open wagons and vans and varied in design detail, and Hornby had modelled two types. The other additions were a new iron ore tippler, a well detailed BR standard brake van replacement and a 60-ft KFA container flat, with containers.

RailMaster was launched in 2011 and provided the means by which, with the Elite controller, you could control your model railway layout from your PC or laptop through a USB port. It allowed you to control up to ten locomotives at a time, each being given tailored default settings. You could action up to twenty-six light and sound functions, set up programmes for the locomotives to perform to, so that it was possible to sit back and watch the 'ballet'. Also available was Track-Master, which was a computer aided design tool that incorporated the full range of Hornby track pieces, enabling them to be reproduced on the PC screen in photo-quality images.

The OTA turquoise timber carrier. (Courtesy Tony Wright)

The 'Tiphook Rail' KFA container wagon.

In the Skaledale building range, a giant ferro-concrete coaling tower of the engine yard, referred to earlier, had been released in 2010 as a limited-edition, and this was followed in 2011 by a limited-edition ferro-concrete ash plant to complete the scene.

On 16 April 2011 James May tried again to run a Hornby model train the ten miles between Bideford and Barnstaple, but this time the British team was challenged by a German one from Miniatur Wunderland. Each ran three trains from opposite directions. The German team won a round with a Rivarossi H0 model of a German DB Class 403 electric train, which beat a Hornby InterCity 125 HST. In another round a Rivarossi model of a German DR Class 58.30 was beaten by James May's original Tri-ang *Flying Scotsman*! The third round featured modified trains driven by any power source the teams could come up with and the British team's *Thomas the Tank Engine*, with an electric motor driven by a hydrogen fuel cell, beat the German standard EuroSprinter ES 64 P electric locomotive, powered by a bank of lithium-ion cells.

2012
STOCK SHORTAGES

The supply problem from China worsened and Hornby were busy seeking alternative sources, but so too were other model companies for which Sanda Kan had stopped manufacturing. Several companies considered returning production to Europe and North America, but it did not make economic sense. Although a Chinese factory worker had his yearly salary increased by nearly five-fold in the previous decade, he still earned four times less than a British factory worker.

During 2012 the re-tooled B17 arrived and the suite of tools allowed for more of this diverse class to be modelled. The earlier tooling of 1980 was limited to the sub-class B17/4 'Footballers', but with the new tooling it was possible to also make the sub-class B17/1 locomotives. The first introductions of the B17 included B17/1 LNER green 2800 *Sandringham* 4-6-0 and BR green 61637 *Thorpe Hall.* To represent the B17/4s there was the BR green 61650 *Grimsby Town.*

Hornby had spent the best part of two years obtaining works drawings for an LNER Class D11 'Director' (compiling information, sourcing images, creating tool drawings, locating a suitable toolmaker) when Bachmann announced that they

Newly tooled LNER Class B17, *Sandringham.*

The re-tooled ex-LNER B17/6, *Grisby Town.*

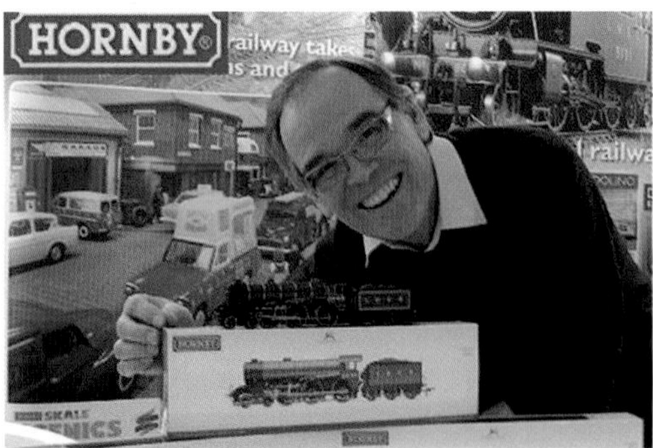

Hornby's Simon Kohler launching the re-tooled B17.

were about to introduce the same model. Hornby had little choice but to abandon the project.

An interesting and completely new subject released during the year was the LNER Class O1 2-8-0, which was a Thompson 1944 rebuild of Class O4s, which had been Robinson's GCR Class 8K of 1911. The first arrivals in plain black were LNER 3755, BR 63670 (weathered) and BR 63789.

The much looked-forward-to 'Brighton Belle' arrived and was available in 1934 umber and cream livery as set 2051 as well as the less popular 1967 blue and grey livery as set 3053. Originally called 'The Southern Belle' these five-car trains arrived on the Brighton Line in 1933. They had been classified as 5PUL, but later as 5-BEL. The two model driving cars were sold as a train pack and the matching three centre cars were in a separate coach pack.

A new RailRoad version of the LNER A1 Class was released, similar to the simplified model of 2007, but with further modifications in order to further reduce its price. The former Lima Classes 31 and 42 'Warship' was released in the RailRoad range, and a specially boxed fortieth anniversary limited edition of *Evening Star* was released, commemorating the arrival of the Tri-ang Hornby model in 1971.

The LNER Class 01.

The 'Brighton Belle'. (Courtesy Hornby)

The Fortieth anniversary of the Hornby *Evening Star* model.

The Class 31, ex-Lima.

The ex-Lima Class 42, *Formidable*.

A new super-detailed Class 67 arrived as a replacement for the one which had been absorbed from the Lima range. It was immediately available as 67001 in EWS livery, 67012 *A Shropshire Lad* in Wrexham & Shropshire livery and as 67018 *Keith Heller* in DB Schenker red.

Following the release of the Gresley LNER suburban coaches the year before, a set of

The re-tooled Class 67 Wrexham & Shropshire (W&S), *A Shropshire Lad*.

A Thompson suburban composite.

The Maunsell pull-push coach pack.

Thompson suburbans arrived in 2012 in BR crimson livery. Thompson had built his with metal sides, but he then made them look like teak to match the Gresley ones. The LNER ersatz teak effect was beautifully recreated on the models by Hornby. Three types were modelled: first/third, all third and brake third, but the LNER versions would not arrive until 2013.

The Maunsell Van B.

There were also three more Maunsell coaches released during the year as well as a Maunsell bogie 'Van B'. The latter was a replacement for the Tri-ang 'Utility Van' of 1958, which was a bit of an embarrassment with its missing buffer stocks. Two of the new Maunsell coaches were for push-pull use, being a driving composite and an all-second. The real coaches had been converted in 1959 from 1935 brake thirds and 1933 open thirds. While they were producing the models, Hornby also made a model of an unconverted open third.

During 2012, Hornby relaunched Pocher kits.

With growing problems at Hornby, Neil Johnson resigned as Chairman of the Hornby Board and was replaced by Roger Canham.

2013
THE GREAT GATHERING AND *THE TITFIELD THUNDERBOLT*

'The Great Gathering' and *The Titfield Thunderbolt* may be a million miles apart, but in 2013 the Hornby management had both to take their minds off more pressing problems at home.

To mark the seventy-fifth anniversary of *Mallard's* record-breaking run, when it reached 126 mph at Stoke Bank near Grantham, making it the fastest steam locomotive in history, the other five surviving Class A4s were brought together with *Mallard* at the National Railway

The 'Great Gathering' at the National Railway Museum, York. (Courtesy Hornby)

Museum in York. *Sir Nigel Gresley, Union of South Africa, Bittern, Dwight D Eisenhower* and *Dominion of Canada* (the last two having travelled 2,500 from the USA and Canada) were lined up with *Mallard* in the Great Hall in July. The event was sponsored by Hornby who released models of all six locomotives in their current liveries. Just 510 of each model were made and, by collecting all six vouchers that came with the models you could claim a free display case for them.

Before they returned to their homes, a further event was held to bring them all together again and this, 'The Great Goodbye', was held at Locomotion, the NRM outpost museum at Shildon. Hornby re-released the six models, but in 'The Great Goodbye Collection' packaging and, again, 510 of each were produced. Because of the importance of the occasion, Hornby wanted to make the models extra special. Consequently, they had enhanced liveries, etched nameplates, numbered certificates, special commemorative packaging as well as the quality cabinet to display them in. Also, the low production number for each was to ensure that they kept their value in the years ahead.

The Ealing Studios comedy *The Titfield Thunderbolt* had been released in 1953 and was inspired by the Talyllyn Railway in Wales, which was the world's first heritage railway run by volunteers and featured in Tom Rolt's book *Railway Adventure.* Four years before, Hornby decided that the film would make a good subject for a sixtieth anniversary pack and while they did not have a model of the *Thunderbolt,* they had a model of the Class 14xx, which was the other locomotive

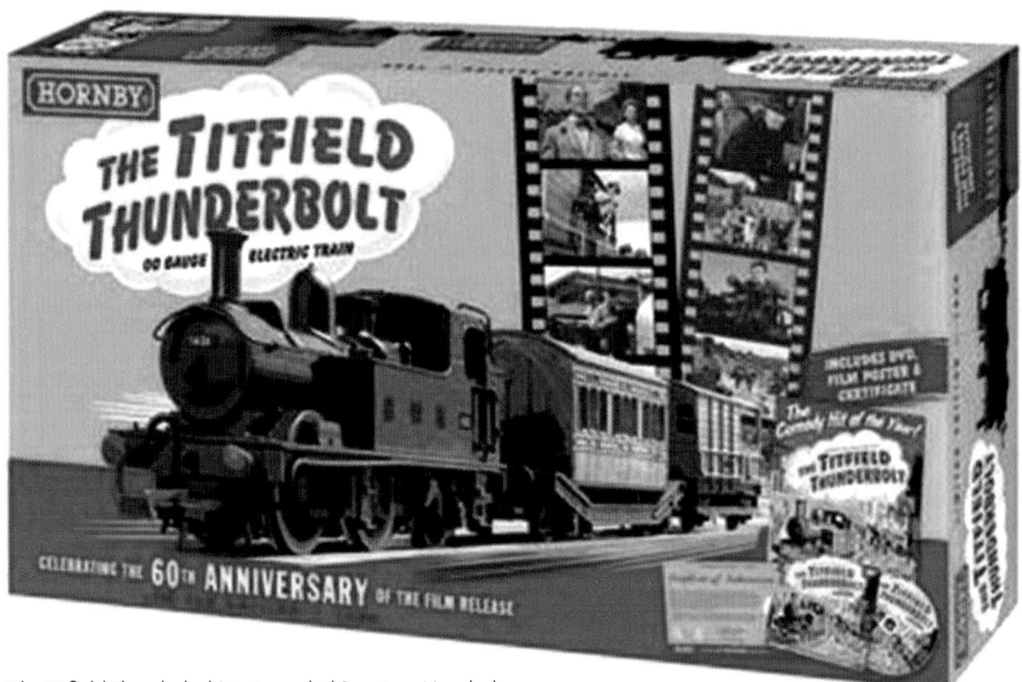

'The Titfield Thunderbolt' train pack. (Courtesy Hornby)

The GWR Class 72xx.

featured in the story. They could also assemble the required rolling stock and a bonus was the inclusion of a DVD of the film in the train pack. This release will be prized by collectors in years to come.

As a follow-up, a fiftieth anniversary train pack of the Beatles film *A Hard Day's Night* was planned for 2014. It was to include a DVD of The Beatles' first film, which had opened with a train scene. All went well, but in October 2013 Apple Corps failed to give their approval and the pack had to be scrapped.

There was a flood of new locomotives in 2013, including the 'Design Clever' GWR 42xx and 52xx 2-8-0T and GWR 72xx 2-8-2T, a GWR 40xx 'Star' Class 4-6-0, a BR Class 8 *Duke of Gloucester*, a Sentinel 4wDM and a 2-BIL EMU. So far Hornby had resisted the temptation to use the new-build *Tornado* tooling to produce original 'Peppercorn' A1s, but in 2013 Class A1 60154 *Bon Accord* in BR blue livery turned up in 'The Majestic' elink digital train set.

The ex-GWR Class 52xx.

The GWR Class 42xx.

The large GWR tank engines, despite the criticisms over lack of detail, were a welcome addition having, for several years, been high on the readers' wishlists of *MREmag* internet magazine. The first batch contained GWR plain green 4283, 5274 and 7202 and BR plain black 4266, 5243 and 7229. Producing three classes from one suite of tools gave welcome variety.

The GWR mixed traffic 4-6-0 'Star' Class was a completely new subject for the main range. It was a George Churchward design dating from 1907 and seventy-three were built at Swindon; the last in 1923. Arriving in 2013 were GWR 4018 *Knight of the Grand Cross*, BR green 4061 *Glastonbury Abbey* and, as a special for the GWR 'Steam' museum in Swindon, there was GWR 4003 *Lode Star*.

The BR Class 8 4-6-2 71000 *Duke of Gloucester* was a one-off locomotive designed by Robert Riddles and built in 1954 as a replacement for a locomotive lost in the Harrow & Wealdstone train crash. It was to be the first of a class of high-powered top-link locomotives, but no more were made. The model was 'Design Clever' and was sold in the RailRoad series.

The Sentinel 4wDM was the first super-detail model of an industrial locomotive to be produced by Hornby. It was a highly detailed model of a diesel shunter introduced in 1963 for use on industrial sites. They were powered by a Rolls-Royce engine and several will be seen on preserved lines. The two model versions delivered in 2013 were NCB No. WL2 in dark blue and Esso Bitumen Plymouth's *Cattewater* in red.

The GWR 'Star' Class, *Knight of the Grand Cross.*

The RailRoad BR Class 8P, *Duke of Gloucester.*

The Esso Bitumen 4wDM Sentinel, *Cattewater.*

The arrival of a former Southern Railway EMU was most welcome and, except for the 5-BEL, was the first in the range since the Tri-ang 4-SUB of 1957 was dropped in 1965. The new model from China was a Class 401 2-BIL and both SR olive green 2114 and BR coach green 2134 units were delivered. The real semi-fast units were introduced in 1935 and fifty-two had been built. They were withdrawn from service in 1969 and one set may be found in the National Collection.

Until now Hornby had made only its original short range of BR Mk 1 coaches, which were first released in 1961 and re-tooled in the 1990s. Those who wanted specific Mk 1 designs had the extensive Bachmann range available.

The SR Class 2-BIL EMU. (Courtesy Hornby)

However, Hornby had decided that it was time that it improved its Mk 1 coaches and extended the range for use in train sets. In 2013 three new types arrived from China and these were a corridor composite (CK), a corridor second (SK) and a replacement corridor brake second (BSK). For these the 'Design Clever' principle had been used.

There were three more completely new models on the wagon pages of the catalogue. These were an LMS CCT parcels van, a BR 'Blue Spot' fish van and a GWR shunter's truck. Unfortunately, Bachmann had also been developing a GWR shunter's truck, but the Hornby model came to the market first.

The BR Insul-fish 'Blue Spot' fish van.

The LMS covered carriage truck.

During the year improvements were made to the Hornby website and these included the ability to see availability dates. Bringing new factories in China online was taking time, and all at Hornby had to endure the complaints arising from missed delivery dates. This must have been hard as there was little that they could do about it.

Hornby's Chief Executive, Frank Martin, resigned at the start of the year after a string of profit warnings and a 70 per cent drop in share value in six years. Chairman Roger Canham, who had replaced his predecessor Neil Johnson just six weeks previously, now needed to find a new Chief Executive capable of repairing the fortunes of the firm, and Richard Ames was appointed.

GWR and BR shunter's trucks.

2014
NEW MARKETING POLICY

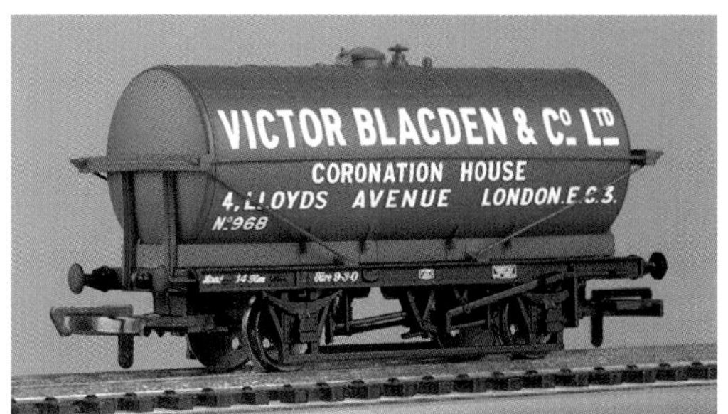

Changes in management had brought changes in marketing that were not always appreciated by the public or retailers. The intention seemed to have been that the new Hornby website (www.hornby.com) should be the focus for modellers and function as an online shop, selling direct to Hornby customers.

Some modellers, who were used to walking into a model shop and buying models off the shelf, were unhappy with a pre-order system Hornby had introduced. This required retailers to take orders from their regular customers in advance of manufacture and only that number would be supplied. The idea was to reduce over-production, but this meant that if a modeller did not order a model in time they would miss out and have to wait for it to be re-released, by which time it could have a different identity and not be the one they wanted.

Another criticism was the blurring of the line between main range models and the RailRoad budget range. New models with greater accuracy, like the BR 'Crosti' Class 9F, the LNER Class P2 and the GWR 'Hall' sat somewhere between the two.

The model railway press had always played an important role in promoting new models, but under the new management models were no longer sent to magazine editors for them to be reviewed. This resulted in less coverage of Hornby models in model railway magazines. The Marketing Department was also showing a special interest in one magazine in particular: the independent *Hornby Magazine* by an independent publisher.

Also, in the past, Hornby had been well represented at exhibitions where they would meet and greet customers and listen to their views and wants. The toning down of this contact meant that the public quickly developed a feeling that Hornby wanted to hold them at arm's length and avoid face-to-face contact. This affected brand loyalty and no doubt added to falling sales, especially when friendly senior staff of their rivals attended shows and answered questions.

One complaint was that letters sent to the company were being ignored. A new emphasis was being placed on social media and a new forum had been set up on the Hornby website. This was where you were expected to ask questions and, it was hoped, receive answers.

It was during these marketing changes that Hornby's Marketing Manager, and previous public face of Hornby, left the company after more than thirty-five years with Hornby. Simon Kohler, now working freelance, was persuaded to write a regular uncensored blog for the website in which he recalled many Hornby achievements in recent years and was able to explain the reason why and how things happened – and admit to failures. These provided an insight into the world of Hornby that had previously been denied the public and did much to win back support. The first of these blogs was posted in May 2014 and many interesting stories followed; they totalled forty-five over a two-year period.

The ex-LNER Class K1.

The LNER Class P2, *Cock O' The North.*

Conscious of the growing dissatisfaction, Hornby held a 'Meet the Team' day on 12 June and the model press was invited to Margate to meet the Hornby personnel. On the day the press was encouraged to ask questions, some of which had been gathered from contributors to internet forums *MREmag* and *RMWeb.*

A series of fortnightly 'Engine Shed' blogs by the model development team at Hornby followed. The blogs (now monthly) keep the public informed of the progress of new models as they approach production and show pictures of the work involved in getting the detail right. Readers are encouraged to comment on illustrated pre-production samples. Recently, a new addition has been 'Signalbox', from an in-house studio, enabling customers to watch 'YouTube' video blogs about new releases and listen to interviews with senior personnel. Another improvement was the development of a better magazine for the Hornby Collectors Club.

The 2014 catalogue made the first mention of Twin Track Sound (TTS), which was a method Hornby had developed to greatly reduce the cost of sound chips in locomotives using an eight-pin decoder. Many models would now be fitted with TTS, including some in the RailRoad range.

For 2014 the first new release was the LNER/BR Class K1 2-6-0. Designed by Arthur Peppercorn, this was a development of Edward Thompson's K1/1, which was a rebuild of Nigel Gresley's K4. The K1s were not ordered until 1947 and so all were released in BR livery. The first batch of models consisted of BR lined black 62024 and 62027.

The much-awaited iconic LNER Class P2 2-8-2 2001 *Cock O' The North,* with its beautiful lines, arrived in 2014 as a RailRoad model, but there was also a fully lined out version and one fitted with a sound chip. Like the 'Duke' the year before, this was a unique subject as the rest of this class of just six were built in different styles, four of them similar to A4s. Designed by Nigel Gresley and built in 1934, they were for passenger expresses between Edinburgh and Aberdeen. All were later rebuilt by Edward Thompson as 4-6-2s.

Following on the heels of the Southern electric 2-BIL EMU came the similar 2-HAL EMU. These were introduced in 1939 and one hundred sets were built. The models were DCC-ready

The SR 2-HAL electric multiple unit.

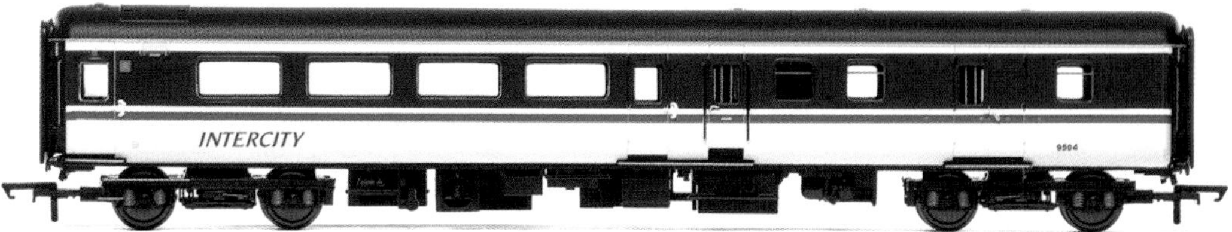

The Intercity Mk 2E brake standard open. (Courtesy Hornby)

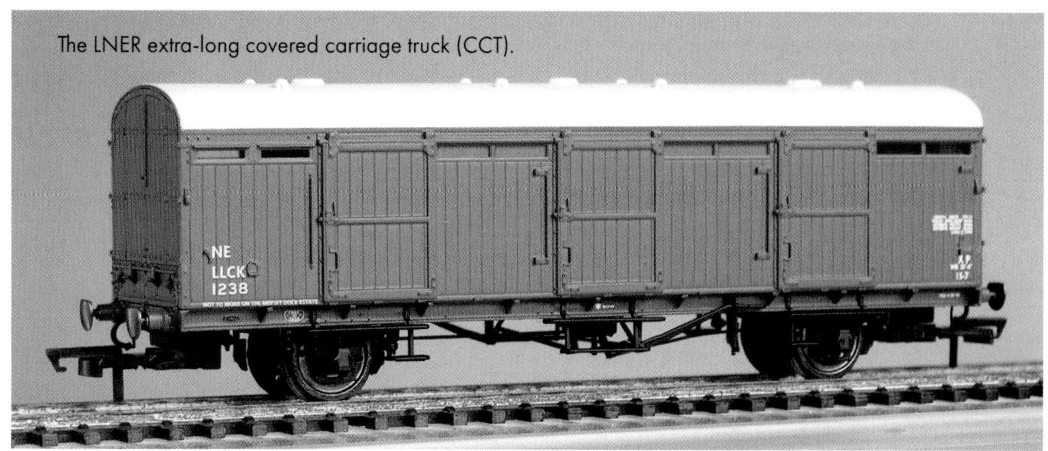

The LNER extra-long covered carriage truck (CCT).

and had sprung buffers, and the first delivery included SR olive green set 2653 and BR coach green sets 2630 and 2639.

At the end of 2014 Hornby introduced a range of Mk2E coaches. While the real Mk2Ds had been successful, there were still improvements to be made and Mk2Es came into use in 1972. More than 200 had been built and entered service on the LMR, WR and ER. There were only three types – TSO, FO and BSO – and all were now modelled by Hornby.

Following the LMS CCT, a new model in 2014 was the LNER extra-long CCT. A total of 117 had been built between 1939 and 1950. Some had survived until the late 1970s. They were used for general freight and, with end access doors opened, could have also been used to carry cars.

Delivery problems continued and the disruption was so bad that during 2013 and 2014 Hornby received only 60 per cent of what it had ordered. After lengthy and complex

Hornby's new distribution base at Hersden.

negotiations resulting in delays in releasing tools and moulds needed for production, Hornby ended its association with Sanda Kan, but had to pay £500,000 to break free. Hornby now received its supplies from three other companies in China: Refined, Talent and Zindart, while Micro Plastics in India were producing the Airfix kits. By the end of the year, together these were supplying 70 per cent of Hornby's goods. The full effect of having several companies working for Hornby would be felt the following year with the arrival of a record number of new releases. The search for further new suppliers continued and Hornby operated through a branch of the company it had established in Hong Kong. Amongst other things, the branch retained control of the tooling in China.

In a move to start disposing of the Margate site, during the year the warehousing and distribution of products was outsourced to a company at Hersden on the A28, near Sturry, west of Canterbury.

2015
FRESH FLOWS

Following on from Hornby's Class A4 'Great Gathering' range, 2015 saw the release of the A4 Silver Jubilee Collection, which consisted of all four of the class that had started life in silver livery for the LNER Silver Jubilee service. These were 2509 *Silver Link*, 2510 *Quicksilver*, 2511 *Silver King* and 2512 *Silver Fox*.

Supplies were now improving as a result of spreading production over more manufacturers in China. On 1 May the Hornby offices were moved to 16,000 square feet of rented space on a science and technology park at Sandwich. The move included the sales, marketing,

The eightieth anniversary 'Silver Jubilee Collection'. (Courtesy Hornby)

The 'Silver Jubilee Collection' *Silver Fox.*

Innovation House, Sandwich, the new home of Hornby plc.

accounts and human resources sections. The administration section moved to the old Pfizer complex at Sandwich. The future location of the Hornby Visitor Centre still needed to be resolved.

Incredibly, there were nine new locomotives delivered in 2015, equalling the record set in 1981. They were a GWR 'Hall', a BR Crosti Class 9F 2-10-0, an LSWR Class 700 'Black Motor' 0-6-0, an LSWR Adams radial tank, an LNER J50 0-6-0T, an LNER 'Claud Hamilton' D16/3 4-4-0, a GER J15 0-6-0, a new GWR 'King' and an SR S15 4-6-0. Note: all of them were models of steam locomotives.

The GWR 'Hall' was advertised as being a RailRoad model, but, as with others, it was also offered with greater detail in the main range. First arrivals were GWR 4901

The new 'Hall' Class model, *Rood Ashton Hall.* (Courtesy Hornby)

The Crosti Class 9F. (Courtesy Phil Parker)

The SR (ex-LSWR) Class 700 'Black Motor' from the '1940 Return From Dunkirk' train pack.

Adderley Hall (RailRoad), ex-Hogwarts GWR red 5972 *Olton Hall* (RailRoad), GWR 4935 *Ketley Hall* (in the 'Western Express' digital e-link train set), GWR 4953 *Pitchford Hall* (in the 'Tyseley Connection' train pack) and, in the main range, BR green 4965 *Rood Ashton Hall.*

The Crosti Class 9F 2-10-0 was another large model supposedly for the RailRoad range. Ten of the locomotives with Franco-Crosti design boilers were built in 1955 and mostly used in the northeast. They were later rebuilt with a conventional blast pipe arrangement.

The LSWR Class 700 'Black Motor' 0-6-0 was to a Dugald Drummond design and thirty of these were built by Dubbs & Co. at the Glasgow works in 1897. The first models to arrive were: SR lined black E695, BR plain black 30693, 30315 and 30316 (weathered). A fifth example, SR black 325, was available in the '1940 Return from Dunkirk' train pack.

The LSWR Class 415 Adams radial tank created some controversy as it was discovered that Oxford Rail was also producing the model, and both were too advanced for either to cancel.

The London & South Western Railway (LSWR) Adams radial tank engine.

The LNER Class J50 tank engine.

The competition law in Britain makes it difficult to avoid this happening. The Class 415 tank locomotive was designed by William Adams in 1882 for the increasing London suburban traffic handled by the London and South Western Railway, and one has been preserved on the Bluebell Railway. The first version of the model to arrive was the preserved 488 in LSWR lined lime green livery.

The powerful LNER J50 0-6-0T was the Great Northern Railway J23 designed by Nigel Gresley in 1913. It had been built for the gradient of lines in the West Riding of Yorkshire. In all, fifty were built. The model has a five-pole motor, eight-pin DCC socket, sprung buffers and removable coal in the bunker. The first delivery from China included LNER black 635, and BR black 68987 and 68971.

LNER 'Claud Hamilton' Class D16/3 4-4-0s were built by James Holden between 1900 and 1903 for the Great Eastern Railway as passenger locomotives. The model has a five-pole flywheel motor, good cab internal detail, sprung buffers and a DCC socket in the tender. First to arrive were LNER lined black 8825, BR plain black E2524, BR lined black 62530 and 62581 (weathered).

The GER J15 0-6-0 class was designed by Thomas Worsdell and modified by James Holden. It was first introduced to the Great Eastern Railway in 1883, and some 289 were built. The model has similar features to the D16/3 above. The first batch included LNER black 7510 and 7524, and BR black 65356, 65475 and 65445.

The new GWR 'King' Class model replaced a super-detail model that had some problems which needed putting right. It has a five-pole

The LNER Class D16/3, *Claud Hamilton.*

The ex-LNER Classs J15.

The re-tooled King Class, *King Richard II.*

skew-wound motor, is DCC-ready and has a well detailed cab interior. So good was the new model that it was voted best steam locomotive in the annual *Model Rail* Model of the Year Awards. The first releases were GWR 6011 *King James I*, BR 6000 *King George V*, BR 6021 *King Richard II* and BR 6029 *King Edward VIII.*

SR 'S15' 4-6-0 was designed by Robert Urie for the London & South Western Railway and twenty entered service in 1920 and 1921. It was a freight version of the N15 'King Arthur' Class. The model was based on the Maunsell modified design and had cab interior detail, removable coal load, sprung buffers, five-pole skew-wound motor with two flywheels and was DCC-ready. The first batch contained SR olive 824, BR plain black 30843 and 30830.

The SR Class S15.

The LMS Stanier suburban third.

A super-detailed 21-ton hopper wagon. (Courtesy Hornby)

Interesting limited-edition train packs this year included 'Sir Winston Churchill's Funeral Train', 'Going Home' (a First World War troop train) and the aforementioned 'Return from Dunkirk', marking the seventieth anniversary of the end of the Second World War.

A new range of coaches this year consisted of LMS 57-foot Stanier suburban first/third, all-third and brake third. They were immediately available in both LMS and BR maroon. There were also two new super-detailed wagons: an LMS horsebox and a BR 21-ton hopper wagon.

The super detailed Type K Pullman cars, which Hornby introduced in 2003, were based on early ones of timber construction. From 1928, the Pullman Car Company had built their cars in steel, while still retaining the K classification. They were built for use in LNER expresses which operated up until the outbreak of the Second World War and in 2015 Hornby released a new range of models based on these. The all-steel design eliminated the need for a truss beneath the underframe and, in this way, the cars were like the 'Brighton Belle' cars produced by Hornby in 2012. The five models released were a parlour third, kitchen third, parlour first, kitchen first and a brake third.

In 2015, a set of six Jersey postage stamps featured Hornby train sets.

Hornby returned to profit for the period December 2014 to 31 March 2015. From this it looked, at least on the business front, that Hornby plc was turning a corner. Hornby announced that it had successfully restructured the UK and European sides of its business, cut back on its products and reduced costs. It revealed that in 2016 it planned to cut more than half of the products it made, as it generated 90 per cent of its profits from only 50 per cent of its range.

The LMS horsebox.

The retooled K type Pullman cars.

Hornby train sets featured on stamps from Jersey.

2016

WHAT! NO CATALOGUE?

Hornby committed an unforgivable sin of not publishing a new catalogue at the start of 2016 and there was a public outcry. The famous Hornby catalogue showed the company's pride in its name and its products. It was eagerly anticipated for the previous year by the Hornby faithful, and had always been where the new models for the coming year were announced, along with beautiful and exciting illustrations. The disappearance of this proud display gave the impression the company had lost pride in itself; it had given up trying. It was the wrong impression to give. In fairness to the management at the time the idea was that the website should be the catalogue, one that could be regularly updated – plus it would save the printing cost, which always exceeded the income generated by sales of the catalogue. In response to the public outcry, a small and unattractive, but free, substitute was hurriedly put together, showing only the new items planned during 2016.

There were three brand new super-detailed locomotive models delivered during the year and a re-tooled one. The LNER Q6 0-8-0 was designed by Vincent Raven as his Class T2 for heavy mineral trains on the North Eastern Railway. They were superheated and 120 were built between 1913 and 1921. Three plain black versions of the model arrived in 2016: LNER 3418 and BR 63443 and 63429.

The second model was of a Class 71 electric locomotive. These were built at Doncaster between 1959 and 1960 as a batch of twenty-four units for BR Southern Region. The locomotives were only able to work on the third rail power system, which ultimately limited their operational scope for passenger and freight work. The model was the subject of another duplication controversy as D. J. Models were also well advanced with a model of the Class 71 when Hornby announced their imminent release. In August 2014 Hornby had laser-scanned the only preserved locomotive, number E5001, at Barrow Hill and

The Hornby 2016 catalogue.

The LNER Class Q6.

The Class 71, first three versions. (Courtesy Hornby)

three BR versions of the model were delivered in 2016: green E5022, blue 71012 and the preserved National Collection locomotive in green as E5001. The model had double flywheel dual bogie drive, a five-pole skew-wound motor, accurate running light modes, cab lighting, changeable headcodes, a removable front valance panel, sprung buffers and working pantograph. However, it was not a good seller.

The new model was a Peckett W4 0-4-0ST design, which represented a classic late-Victorian four-coupled, medium range, industrial saddle tank. The locomotives were built by Peckett & Sons Ltd. at the Atlas Engine Works in St. George, Bristol between 1885 and 1906, and some 140 were produced. Originally planned for release in 2017, the model was brought forward to 2016 to meet a growing demand for a small industrial steam locomotive. They have a four-pin DCC decoder socket, fully detailed cab interiors and die-cast parts for extra weight. The Peckett W4 was voted best new 00 steam locomotive model in the 2016 British Model Railway Awards.

The re-tooled model was the LNER Class B12 4-6-0; the original Tri-ang model it replaced dated from 1963. The B12 was a large mixed-traffic locomotive and was developed by James Holden of the Great Eastern Railway in 1911 as the Class S69. Taken over by the LNER in 1923,

The 'Huntley & Palmers' Peckett W4.

The re-tooled LNER Class B12.

it became one of the LNER's standard designs. Three versions were in the first batch of models from China: LNER green 8573, early BR lined black 61533 and late BR lined black 61580.

A limited-edition during the year was the Sir Nigel Gresley locomotive pack. This contained four of his express locomotives: Classes A1, A3, A4 and P2. All were in LNER green livery.

The year 2016 also saw further growth in the range of coaches available. As previously explained, in 1991 Bachmann had released a range of 1938 Collett GWR coaches and so when the Hornby team were considering a high-quality GWR range they went for the later Hawksworth design, which had topped the *MREmag* wishlist poll at the time. However, the real coaches barely saw a coat of GWR paint as they had been built too late. Hornby still had a gap to fill and so decided to produce a range to an earlier Collett design of 1925. This was bow-ended 57-ft stock, produced in order, to modernise the mainline services. The bow ends reduced the length of corridor connections and they ran on distinctively short 7-ft bogies They had either left- or right-hand corridors and both types are modelled by Hornby. The models were voted the best 00 coaching stock in the 2016 *Model Rail* Model of the Year Awards.

Hornby also wanted non-corridor SR coaching stock. By 1934, Maunsell, CME of the Southern Railway, had recognised that the short 48-ft ex-LSWR stock it had needed some major attention, as it was nearing the end of its working life. Much of it was built on wooden underframes,

The Hornby 'Sir Nigel Gresley Collection', 2016.

A Collett brake third. (Courtesy Hornby)

An ex-LSWR coach rebuilt as a 58ft SR 3rd class coach.

and some were still gas-lit, and so a programme of refurbishment was undertaken. They were rebuilt onto standard 58-ft underframes with extended bodies. The vehicles were formed mainly into two-car sets. Hornby modelled four different types and they went on to be winners of the 4 mm-scale coaching stock category in the 2016 British Model Railway Awards.

A SR cattle truck.

New super-detailed wagons released this year were an LMS coke hopper, an SR cattle truck and a commissioned biomass hopper. The amount of detail now provided on new wagon models was outstanding.

The seventieth anniversary of *Thomas the Tank Engine* was celebrated with a metallic blue limited edition.

From 2015, Hornby plc had begun to announce a series of declining financial results. After the PLC shares dropped by more than 50 per cent in a year, at the 2016 results, Hornby declared that it planned to cut more than half of the products. In the year to 31 March 2017, revenues fell further to £47.4 million from £55.8 million, while underlying losses widened to £6.3 million from a £5.7 million deficit in 2016.

In February it was reported that Hornby's Chief Executive, Richard Ames, had quit his post as Hornby's CEO less than a week after Hornby issued a third profit warning in five months and said it risked breaching a lending agreement with Barclays Bank. Ames had been less than two years in the job. Roger Canham, the Chairman, took over CEO duties until Ames could be replaced. Steve Cooke became the next CEO. There was a risk of the bank calling in the debt and that threatened Hornby with collapse.

The seventieth anniversary 'Thomas the Tank Engine' limited edition. (Courtesy Hornby)

2017

THE RISE OF THE PHOENIX

At a shareholders' meeting in July 2017, the financial declines culminated in the second-largest owner of shares, New Pistoia Income (NPI), proposing that the Chairman of the Hornby Board be replaced. The motion was defeated, but the largest shareholder, Phoenix Asset Management (PAM), agreed to buy the 17.6 million Hornby shares held by NPI. This gave PAM a 55.2 per cent holding in the company and effected a takeover of Hornby plc. The Hornby Chairman, Roger Canham, resigned in August 2017, followed in September by the Chief Executive, Steve Cooke.

In October 2017 PAM announced the new management team who were joining the company to steer through a turnaround. They were Lyndon Davies, former Mettoy employee and owner of LCD Enterprises and Oxford Diecast; Tim Mulhall, from Oxford Diecast and credited with knowledge of the international market, having been the former importer for Hornby International brands in the UK; and Simon Kohler, ex-Hornby Marketing Manager. Lyndon Davies became Executive Chairman and CEO and Simon Kohler became the Marketing and Product Development Director. In November 2017 Hornby entered into an acquisition agreement through which it bought 49 per cent of the shares of LCD Enterprises for £1.6 million.

Lyndon Davies outside the Oxford Diecast factory in China.

Early in the year, multi-millionaire Jeremy Hosking, who founded Locomotive Storage Ltd. and owns thirteen mainline steam locomotives, bought the Westwood site of the former Hornby factory and warehouse at Margate. As his

The South Eastern & Chatham Railway (SE&CR) Class H tank engine. (Courtesy Hornby)

company did not need all the space it meant that Hornby, if they so wished, could move back into the offices, something they did at the beginning of 2019. It also meant that the Hornby Visitor's Centre no longer needed to move out.

There were three new models from the suppliers in China and two were completely new subjects. One of these was Wainwright's SE&CR H Class 0-4-4T. This had originally been Harry Wainwright's solution to updating the ageing 2-4-0 and 0-4-2T stock running on the South Eastern and Chatham Railway at the turn of the twentieth century and sixty-six were built at Ashford. The models were DCC-ready and powered by a five-pole skew-wound motor and the first batch contained SE&CR lined green 263 and early BR black as 30129.

Ever since Hornby released their rebuilt 'Merchant Navy' Class locomotive in 2000, Hornby fans had been waiting for the un-rebuilt version to be modelled. Now, seventeen years later and after having been announced in the late spring of 2015, it had arrived and what a beautiful model it was. Conceived in 1937 when Oliver Bulleid became CME of the Southern Railway, his vision was for a 4-6-2 fast mixed-traffic engine with quick acceleration, equally capable of hauling services such as the Golden Arrow and Atlantic Coast Express and for freight workings to a speed of around 75 mph. Despite the onset of war in 1939, Bulleid's design was accepted by the wartime Railway's Executive Committee and production commenced through November 1940 at Eastleigh Works. The first locomotive, 21C1 *Channel Packet* was named on 10 March 1941. All were later rebuilt by British Railways. The first batch of models to arrive in 2017 included SR malachite 21C1 *Channel Packet* and 21C3 *Royal Mail* as well as early BR green 35028 *Clan Line* and 35023 *Holland-Afrika Line* (with TTS sound).

There was also a completely re-tooled super-detailed model of the 'Duchess', which was DCC-ready with a five-pole skew-wound motor, provision for a speaker in the tender, and the locomotive and tender had semi-permanent coupling. The body was even better detailed than the last version and the suite of tools allowed for Ivatt's modifications to 46156 and 46257. Models released in 2017 were LMS maroon 6231 *Duchess of Atholl* (without smoke deflectors), BR green 46237 *City of Birmingham* (with TTS sound) and BR maroon 46256 *Sir William Stanier F.R.S.*

The SR un-rebuilt 'Merchant Navy' Class, *Royal Mail.*

The new LMS *Duchess of Atholl.* (Courtesy Hornby)

A super-detailed GWR freight brake van was also released. The 'Thomas & Friends' range had been drastically reduced and there were hints that Hornby would not be renewing its licence.

In 2017, to mark the seventieth anniversary of the final year of the 'Big Four' railway companies, Hornby selected four locomotives (one from each company) that were in use on the final day (31 December 1947) before the nationalisation of the railways. Models of them, in the liveries they carried at the time, were produced as limited editions and a potted history of each locomotive was given in the 2017 catalogue.

The four models were an SR 'Battle of Britain' 21C168 *Kenley*, GWR 'King' 6004 *King George III*, LMS rebuilt 'Royal Scot' 6108 *Seaforth Highlander* and LNER Class A3 108 *Gay Crusader*. The models were sold individually.

A re-tooled ex-GWR 'Toad' brake van. (Courtesy Hornby)

The GWR, *King George III*. (Courtesy Hornby)

The LMS re-built 'Scot', *Seaforth Highlander*. (Courtesy Hornby)

2018

UNDER NEW MANAGEMENT

The end of year Annual Report for March 2018 revealed how serious the position was for the company, showing further slumps in revenue down to £35.7 million and a widening pre-tax loss of £7.6 million.

There were four new locomotives and two of them were new subjects. One was the 0-6-0 North British Railway Class C, which in 1923 became LNER Class J36, and the other was the Hitachi Class 800/0 IEP. The other two new locomotives were a fourth version of the 'Coronation' design and a new super-detailed West Coast Main Line Class 87 electric locomotive, replacing the former Lima model with a high-quality alternative. There was also a new toy train set from new tooling and called the 'Junior Express'.

The ex-NBR Class C was no doubt chosen to please Scottish modellers who had complained

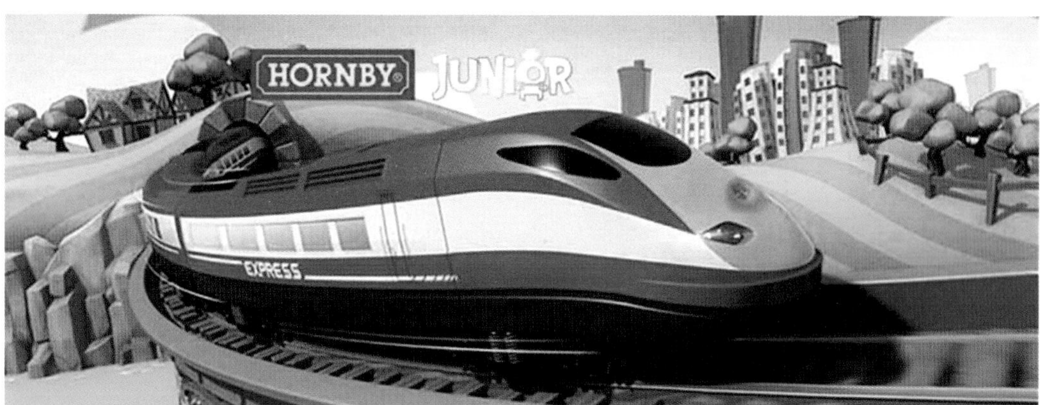

The 'Junior Express' train. (Courtesy Hornby)

The LNER Class J36 (ex-North British Railway Class C).

The Hitachi IEP bi-mode Class 800/0 test train. (Courtesy Hornby)

that there was little of local interest for them in the Hornby range. Designed by Matthew Holmes for the North British Railway, the first six NBR Class C locomotives were introduced in 1888 and such was their success that, by 1900, 168 locomotives had been built. During the First World War, the Railway Operating Division (ROD) sent twenty-five members of the class to France and survivors returning in 1919 were awarded commemorative names. The first model to arrive was NBR lined black 673 *Maude*.

The Class 800 units have been built by Hitachi since 2015, at Newton Aycliffe, and are based on the Japanese Hitachi A-train. The first Great Western Main Line units entered service in October. The bodyshells were shipped from the Kasado plant in Japan. The Class 800 units are part of the Intercity Express Programme (IEP). In 2018, Hornby introduced their GWR model in five-car packs with eight-pin DCC sockets fitted in both driving cars. The socket in the motorised car was for motor and light functions while that in the non-powered driving car was for lighting control. The driving cars were sold together in a train pack and the three trailers in a coach pack. There were three train packs originally available: the limited-edition white test train 811002 and 815002; in GWR dark green 800004 *Sir Daniel Gooch* and 811004 *Isambard Kingdom Brunel*; and 800010 *Paddington Bear* and 811010 *Michael Bond*.

The new 'Coronation' Class locomotive by Hornby is the fourth and is even more detailed than the super-detailed model of 2001. Features include a sliding cab roof vent, flanges over the front bogie (where the cylinder bypass valves had to be hidden), the Hudd ATC apparatus, speed recorders, different handle positions on the front casing, streamlined lamps, the correct sandbox filler caps, brake blocks, different chimneys, slotted front steps, the extra catch on the front casing for those which needed it and extra access panels. Models delivered in 2018 were LMS blue 6221 *Queen Elizabeth*, LMS red 6229 *Duchess of Hamilton* and 6244 *King George VI.*

The pre-production re-tooled 'Coronation' Class. (Courtesy Hornby)

The BR Class 87, *Robert Burns*. (Courtesy Hornby)

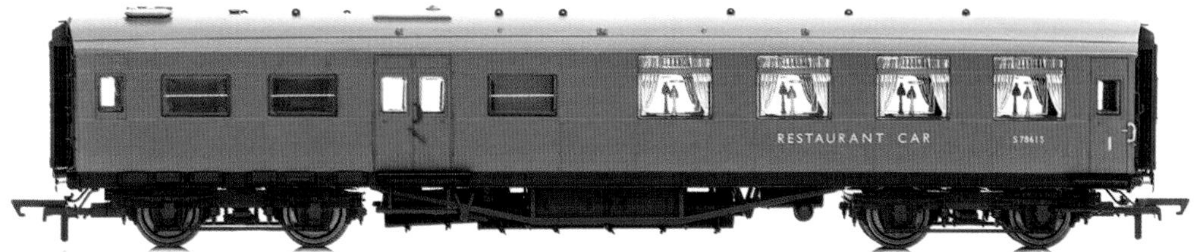

A BR (ex-SR) Maunsell kitchen-dining first. (Courtesy Hornby)

An ex-LNER 'Toad E' brake van. (Courtesy Hornby)

The 25 kV Class 87 locomotives were needed to cope with the route gradients of the West Coast Main Line between Weaver Junction and Glasgow. Electrification was scheduled for completion by May 1974, leaving little time to design a completely new locomotive from scratch and so British Rail decided to base the new class on the existing Class 86 locomotives. The first models to arrive were BR blue 87035 *Robert Burns*, BR Inter-City Swallow 87010 *King Arthur* and Virgin Trains red and black 87019 *Sir Winston Churchill*.

Also new in 2018 was a 59-ft first class kitchen/dining car, which had been missing from Hornby's extensive range of Maunsell coach types. The go-ahead to construct six first class dining cars had been given on 6 August 1925. They were for use on the London–Bournemouth, London–Plymouth and London–Exeter services. The model released by Hornby is highly detailed inside and out.

Having re-tooled the GWR guard's van in 2017, this year it was the turn of the LNER short 'Toad B' and 'Toad E' to have high-quality tooling. There was also a sound-fitted goods van.

A limited-edition model of LNER 4468 *Mallard* in Garter Blue with 18-ct gold-plated metalwork was sold during the year in an attractive presentation case. This was to commemorate the eightieth anniversary of the real locomotive breaking the world speed record for a steam railway locomotive.

There was also a commemorative train pack to celebrate the '15 Guinea Special', which was a final steam tour on 11 August 1968, marking the official end of steam. The pack held BR 'Britannia' Class 70013 *Oliver Cromwell* and three coaches.

2019
NEW HOPE

As said earlier, the Westwood site of the former Hornby factory at Margate was bought by multi-millionaire, Jeremy Hosking, who runs Locomotive Storage Ltd. and owns thirteen mainline steam locomotives. The site was bought early in 2017 and during the following year the first of the real locomotives that were to occupy the warehouse next to the Hornby Visitor Centre started to arrive. The first was A4 4464 *Bittern,* which has two tenders and is in Garter Blue livery. Known as the '1:1 Collection', there are twenty-four items including locomotives and fully restored rolling stock. The intention is to keep space for visiting subjects from other collections and the first of these is 'Black 5' BR 45379 from the Mid-Hants Railway. Hornby have released models of this locomotive and *Bittern* in a new '1:1 Collection' series.

The Hornby 'One to One' collection. (Courtesy Hornby)

The LNER A4, *Bittern,* with two tenders. (Courtesy Hornby)

The LNER Hitachi EP bi-mode, *Azuma*. (Courtesy Hornby)

Following on from the GWR 800 units, in 2019 the East Coast Main Line 800/1 *Azuma* unit was in the catalogue. 'Azuma' is the Japanese word for 'East'.

The SR 'Lord Nelson' locomotives planned for the previous year arrived early in 2019. Designed by the Chief Mechanical Engineer (CME) of the Southern Railway, Richard Maunsell, the first 'Lord Nelson' locomotive, E850, was completed on 11 August 1926, and orders for a further fifteen engines soon followed. All members of the class were named after naval leaders and the Southern Railway's publicity department went to work promoting the new class, calling the 'Lord Nelson' *'the most powerful express locomotive in Britain.'* A very extensive suite of tools was made for this model to allow for virtually every design variation and modification. The first wave of models released by Hornby contained SR olive green 851 *Sir Frances Drake*, BR green 30863 *Lord Rodney* and 30850 *Lord Nelson*, which included a TTS sound decoder.

A re-tooled LBSCR 'Terrier' tank engine was released at the start of the year and straight away came in six versions: LB&SCR Stroudley's 'New Engine Green' ochre livery as 655 *Stepney*, SE&CR green 751, K&ESR blue 5 *Rolvenden*, SR olive green 2662, early BR lined black 32655 and late BR lined black 32636.

Hornby had been working their way through their larger locomotive models re-tooling them to make them even more detailed and giving them a larger suite of tools to allow for more variations. This year it was the turn of

The SR Class LN, *Sir Francis Drake*.

The re-tooled ex-London, Brighton and South Coast Railway (LBSC) 'Terrier' tank engine. (Courtesy Hornby)

Pre-production sample of the new 'Princess' locomotive. (Courtesy Hornby)

the 'Princess Royal' Class and the first batch of models for release at the end of the year included LMS 6201 *Princess Elizabeth*, BR 46206 *Princess Marie Louise* and BR 46207 *Princess Arthur of Connaught*. The year 2020 will be the seventieth anniversary of the release of the original model of *Princess Elizabeth* by Rovex.

Hornby's GWR Class 61xx large prairie tank was the improved 1977 Airfix model, acquired by Hornby and re-introduced by them in 1999. The tools have now been replaced by new super-detailed tooling, which can be used to produce both the Class 61xx and the Class 5101. Released this year were GWR 4154 and 6110 as well as BR 6145 and 4160.

Following the success of the Peckett W4 industrial 0-4-0ST in 2016 (some versions of which had sold out before any models arrived),

The re-tooled GWR Class 5101 large prairie tank. (Courtesy Hornby)

The National Coal Board (NCB) Peckett B2. (Courtesy Hornby)

Hornby have followed up with the larger Peckett B2 industrial 0-6-0ST in three different liveries. Also new is another industrial locomotive, which is the smallest Hornby have produced so far. It is a Ruston Hornsby 48DS 0-4-0 forty-eight horsepower diesel shunter, which is supplied with a 'Conflat' wagon to supplement power collection (due to the shortness of the locomotive's wheelbase). This was launched during the year with a choice of four liveries.

For those who had been enjoying the locomotive sounds that Hornby's Twin Track Sound (TTS) decoders provide, the idea had been taken a step further in the 2018 range with the release of a TTS Sound Van. This was a goods van, which could be parked in a siding and emanate a whole range of sounds, controlled by the operator. The sounds were grouped into 'areas' that included workshop, station platform, station yard, signal box and general atmosphere. The sounds of each of the areas were on a loop and so could be left to play continuously. A second van with a different assortment of sounds was released at the end of 2019.

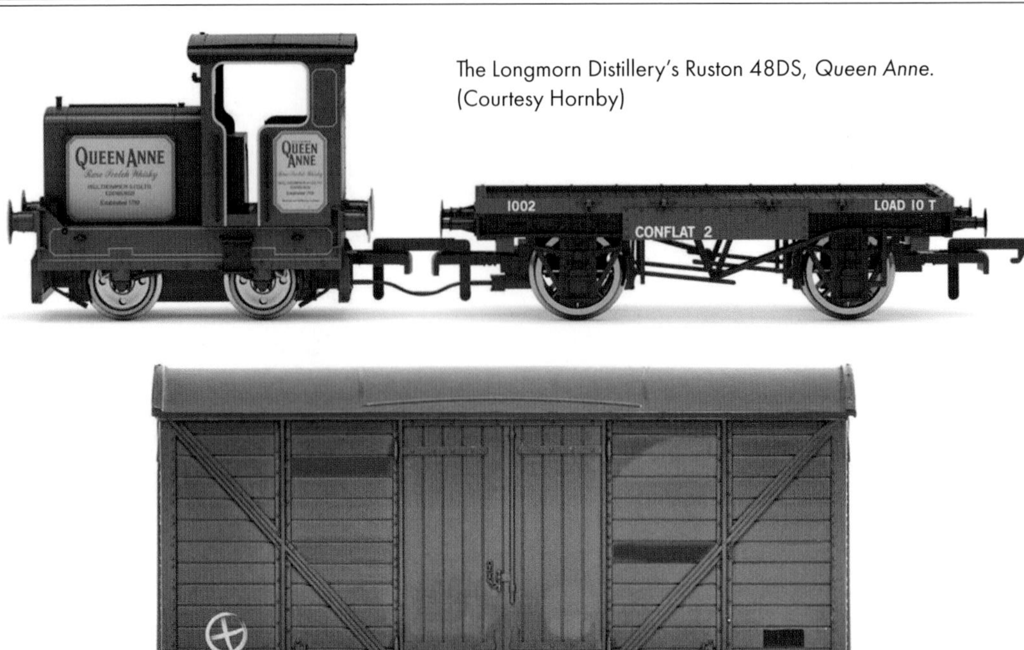

The Longmorn Distillery's Ruston 48DS, *Queen Anne*. (Courtesy Hornby)

A vent van with sound. (Courtesy Hornby)

A Collett 57-ft bow end suburban brake third. (Courtesy Hornby)

So far Hornby have produced LNER, LMS and SR non-corridor coaches, which might be used for suburban trains and other stopping services. This year it was the turn of the GWR and 57-ft Collett bow-ended suburban coaches to be chosen. These featured in Charles Collett's coach improvement programme between 1927 and 1929. Hornby modelled both left- and right-hand examples of a composite coach and a six-compartment brake third.

Also modelled for release in 2019 was a range of 59-ft Bulleid coaches for the Southern Railway. Work on the designs of the real coaches started in 1938, but, owing to the Second World War, orders were not placed until 1944. The first coaches left Eastleigh Works towards the end of 1945. Hornby have modelled a corridor composite and a corridor brake third with enough variations in the first batch to make up into two three-car SR sets and two three-car

The SR Bulleid 59-ft composite coach.

The GWR Mk 3SD TGS. (Courtesy Hornby)

Mk 2F coaches. (Courtesy Hornby)

BR sets appropriately numbered. These arrived during the summer.

Also released in 2019 was a set of models of both the BR Mk 2F and Mk 3SD coaches. The real Mk 2F coaches were the final development of the Mk 2 design and were introduced in 1973. The Mk 3SD coaches are an update of the Mk 3, which did not meet with today's standards for people with limited mobility. The Mk 3SDs have sliding doors, modified toilets and new seating. Some 200 were being modified for GWR, ScotRail and Cross-Country, and the planned Hornby range would cover all three liveries. The models had been scheduled for the end of the year.

A re-tooled LMS brake van. (Courtesy Hornby)

The introduction of super-detailed brake vans continues with the LSWR and LMS designs and a selection of liveries.

The year saw the return of the *Harry Potter* series along similar lines to the original range, but in new packaging. There was a train set with the locomotive in red as *Hogwarts Castle* (now correctly a 'Hall' Class model instead of the 'Castle' used before) and two maroon Mk 1 coaches. Also, *Hogwarts Castle* was available

The new 'Hogwarts Express' train set. (Courtesy Hornby)

The fiftieth anniversary of the *Flying Scotsman*'s USA tour. (Courtesy Hornby)

The Hornby Arnold N-gauge 5-PUL, 'Brighton Belle'. (Courtesy Hornby)

separately in two formats, one fitted with TTS sound and one without. Also available separately were the Mk 1 SK and BSK coaches with a choice of two running numbers for each, which were different from the numbers used on the coaches in the set. There were also available again the model of Platform 9¾ and the Skaledale Hogsmede station buildings, platforms and bridge, all based on Goathland station, which was used in the films.

The year 2019 was the fiftieth anniversary of *Flying Scotsman's* tour of the USA, which ended up with the locomotive stranded at the Stockton US Army Base, with no funds to bring her home and the owner, Alan Pegler, bankrupted. It was the double-tender version of the locomotive that went abroad, and Hornby commemorated the event by producing a model of the locomotive as it would have looked with its cowcatcher, bell and headlamp fitted. The only difference was that the Hornby model had 18-ct gold-plated metalwork!

The Class 156, *Spirit of the Royal Air Force*. (Courtesy Hornby)

During the year the Class 156 DMU was released in Northern Rail's special RAF commemorative livery and the N-gauge 'Brighton Belle' EMU, made in 2014 by Hornby's German company, Arnold, is due to return with the identity of another of the sets.

2010s – A DECADE SUMMARY

The story of Hornby has been a rollercoaster ride on the peaks and troughs of the international toy and hobbies industries. Catering for both the toy and model markets has counted in its favour. In the last twenty-five years this has allowed the company to withstand the decline in demand for traditional toys by increasing concentration on the demands of model railway enthusiasts. Hornby has proved time and again that it is the Great Survivor!

Although the models are no longer made in Great Britain, the perception, design and quality control are still provided by British expertise. That is important when it is British models for British modellers, and no one does it better than Hornby. However, let us not forget that the models also benefit from the skill of Chinese engineers, toolmakers and assemblers, who are among the best in the world.

After a glowing first decade in the new millenium, during the second decade Hornby was made to suffer for the decision it had taken to risk its future with just one manufacturer, when it moved production to China. The second decade has been dogged by delays in deliveries, resulting in promised models often arriving a year or two years after being announced in the catalogue. It has also meant that, while the company continued to have its usual overheads, it did not have enough stock to sell to meet those costs. The problem was worsened by the rising cost of the models themselves, which upset Hornby's customers and meant they could not afford to buy as many items. In the background, the UK pound was losing value against the US dollar and Chinese businesses want to be paid in dollars.

All of this was a recipe for disaster and led to falling share prices and several changes in top personnel – and yet, through it all, Hornby has survived. It bought itself out of the contract it had with its original Chinese manufacturer and now spreads its business over several companies in China.

It has also survived a new approach to marketing and customer relations, which initially upset retailers, the model press and Hornby's customers. Perhaps the biggest protest followed the decision not to print a catalogue in 2016, the annual catalogue being

looked forward to all year by Hornby's customers. The marketing emphasis was to be the Hornby website, which was an ever-changing catalogue of what is available to buy at any particular moment. It also, of course, provided the means by which the company could sell direct to the public, which upset retailers. However, the company quickly learnt by its mistakes and while the new arrangements are still in place, the problems they created have been addressed, even at the cost of further management changes. One of the biggest changes has been the company's efforts to talk to the public about what it is doing and how it does it; this is through regular blogs and YouTube video chats.

Throughout the decade Hornby has produced many splendid new models and has fulfilled its promises, despite the obstructions put in its way. It has constantly tried to improve its existing models whilst introducing new subjects to the market. The decade has seen new rivals emerge, including larger retailers now commissioning new tooling for their exclusive use. Hornby ends the decade with a new skilled and enthusiastic management team, a big job in turning the business around, but hope in the future.

The year 2011.

The year 2010.

The year 2012.

The year 2013.

The year 2014.

The year 2015.

The year 2017.

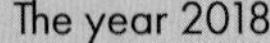
The year 2018.

The year 2019.

The year 2016.

2010s MILESTONES

2010 – 'Design Clever', LNER Class L1, Hawksworth coaches, Mk 3 DVT, new 'Castle', new 28xx/38xx, Class 33, GWR175, Barry J. Freeman, London Olympic preparations, Hornby Visitor Centre and delivery delays.

2011 – Royal Mail series, end of 'Live Steam', end of Bassett-Lowke, Class B1, *Tornado*, 4-VAP, Brush Bagnall 0-4-0DS, *Murdoch*, *Toy Story 3*, 'Legends' range, Class 40, 1908 and 1948 London Games packs, 'Trout', GWR horsebox, OTA, KFA, RailMaster, Track-Master, coaling tower and James May's Anglo-German race.

2012 – Delivery problems, search for new suppliers, B17/1, B17/4, O1, 5-BEL, Class 67, *Evening Star* 40th, Thompson suburbans, Chairman resigns and replaced.

2013 – The Great Gathering, *The Titfield Thunderbolt*, 42xx, 52xx, 72xx, 'Duke', 'Star', Sentinel 4wDM, 2-BIL, new Mk 1s, 'Blue Spot', shunters truck, LMS CCT, CEO resigns and replaced.

2014 – New suppliers in China, dispatching outsourced, TTS, K1, P2, 2-HAL, Mk 2E coaches, LNER CCT and break with Sanda Kan.

2015 – Offices move to Sandwich, new 'Hall', Crosti 9F, 700 'Black Motor', Adams tank, J50, *Claud Hamilton*, J15, new 'King', S15, steel K Pullmans, LMS non-corridor, BR hopper wagon and LMS horsebox.

2016 – No catalogue, Q6, Class 71, Peckett W4, new B12, new Collett coaches, re-built LSWR coaches, LMS coke hopper, SR cattle truck, biomass hopper, falling profits, CEO resigns and replaced.

2017 – PAM take-over, Chairman and CEO resign, new management team, factory site sold, Locomotive Storage Ltd. move in, H Class, original MN Class, new 'Duchess', new GWR 'Toad' and 'Final Day' collection.

2018 – J36, new 'Coronation', new Class 87, Class 800, eightieth anniversary of World Speed Record, 15 Guinea Special, SR dining car and LNER brake vans.

2019 – 1:1 Collection, 'Lord Nelson', *Azuma*, new 'Terrier', new 'Princess', new GWR 'Large Prairies', Pecket W4, Ruston Hornsby Shunter, TTS vans, GWR non-corridor, Bulleid coaches, Mk 2F, Mk 3SDs, LMS and LSWR brarke vans, return of *Harry Potter* and *Flying Scotsman*'s US tour.

EXHIBITIONS IN THE 2010s

Hornby at the Ally Pally, 2017.

The team.

Hornby at Model Rail Scotland, 2017.

Hornby Real 0-4-4T H Class at Warley, 2017.

Hornby win five British Model Railway Awards, 2016.

CONCLUSION

The Hornby brand has come a long way since it first appeared on a train set from the Meccano factory in Binns Road, Liverpool in 1920. It has been through some very rough waters with the substantial pressures on the home toy industry caused by cheap imports and changing fashions in what children wanted. More often than not it has been the public's faith in the Hornby brand that has kept its products flowing over the counter despite the competition.

The years have seen many good decisions taken and sheer luck experienced in other cases. There have also been mistakes – but let us not dwell on them. Better to remember the right decisions, such as the quick expansion of the 0-gauge system, which gained the public's attention and interest, and the early move into electric-powered locomotives in the mid-1920s, which found a new market amongst those who already had electricity in their homes. Then there was the use of *Meccano Magazine* and the 'Hornby Railway Company' to gain customer loyalty and the bold launch of Hornby Dublo giving us an entire system in two years and setting standards for others to follow. Also, the realisation that the future lay in 00-scale and the investment in quality engineering in the 1950s, plus the heavy investment in new tooling by Rovex in the early 1960s, which carried Tri-ang Hornby through the toy industry recession of that decade. The strength of Rovex, enabling it to survive the liquidation of its owners on two occasions over a ten-year period, and the decision to make authentic models with paint finishes to beat off three new rivals. An opportunity was provided by the floatation of an independent Hornby company in the mid-1980s, which funded new tooling, allowing it to survive through the lean years of the late-1980s and early 1990s. There were changes in railway policy, which created many new liveries to model at a time when money for new tooling was in short supply. And there was the decision in the late-1990s to lead the industry in model authenticity and performance in the new century. These are what ensured the survival of the Hornby brand when others fell by the wayside and it was the failure of those rivals that showed what a survivor Hornby is.

The year 2017 was an important one in Hornby's history and created hope for the future. Hornby are back in their home where models have been designed and created for over sixty-five years, the Hornby Visitor Centre no longer needs to move and the company is being run by people who understand the business of designing, making and marketing models for an enthusiast's market. The people who make Hornby models are passionate about what they do. The icing on the cake is the collection of real railway locomotives displayed in the buildings that once formed the Hornby factory and warehouse, allowing the company to return. It is like the final chapter of a good novel when everything comes together as it should be.

The Hornby brand is one hundred years old and that is a major achievement. It is part of Great Britain's heritage and long may it be so.

HORNBY'S OTHER BRANDS

Scalextric

Minimodels Ltd. was founded in 1947 at Tennyson Road, London, and moved to Havant in 1954. The company developed a range of miniature racing cars, which they electrified in 1957, and produced a slot-car system that they called Scalextric. In November 1958, Lines Bros. purchased the company and, in May 1961, moved it into a brand-new factory in Havant where the Scalextric slot-car system continued to develop as the market leader of world renown. As the Lines Group shrank under a toy industry recession, production of Scalextric was moved to the Rovex factory at Margate in 1970 and gave Rovex two very strong products for the 1970s – Hornby Railways and Scalextric. These have remained the kingpins of the company to the present day. Adopting new products was not a new experience for the staff at Rovex, who had taken over plastic kit development in 1963 and 1966 followed by the Minic Motorway slot-car system in 1967.

In the final years of the Lines Group, Rovex had become Rovex Industries Ltd. in 1967, as the model-making division of the Lines Group. From that time several semi-independent companies within the group were welded together into a single company with factories in Margate and Canterbury, and this was the company that DCM bought in 1972.

Rivarossi

Rivarossi was founded in 1945 by Alessandro Rossi and Antonio Riva, hence the name Riva-Rossi. The company produced very high-quality models and its main market has been the USA, where they were briefly marketed by Lionel. After a fall-out and parting, Athern took over importing Rivarossi's products and later the dealership moved on to AHM. In 1992 Rivarossi acquired the Italian model manufacturer, Lima, and in 1997 added the French firm Jouef and the German N-gauge manufacturer, Arnold, to what became known as the Lima Group. In 2003 the group went into receivership and its tools and intellectual assets were bought by Hornby plc for €8 million.

Lima

Lima was founded in 1946 as a parts supplier for the Italian state railway and in 1948 turned to producing toys. By 1962 it was providing French, Belgian, Dutch and German models and, less than ten years later, Lima was one of the largest model manufacturers in the world, also supplying Australia, Great Britain, South Africa and the USA. In 1967, Lines Bros. agreed to market Lima N gauge through their subsidiary G&R Wrenn. It was sold as Wrenn Micromodels.

In 1976 Lima started a British 00 model range (as opposed to its earlier unsuccessful H0 British range) and from 1982 gradually moved into the higher quality market. In the late 1980s it was producing batches of 500 of its many diesel and electric locomotive classes in a wide variety of liveries. By the mid-1990s, Lima had a UK product range of over 300 models, producing five or more new ones each month. Their distributor, Riko International, went into receivership in 1999 and together with this and the production of some bad models left the company in difficulty. As a subsidiary of Rivarossi, Lima was an important part of the group bought by Hornby plc in 2004 and its British models have nearly all been absorbed into the Hornby range. The Lima Group's Continental models are marketed through Hornby International.

Jouef

Georges Huard founded Jouef in 1944 at its traditional home in Champagnole, France. The company's first offering had been a toy-like tinplate 'Trans Saharan Express – Algiers to Timbouctou'. In the early 1950s, Jouef moved into plastic injection moulding. During the 1960s they marketed a limited H0 range of British outline model railways under the brand name 'Playcraft', through the British company Mettoy (manufacturers of Corgi toys). Because of their low price, they were a serious competitor for Tri-ang Railways and Hornby Dublo. The Playcraft range petered out in the late 1960s. In 1977 Jouef produced an excellent 00 model of a Class 40 diesel and some BR Mk 3 coaches, which were well received. In 1979 a factory was opened on the Shannon Airport trading estate at Limerick in Ireland, but the ill-fated venture closed in 1981. By 1997 Jouef was in financial difficulty and was bought by Rivarossi and was acquired by Hornby plc in 2004 as part of the Lima Group.

Arnold

K. Arnold & Co. was founded in Nürnberg in 1906 by Karl Arnold and produced an extensive line of model ships, doll house items and other toys. In 1935, K. Arnold & Co. hired Max Ernst as Managing Director. At the end of the Second World War, all the Arnold facilities were in ruins. The factory buildings in Nürnberg were re-built and the Arnold company continued to grow. In the post-war years, under Max Ernst's direction, Arnold developed the first successful N gauge system, called Arnold Rapido, and today Arnold holds the world patent for the N gauge coupling. Karl Arnold died in 1946 and Max Ernst retired in 1976, at which time Arnold was using three facilities in the Nürnberg area. The company continued under family control until 1995, when Arnold went into bankruptcy and was sold to Rivarossi and, as such, was acquired by Hornby plc in 2004.

Electrotren

The company was founded in Spain in 1951 and began with the production of 0-gauge model railways. In 1954 it started an H0 range, going on to also develop N-gauge trains. The models are of a high quality and were mainly of Spanish prototypes, but there were also models of French, German and Swiss railways in the range. The company was the Spanish importer of Scalextric and in April 2004 it was mutually agreed that the company should become part of the Hornby Group. Hornby plc bought the company for €7.5 million.

Humbrol

Since Humbrol (Humber Oil Company) was founded in 1919 the brand has been under several owners. In 1976 Humbrol became part of the Hobby Products Group of the International Borden group and then later, in 1986, the Airfix brand also joined the group. In 1994, the group was acquired by an Irish investment company, Allen & Maguire, and in November 2006 the Humbrol and Airfix brands were acquired by Hornby.

Airfix

Airfix was founded in 1939 by a Hungarian, Nicholas Kove, initially to manufacture inflatable rubber toys. In 1947 Airfix started injection moulding and in 1949 produced a kit of a Ferguson TE20 tractor, which was sold in Woolworth's. They went on to produce many kits, including aircraft, soldiers, cars, ships and 00-scale railway accessories. They launched *Airfix Magazine* in 1960 and bought up Kitmaster railway kits in 1962. In 1963 Airfix launched its slot car system and, with the collapse of Lines Bros. in 1971, bought Meccano Ltd. In 1975 Airfix launched a new 00 model railway system later renamed GMR. Having spent £7 million trying to rescue Meccano Ltd., in 1981 they called in the Receiver. It was bought by the US giant General Mills through its UK Palitoy subsidiary.

General Mills had bought Meccano (France) in 1971 along with the Lines factory in Calais, to which Airfix and British Meccano were moved. Four years later, General Mills withdrew from the toy market in Europe and Airfix was bought by the Hobby Products Group of Borden, Inc., who owned Humbrol and kit-maker Heller in France. With the collapse of Heller, Humbrol (with Airfix) went into administration on 31 August 2006 and was bought by Hornby plc for £2.6 million.

Pocher

Following the Second World War, an Italian, Arnaldo Pocher, became interested in railway modelling and in 1951 he formed Pocher Micromeccanica S.n.c. alongside Corrado Muratore, producing train signals, points and platforms. They produced finely detailed models of freight and passenger carriages in white metal and later locomotives and power cars. In 1966, at the International Toy Fair of Milan, Pocher exhibited a highly detailed 1:8 scale model of the Fiat F2 130 HP, the car, driven by

Felice Nazzaro, which won the 1907 French Grand Prix. The company went on to produce ever more detailed models of motoring classics and continued to do so under Rivarossi from 1981 until the organisation became part of Hornby plc and was re-launched in 2012.

Corgi

The Mettoy company was founded in 1933 by Philip Ullmann in Northampton where he was later joined by Arthur Katz, who had previously worked for Ullmann at his toy company Tipp and Co. of Nürnberg, Germany. They initially produced tinplate toys. In July 1956 they introduced a range of die-cast road vehicle models ('the ones with windows') to compete with Dinky Toys. For twenty-seven years these were manufactured in Swansea before the company went into liquidation. In March 1984, a management buy-out was successful and the company Corgi Toys Ltd. was formed. In 1989, the management sold the Corgi brand to Mattel and the factory was retained under the name of Microlink Industries Ltd. In 1995, Corgi regained its independence from Mattel and moved to Leicester as Corgi Classics Ltd. On 1 May 2008, once more in financial difficulty, Corgi Classics was bought by Hornby plc for £7.5 million.

Bassett-Lowke

Bassett-Lowke was a model trading company, based in Northampton, and founded by Wenman Joseph Bassett-Lowke in 1899. Initially, Bassett-Lowke depended on German companies such as Bing, Carette and Märklin to build British-type railway models for him, but after the First World War he started building them himself. His locomotives were built in gauges 0, 1 and 2, and he also built locomotives for miniature railways up to 15-in. gauge. The company built model boats, miniature ships and large industrial models, including the feasibility models of the Mulberry harbours for the D-Day landings.

Bassett-Lowke's decline started in the late 1950s, due largely to the reduced popularity of 0 gauge. In 1964, the company ceased retail sales and sold its shops, going out of business in 1965. The company was acquired by Messrs Riley and Derry and around 1969, Ivan Rutherford Scott, Allen Levy and Roland Fuller made efforts to revive the model railway business. In the late 1980s Northampton businessman, Nigel Turner, bought the business and in 1993 the name was revived with short-run white-metal traction engine models. The name was acquired in 1996 by Corgi, who revived the 0-gauge railway locomotives. After the purchase of Corgi by Hornby plc, Bassett-Lowke was transferred from Corgi to Hornby Hobbies Ltd.

ACKNOWLEDGEMENTS

Fitting together the Meccano story with those of Rovex and Hornby Hobbies has been like a jigsaw puzzle. It has required combining bits of information taken from books, manufacturers' catalogues, newspaper stories, company annual reports, correspondence, auction catalogues, production records, minutes of meetings, private archives, memories of staff, the internet and magazines.

The writing of this book would have been very difficult without two volumes published by New Cavendish Books – namely Chris and Julie Graebe's *The Hornby Gauge 0 System* (ISBN 0 904568 35 0) and Michael Foster's *Hornby Dublo Trains* (ISBN 0 904568 18 0). Both are classic works which record each story in detail and are highly recommended. Together they cover the first 45 years of the Hornby century.

I am also grateful to Richard Lines who gave me so much of his time when I was undertaking research for the *Rovex Trilogy,* which was also published by New Cavendish Books. The second on Tri-ang Hornby (ISBN 1 872727 58 1) and third volumes on Hornby Railways (ISBN 1 904562 00 0) cover the middle period of the story (30 years). For the final 25 years of the century, which I believe have not previously been recorded in a book, I must thank Simon Kohler for our discussions, for the many blogs he published on the Hornby website and for allowing me to tell the uncensored story – warts and all.

I am also grateful to Tom Carfrae, the head of the Research and Development Department at Hornby before he retired, and to John Stansfield for access to old records.

For the early part of the story much use was made of *The Meccano Magazine Comprehensive Index* online, which is a great resource for those wishing to read issues of *Meccano Magazine* and freely download individual pages and articles. It was compiled by the Internet Meccano Magazine Scanning Group. The earliest issue available is September 1916 and the most recent is the final issue of April 1981. It is very nearly a complete collection.

Over the last 40 years I have been compiling a picture archive with many of the pictures, in recent years, being downloaded from online auction catalogues. This archive has been donated to the Train Collectors Society (TCS) for use by its members. I am grateful to auction houses and online retailers for allowing me to use their pictures and I am particularly indebted to Vectis Auctions, SAS, Lacy, Scott & Knight (LSK), Wallis & Wallis (W&W) and UK Toy & Model Auctions (UKT&M); also the websites of Rails of Sheffield and Hattons.

Various people have donated pictures to the TCS Digital Archive or to me personally, that may have been used in the book. Among the donors of pictures in my original selection were Tony Wright, Tony Pritchard, Graeme Hearn, Mike Fowler, David Busfield, Tom Bell, Bob Leggett, John Agnew, Tony Penn, Dave Clark, Barry Potter, Phil Parker, Tony Cooper, Darren Cooper, Matthew Petzold and Rolande Allen.

Where borrowed pictures have been used the source is acknowledged in the caption. Other pictures are by the author.

The jigsaw puzzles used were by Gibsons.

Finally, my thanks to my daughter Milly Riley for proofreading the book; a job I am no good at!

INDEX

HORNBY SERIES / HORNBY TRAINS 0-GAUGE 1920–1962 (BY MECCANO)

Train Sets

Locomotives

Coaches

Wagons and Loads

Lineside

Power and Track

Miscellaneous

HORNBY DUBLO 00-GAUGE 1938–1964 (BY MECCANO)

Train Sets

Locomotives

Coaches

Wagons and Loads

Lineside

Power and Track

Miscellaneous

TRI-ANG HORNBY 00-GAUGE 1965–1971 (BY ROVEX)

Train Sets

Locomotives

Coaches

Wagons and Loads

Battle Space!

Lineside

Power and Track

Overseas

Miscellaneous

HORNBY RAILWAYS INCLUDING 'HORNBY' (1997–2020) 00-GAUGE 1972–2020 (BY ROVEX/HORNBY HOBBIES)

Train Sets and Train Packs

Locomotives

Referred to Network Locomotive Classes

Referred-to Named Locomotives

County of Radnor – 2011
County of Somerset – 1997
Defiance – 2003
Derwent Grange – 2005
Dominion of Canada – 1994, 2013
Dominion of New Zealand – 2009
Dorchester – 2010
Duchess of Atholl – 1982, 2017
Duchess of Buccleuch – 2002
Duchess of Gloucester – 2001
Duchess of Hamilton – 2008, 2018
Duchess of Rutland – 2002
Duchess of Sutherland – 1977, 2010
Duke of Edinburgh Award – 1988
Duke of Gloucester – 2013
Duke of Sutherland – 1979
Dwight D Eisenhower – 2013
Earl Cairns – 2009
Elgar – 1995
Eton – 1986
Evening Star – 1977, 1988, 2000, 2011, 2012
Excalibur – 2007
Exeter – 1995
Fighter Pilot – 1987
Firth of Tay – 2006
Flying Scotsman – 1981, 1993, 1996, 1999, 2000, 2005, 2007, 2008, 2010, 2011, 2019
Freshwater – 1998
Gay Crusader – 2017
Glasgow Yeomanry – 1973
Glastonbury Abbey – 2013
Golden Plover – 2004
Great Northern – 2005
Great Western (4-2-2) – 2010
Great Western (4-6-0) – 2010
Greyfriar's Bobby – 1988
Grimsby Town – 2012
Guillemot – 1997
Hardwick Grange – 2005
Hogwart's Castle – 2001, 2019
Holland-Afrika Line – 2017
Ince Castle – 2010
Isambard Kingdom Brunel – 2018
Iron Duke – 1974
Keith Heller – 2012
Kenley – 2017
Ketley Hall – 2015
Kidwelly Castle – 2010
King Arthur (Class N15) – 2007
King Arthur (Class 87) – 2007, 2018
King Edward I – 1978
King Edward VIII – 2015
King George III – 2017
King George V – 1985, 2015
King George V (0-4-0T) – 1991
King George VI – 1983, 2003, 2018
King Henry VI – 1996
King Henry VIII – 1978, 1980
King James I – 2015
King Richard II – 2015
King Stephen – 2003
King Uther – 2007
King William IV – 2003, 2011
Kingfisher – 2010
Kneller Hall – 1978
Knight of the Grand Cross – 2013
Lady Diana Spencer – 1981
Leeds United – 1982
Lode Star – 2013
Lord Beaverbrook – 1995
Lord Nelson – 2019
Lord of the Isles – 1981
Lord Rodney – 2019
Lord Westwood – 1973
Mallard – 1979, 2003, 2004, 2008, 2011, 2013, 2018
Manchester United – 1980
Michael Bond – 2018
Morning Star – 1981
Nunney Castle – 2011
Oliver Cromwell – 1973, 2006, 2018
Olton Hall – 2015
Overton Grange – 2005
Paddington Bear – 2018
Papyrus – 2005
Pendragon – 2007
Phoenix – 1981
Pitchford Hall – 2015
Planet – 2007
Plymouth – 2006
Princess Alexandra – 2002
Princess Arthur of Connaught – 2001, 2019
Princess Beatrice – 1992
Princess Elizabeth – 1984, 2009, 2019
Princess Helena Victoria – 1997
Princess Margaret Rose – 2001
Princess Marie Louise – 2019
Princess Victoria – 1974
Queen Elizabeth – 2018
Queen Mary – 1991
Resolution – 2003
Resolven Grange – 2005
Robert Burns – 2018
Robin Hood – 1983
Rocket live steam – 1979, 1980
Roedeer – 2011
Rood Ashton Hall – 2015

Coaches

Wagons and Loads

Lineside

Thomas & Friends

Power and Track

Overseas

Miscellaneous

BASSETT-LOWKE 0-GAUGE 2008–2009 (BY HORNBY HOBBIES)